Showing forth the Virtues of God

Showing forth the Virtues of God

Compiled by Rob Lawson

The Christadelphian
404 Shaftmoor Lane, Hall Green, Birmingham B28 8SZ, UK

2018

First published 2018

ISBN 978 0 85189 406 5 (print edition)
ISBN 978 0 85189 407 2 (electronic edition)

Printed and bound in the UK by
CMP (UK) Limited

Scripture references are mostly from the King James (Authorised) Version.

Contents

Preface

THE Apostle Peter wrote his first epistle to "the strangers scattered throughout Pontus, Galatia, Cappadocia, Asia, and Bithynia". Greeting the brothers and sisters as "strangers" to the world around them he set the tone for the letter as a whole, one of its main emphases being how to live a godly life in an ungodly world. Nowhere is this contrast between believer and unbeliever more stark than in the second chapter where the world around about is described as "foolish", "ignorant" and "disobedient". His brothers and sisters in Christ, however, are described as a "chosen generation, a royal priesthood, a holy nation". To this honourable status is added the purpose of their election – "that ye should shew forth the praises ('virtues', KJV margin) of him who hath called you out of darkness into his marvellous light".

The task of reflecting God's character is as challenging now as it was then. The doctrine of "God Manifestation" was a key that helped Brother John Thomas delineate anew the apostolic Gospel. In recognition of this heritage, the first section of this book is dedicated to themes with which he would have been familiar. Nine short studies by various brothers attempt to, amongst other things, explain the Yahweh name, decode the imagery of the cherubim, and examine the angels' work as God's representatives. The publishers wish to thank Brother Jason

Hensley for his permission to abridge a chapter from his book *Unlocking the Mystery*.

Having recognised the duty to manifest God in our lives, it is imperative to know Him clearly. The second section consists of articles by Brother John Morris, originally published in *The Christadelphian* from January 1994 to March 1995. Taking a cue from Yahweh's great self-declaration in Exodus 34, the author explores Bible teaching on fourteen aspects of His character.

The final section is an abridgment of *Names and Titles of the Deity*, written by W. H. Boulton in 1922. Differences between the original text and the one provided here are explained in the section introduction. It is hoped that it will provide a useful quick reference for those studying this exalted theme.

May these studies instil in us a sense of thankfulness that God has "given unto us all things that pertain unto life and godliness, through the knowledge of him that hath called us to glory and virtue" (2 Peter 1:3).

Rob Lawson
Birmingham, March 2018

Section 1

God Manifestation: principles and symbols

Manifestation | noun | 1. A thing that represents or stands for something or someone else, especially a material object representing something abstract.

Principle | noun | 1. A fundamental truth or proposition that serves as the foundation for a system of belief or behaviour or for a chain of reasoning.

Symbol | noun | 2. A thing that represents or stands for something else, especially a material object representing something abstract.

---

1 |

God Manifestation in the Old Testament

(Richard Morgan, 1995)

The doctrine of God Manifestation is, as Brother Richard Morgan notes below, an all-embracing concept. It involves God, His creation and all its history. A subject of this magnitude can be studied at great depth; however before beginning detailed study an introductory overview of key elements can be useful. This is provided by the first two articles in the present volume.

On February 25, 1995 a seminar was held in Bristol (UK) under the theme "Contending for the faith". As the overarching idea of the Biblical faith, two sessions were devoted to discussing God manifestation. The sessions were led by two young brethren, Richard Morgan looking at the Old Testament and Justin Robinson the New Testament. The articles, like the two Testaments, complement each other to show God as manifest in the angels, the saints, and above all in the person of the Lord Jesus Christ. They were first published in *The Christadelphian* in May and June of 1995.

GOD Manifestation is the theme of the Bible. It is that all embracing doctrine that describes the eternal purpose God has with mankind upon the earth. As Brother John Thomas wrote, "Man was not ushered into being for the purpose of being saved or lost; God Manifestation, not human salvation is the doctrine of the Bible". The work of salvation wrought in the

Lord Jesus Christ, vital though it is, is merely the means to the end of God's ultimate purpose of His manifestation.

So what is God Manifestation? The word "manifestation" as such is only found in the New Testament where it is translated from the Greek word *phanerosis*. The basic meaning of this word is 'to make something visible, or clear, to make something known, to reveal something'. The root word of *phanerosis* is *phos*, meaning 'light'. For something to be revealed, or made visible, there must be light, the source of which must be God. Therefore God Manifestation can be briefly described as the enlightenment about God, making Him known or revealing Him in some form.

Before looking at specific examples of God Manifestation in the Old Testament it is first necessary to describe God Himself. A verse in one of Paul's epistles will suffice, "But to us there is but one God, the Father, of whom are all things, and we in him" (1 Corinthians 8:6). God is one, He is a Unity – that is one of the first principles of Truth. He is the One source of all power and creation in the universe and without Him there is no life.

Revelation through angels

One of the various ways in which God has been manifested, or revealed, in the Old Testament is through His messengers, the angels. One such angel spoke to Hagar when she fled from the face of Sarah. At first sight the words of the angel are confusing, "And the angel of the LORD said unto her, I will multiply thy seed exceedingly, that it shall not be numbered for multitude" (Genesis 16:10). The angel spoke as if he were God Himself referring to a promise only God could perform. The words of Hagar are similarly confusing, "And she called the name of the LORD that spake unto her, Thou God seest me" (verse 13). The angel is referred to in the text as "the LORD" and by Hagar as "God". How can we reconcile this in the light of there being only one God? The answer lies in the doctrine of God Manifestation.

Firstly note that the angel is referred to as "the angel of the LORD". He was of the Lord because he was representing God to Hagar. An everyday example will help to explain the principle. Imagine there is a knock at your door and when you answer it, a man announces himself and says, "Smith and Co." Obviously the man at the door isn't literally the company "Smith and Co." but a representative of it; he calls himself by the name of the company. As a representative of God, the angel was called by His name ("the LORD" of verse 13) and spoke the words of God to Hagar, not his own words. This is a principle used throughout the whole of scripture.

It would be wise to have a look at the actual word "God", for that word in no way describes the real meaning. There are basically three words translated "God" in the Old Testament and they are all related. Firstly there is the word "El". The idea behind this word is of power or might. It describes God in His very being. He is the only source of all power, the great omnipotent one. Therefore there is only one El. Another word used is "Eloah", derived from El and meaning 'Mighty One'. God is the supreme Eloah, but each of the angels is also an Eloah because they derive their power from God. Finally the word "Elohim" is the plural form of Eloah and means 'Mighty Ones'. This describes God and the angels in collection.

Three Eloah, or a group of Elohim, were the angels who appeared to Abraham in Genesis 18:

> "And *the LORD* appeared unto him in the plains of Mamre: and he sat in the tent door in the heat of the day; and he lift up his eyes and looked, and, lo, *three men* stood by him." (verses 1,2)

The principle is the same as before: the three angels are referred to as "the LORD" because they represent God. However, here there are more than one and this presents us with an important principle that actually describes the very purpose of Almighty God: the One God is manifested in a multitude of Mighty Ones. As we hope to show, this is the purpose which God had right back in the beginning.

Before looking at this in detail we need to consider another reference dealing with an angel. In their wilderness wanderings the children of Israel had a powerful guide and protector:

> "Behold, I send an Angel before thee, to keep thee in the way ... Beware of him, and obey his voice, provoke him not; for he will not pardon your transgressions: for my name is in him ... thou shalt indeed obey his voice, and do all that I speak."
>
> (Exodus 23:20-22)

There are two things to note about this angel: the children of Israel were not to provoke his voice, but this was also what God Himself spoke – "I speak". In verse 21 we are told that the name of God was in the angel, again signifying that he represented the one God. God delegated power and authority to the angel to withhold the forgiveness of sins according to the righteousness of God. The significance of God's name being in the angel will soon be made clear.

But how does all this relate to mankind and the purpose of God? A verse in Luke will show the connection, "They which shall be accounted worthy to obtain that world ... are equal unto the angels" (Luke 20:35,36). This is speaking of the saints in the kingdom of God, and they are said to be equal unto the angels. We should therefore be able to take the principles of God Manifestation as seen in the angels and apply them to the children of God.

God's appointed representatives

And so we can. The term "Elohim" is not only applied to God and the angels in the scriptures, it is also applied to men. One such passage is found in a law to do with theft: "If the thief be not found, then the master of the house shall be brought unto *the judges*" (Exodus 22:8). Obviously the "judges" in this verse were men, specially appointed to the task. However, the word translated "judges" is actually "Elohim", Mighty Ones; the word can be applied to men as well as to angels. Psalm 82 is directed to the judges in Israel and shows how applicable to their role the term is. In verse 6, God says, "I have said, Ye are gods [literally, Elohim]". This is without doubt speaking of men, for the Lord Jesus quoted this verse and applied it to them "unto whom the word of God came" (John 10:34,35).

The Psalm also tells us of the judgement they were to carry out:

> "Defend the poor and fatherless: do justice to the afflicted and needy. Deliver the poor and needy: rid them out of the hand of the wicked." (Psalm 82:3,4)

However, these judgements are the judgements of God; there are many passages in the scriptures that speak of God acting in this way. The judges in Israel were therefore called *Mighty Ones* because they were carrying out the judgements of God Himself; like the angels they were God's representatives and the One eternal God was manifest in them.

All of these principles governing the purpose of God in manifesting Himself in a multitude are memorialised in the name of God. It is called the memorial name because it is revealed so that we can remember the purpose of God.

The memorial name

The name was revealed to Moses at the burning bush when he asked:

> "Behold, when I come unto the children of Israel, and shall say unto them, The God of your fathers hath sent me unto you; and they shall say unto me, What is his name? what shall I say unto them?" (Exodus 3:13)

In other words, Moses wanted to know how he should refer to God when the children of Israel wanted to know who He is.

The answer was immediately given, "I AM THAT I AM: and he said, Thus shalt thou say unto the children of Israel, I AM hath sent me unto you" (verse 14). As it says in verse 15, this is the memorial name, "I AM". The verb *ehyeh* is also used in verse 12, explaining its true meaning, "And he said, Certainly *I will* be with thee". The future tense aspect of the memorial name is shown here. What God was really saying to Moses is, "I WILL BE WHAT I WILL BE". In the third person the name becomes the more familiar "LORD" or "GOD" (capitalised in our English translations); in the Hebrew "Yahweh" and meaning 'He will be'.

This is the name by which God wishes to be remembered. But what exactly does God intend to be? There are many times when God states He is to be something. One such case is in a verse already cited, "I will be with thee", the promise of God that He would care for Moses. However, in considering the ultimate purpose of God with mankind a look at the first occurrence of the memorial name in scripture will show what God intends to be in the future. It is found in the early chapters of Genesis:

> "These are the generations of the heavens and of the earth when they were created, in the day that the LORD God made the earth and the heavens." (Genesis 2:4)

In this passage the memorial name Yahweh is joined on to the word "God" (Hebrew, *Elohim*). This compound title neatly sums up the eternal purpose of God, "Yahweh Elohim", or "He will be Mighty Ones". It is very helpful to think of the words "He will be" when reading "LORD" or "GOD" in the common version.

At first glance Yahweh Elohim (LORD God) seems to be a very common title in the book of Genesis. It occurs eleven times in chapter 2 and eight times in chapter 3 alone. However, when we look at the rest of Genesis we see that it only occurs another seven times in total! There must be some intention here in the concentration of the title in the first three chapters. The reason has to do with the fact that the last forty-seven chapters of Genesis record events which occurred after the entrance of sin and death into the world. Until then, God's purpose of being manifested in men and women was working out, for Adam and Eve were without sin, and in harmony with His purpose. But as soon as they sinned God could no longer be manifested in them. This is not to say that God's purpose has changed. It is still His ultimate intention to be manifested in a multitude of people.

The testimony of creation

The first words of scripture read, "In the beginning God created the heaven and the earth". Why? What purpose did God have in creating this earth? A verse such as the following in Isaiah will introduce the reason:

> "For thus saith the LORD that created the heavens; God himself that formed the earth and made it; he hath established it, he created it not in vain, he formed it to be inhabited."
>
> (Isaiah 45:18)

God formed this world that it might be inhabited, and so He created the plants and the animals to fulfil this. And isn't the creation of God that we see around us a testimony to His power and beauty!

The creation is indeed a manifestation of God. It is when we come to the creation of man that we see the main reason why God created this world to be inhabited, "And God said, Let us make man in our image, after our likeness" (Genesis 1:26). The importance of these words cannot be over emphasised. Mankind was created in the image and likeness of the Elohim. The word "image" means 'form' or 'appearance'. Man was made to appear like God, in other words to manifest Him. As Paul says of man, "He is the image and glory of God" (1 Corinthians 11:7). Man was made in the glory of God! This is something wonderful when we consider what the glory of God actually is.

What is meant by the word "glory"? It literally means 'to be heavy', and is anything that renders a nation, person, or place weighty. A man who is very strong has his glory in his strength, because it is that attribute which gives him weight, that makes him of some note. A nation might have its glory in the size of its population.

What then are the attributes of God that give Him weight? Moses wanted to know this when he asked to see a manifestation of God, "Now therefore, I pray thee, if I have found grace in thy sight, shew me now thy way, that I may know thee" (Exodus

33:13). In a final plea he says in verse 18, "I beseech thee, shew me thy glory".

God's attributes

The answer God gave to this request shows us what makes Him of such weight, "And he said, I will make all my goodness pass before thee" (verse 19). The glory of God is seen in His wonderful character of goodness, detailed in the next chapter as –

> "merciful and gracious, longsuffering and abundant in goodness and truth, keeping mercy for thousands, forgiving iniquity and transgression and sin, and that will by no means clear the guilty; visiting the iniquity of the fathers upon the children, and upon the children's children, unto the third and to the fourth generation." (Exodus 34:6,7)

These characteristics of God are what should have been reflected by the mighty ones in Israel as they administered the judgements of God, defending the fatherless and the widow.

Man, created in the appearance of God and given the ability to manifest His glory, was placed on this earth so that the character of God could be revealed in a multitude. One of the most important verses in the Bible is Genesis 1:28. It is so important because it contains the very first instructions of God to man: "Be fruitful, and multiply, and replenish the earth, and subdue it: and have dominion ..." A careful consideration of these words will further enhance our understanding of God's purpose.

Man was told to be fruitful, that is, to bear children. His children were likewise to be fruitful. In doing this he would replenish, or fill the earth. In other words, God's intention was that man should inhabit the whole earth and eventually rule over His creation, being the pinnacle of it. Man has been fruitful, he has multiplied and he has filled the earth. But when sin and death came into the world he could not manifest the glory of God. What would have happened if man had lived up to his being made in the image and glory of God?

A number of verses tell us the answer, "But as truly as I live, all the earth shall be filled with the glory of the LORD" (Numbers 14:21; see also Isaiah 11:9; Habakkuk 2:14). This sums up the purpose of God, that, being manifested in a multitude of Mighty Ones, His glory or character should fill the earth as men and women reveal it in the way they live their lives.

When it comes down to it, this is all very simple. Our task, as part of the creation of God, is to manifest His character. Consider the parallel Psalms 111 and 112. Verse 4 of the former Psalm reads, "the LORD is gracious and full of compassion", and so He is. In verse 4 of Psalm 112 we read similar words, "he is gracious, and full of compassion, and righteous". But now the subject is not God, but "*the man* that feareth the LORD" (112:1). In both Psalms we read of God's character, part of God's glory, manifest in those men and women who will be in His kingdom.

God's glory manifest in His saints

The only problem comes in how we can manifest the glory of God when it is entirely unnatural to us, for as Isaiah said:

> "All flesh is grass, and all the goodliness thereof is as the flower of the field: the grass withereth, the flower fadeth."
>
> (Isaiah 40:6,7)

There is no goodliness (one of the characteristics of God) in man; there is no glory on him that gives him weight. Therefore we cannot manifest the glory of God unaided. But as the prophet goes on to say, "the word of our God shall stand forever" (verse 8). The only way is to have the seed of the word of God planted in our hearts and minds so that it can bear fruit. Then when the word is multiplied in its effect the whole earth shall be filled with the glory of God.

The principles of God manifestation in the Old Testament are continued in the New Testament where the Lord Jesus Christ is the fulfilment of Isaiah's words, "the glory of the LORD shall be revealed". The link between the Testaments is seen in the birth of the Son of God, "Thou shalt call his name Jesus: for he shall save his people from their sins" (Matthew 1:21). The name of Jesus means 'He shall save', thus giving us a clear definition of the memorial name of God. In Jesus God was manifest to perfection, that he might be the representative sent to save us from our sins so that God's glory might eventually fill the earth.

God said to Moses, "I will be with thee", a promise confirmed in the Lord Jesus, called in verse 23 "Emmanuel", God with us. The supreme manifestation of God in Christ and God manifestation in general in the New Testament will be dealt with in the next chapter.

2|

God Manifestation in the New Testament

(Justin Robinson, 1995)

IN this article we turn our attention to the Lord Jesus Christ and his manifestation of the Father. The attributes which the faithful of Old Testament times had seen in the God of Israel and His angels were now revealed in their fulness in His only begotten Son. Though we may only dimly appreciate the deep and intimate relationship between the Father and the Son, we can learn from his example of showing forth God's attributes the part that we have to play in the manifestation of God's character and purpose.

In Hebrews 1 we see the uniqueness of Jesus in his declaration of God's character and how, as the Son of God, he was better than that which had gone before. Verses 1 and 2 contrast how God spoke in many ways through the fathers in times past, but has revealed Himself in these last days through His Son ("in a Son", RSV). Jesus was the prophesied Immanuel, "God with us", and being the Son of God showed three distinct features:

1. He is the heir – He was to have complete supremacy over all things, which was only possible as the Son of God (Hebrews 2:8).
2. He is the foundation – The worlds (or ages, RV) are founded in the Son. This is expanded in words taken from Psalm 102:13-16, referring to the age to come, made possible by the Son (Hebrews 2:10).

3. He is God's brightness – The Greek idea was of light coming out from the original source, forming a similar light body.

God is light (John 1:6; 1 Timothy 6:16), and Jesus was the light of the world (John 8:12). Therefore he was able to say, "I and my Father are one" (John 10:30). Being the "brightness of his [God's] glory", Jesus showed the seven moral attributes of God's perfection as proclaimed in Exodus 34. The light expressed moral perfection with its seven aspects, as there are seven colours that make up natural white light.

Jesus is also described as the "express image of his [God's] person". This can also be rendered, "exact representation". Christ was pressed into the mould of God's moral attributes, as he was born of a mortal woman. However, he had the stamp of His Father's will on his mind. The use of language here is similar to our experience of photography. We look at a photograph and say: "That's John". It is not really John but is an exact representation of him, to the extent that we refer to the photo as if it were the very thing it represents.

"Declared to be the Son of God"

So Jesus was not God, but in his character he represented the Lord exactly. "Upholding all things", he kept God's purpose by this word of power. This was only achieved through Jesus' obedience. God's objective was that we might be brought back to Him. Christ was sinless, and God raised him from the dead to uphold His righteousness. Through Christ's resurrection, God declared him to be His Son (Romans 1:4). Jesus during his ministry manifested the attributes of his Father mentally and morally. When he was immortalised, God was manifested physically in His Son, who now sits at the Father's right hand.

In Hebrews 1:8, Christ is called God as he will reign on God's behalf: he will be God's representative. This is a quotation from Psalm 45:6 where the word *Elohim* is singular, allowing us to identify it with the Lord Jesus Christ. The manifestation of his Father which he had shown before on the earth will be revealed again. Previously he had shown the Lord in three aspects of his life: in will, in word and in works.

Jesus declared the first of these in his answer to Philip's desire to see the Father (John 14:9-11). Jesus was not claiming to be the Father physically, but that they were one in will and purpose. Jesus' will was only to do "the will of him that sent me" (John 4:34) and to finish God's work of redemption. Paul described this when he wrote:

> "God was in Christ reconciling the world unto himself, not imputing their trespasses unto them; and hath committed unto us the word of reconciliation." (2 Corinthians 5:19)

In Jesus' words he displayed the Father: he never had to qualify his speech by "Thus saith the LORD", for his speech was never his own. He was always an ambassador representing the Father (John 12:49,50).

Nor were his actions his own (John 14:11). They were the third witness that he called, that they might believe that he had made known the Father. In John 5:36 he identifies his works again in response to the accusation that he was making himself equal with God (John 5:17,18).

Collectively all three aspects manifested the name of God, which Christ declares to be his purpose elsewhere in John when he says, "I have manifested thy name". We can see the three ways in which God is in Christ in the account of his healing of the palsied man (Matthew 9:1-8). It was only possible to speak such words as God's words, as only God can forgive sins. This work was only possible with the Father's power, therefore it was the Father's work. The people recognised the Saviour whose will it was, observing the means by which "The LORD is my salvation".

John was an eyewitness to the Son of God (1 John 1:1); he saw, heard and handled the "word of life", the word that was made flesh. In John 1, Christ is referred to as a revelation of the light. He existed from the beginning as the Word with God, which was an expression of the mind of God, a channel by which His power is exercised for a purpose. The will was the word which was the work, for word and work are interchangeable: both are His will (Isaiah 55:11).

The word was made flesh by the Holy Spirit working on Mary and was a fulfilment of God's promise to David. "I will be his father and he shall be my son" referred to an event in the future. This illustrates that Christ was not in existence at the beginning of time. He was only in the mind and plan of God.

"Full of grace and truth"

The "word ... dwelt among us" (John 1:14), so that the people could behold the glory of the Father, as Christ was full of grace and truth. He was a living embodiment of God's own mind, a perfect expression of the Lord's glory. He manifested a fulness of grace and truth, showing the balance of God's character. These two attributes in John 1:17 were revealed clearly by Jesus Christ, His anointed. But verse 18 stops us thinking that we might have seen God: "No man hath seen God at any time", but in Jesus we have the declaration of God's character, the exact representation.

Let us consider how grace and truth were shown by Jesus. Grace, in the Greek, means 'a favourable regard, a favour that is undeserved'. Jesus was gracious and, motivated by love (1 Peter 2:3), showed grace in healing many. The greatest act of grace was the gift of himself, for our healing, out of a selfless love that could be no greater. Grace brought a way of salvation through the second Adam:

> "For if through the offence of one many be dead, much more the grace of God, and the gift by grace, which is by one man, Jesus Christ, hath abounded unto many." (Romans 5:15)

Truth expressed the faithfulness of God's consistency. Jesus manifested this and therefore was able to say, "I am the truth". He possessed a love that was morally strong and was shown in truth, in purging the temple and reproving the leaders. The greatest display of truth was in his death and resurrection, because he displayed what sin deserves, but conquered death as he was sinless. He showed God's faithfulness to mankind in bringing redemption for God's creation. This is inferred in John 8:32: "If ye continue in my word, then are ye my disciples indeed: and ye shall know the truth, and the truth shall make you free."

Grace and truth were also declared by God through the atonement. The purpose of the word made flesh is described in Romans 3:23-25. Sin is the failure to show forth God's glory. Being made righteous is God's undeserved gift (His grace) to us. It came by Christ's sacrifice, that we may fulfil God's purpose in showing forth His glory. His faithfulness is declared by His righteousness; none of God's principles were bent or changed. The shedding of the blood of a righteous man allows, through faith, a way of salvation by which we might be reconciled to God.

Salvation was an expression of God's righteousness. Grace was counterpoised by truth in the Lord's act of redemption, "that we might be made the righteousness of God in him" (2 Corinthians 5:21).

What has been considered so far is summarised in Philippians 2, which leads to how the Son is glorified. As a consequence of declaring his Father in his ministry and in its climax on the cross, Jesus is given a name which is above every name (verses 10, 11). 'Yah saves' is supreme because he is the means by which the "LORD" ('He who will be') is revealed through an immortal family of sons and daughters.

Such honour and exaltation adds to the glory of the Father, for the Lord will have His purpose accomplished in a people who manifest His name and His attributes. Honouring the Son brings even greater honour to the Father. The same principle is shown in John 17 when Jesus prays, "Glorify thy Son, that thy Son also may glorify thee" (verse 1). The Son's glory did not diminish the glory of God – it enhanced it.

The name was glorified by Christ before his death: "Father, glorify thy name", he said, when Gentiles asked to see him (John 12:28). It was also glorified by his resurrection to life eternal as Christ is now at the right hand of the Father developing a family with godly characteristics, waiting for the establishment of the kingdom. These two aspects of his work after his resurrection were promised to David (2 Samuel 7:13): "He shall build an house for my name and I will stablish the throne of his kingdom for ever." A house of people would be established that would bear the name of God for ever, as they had tried to manifest Him in their lifetimes. This introduces what our response should be!

God Manifestation and discipleship

God Manifestation is the purpose of our lives, as expressed in the epistle to Titus (2:11-14). Grace brings salvation; it is not deserved, and it comes by Jesus Christ to redeem a people by his blood through faith and works. What we must strive to do is to deny ourselves and develop godly attributes. We must overcome the lust of the flesh, the lust of the eyes and the pride of life, and live with self-control, replacing the natural mind with the spiritual mind. The two aspects of discipleship involve destroying the "Old Man" and building up the "New Man". We should be manifesting God in our lives now, living righteously and soberly in this present world. We are to have a vision of the kingdom and the fulfilment of God's purpose: "For the earth shall be filled with the knowledge of the glory of the LORD as the waters cover the sea." Only in the kingdom will this be finally accomplished.

We shall be judged by our Lord on our desire to deny ourselves and exalt God in our lives. The Lord Jesus emphasised the importance of God Manifestation to his followers when he summarised it in the words: "Seek ye first the kingdom of God and his righteousness." The motivation for this transformation is found in Ephesians 5:1,2. It is the same motivation, love, which caused God to provide a Son and which motivated the Son to accept His purpose. We are to be followers, or more powerfully, "imitators" (RV) of our Father, as His children of light. To do this we have to know God and have an intimate knowledge of Him through the word, revealed more perfectly through his Son Jesus Christ. To imitate God is to do His will, not our own, manifesting grace and truth in speech and action, governed by the mind of Christ.

God manifestation, as we have indicated, is a way of life. There is no neat division between doctrine and conduct. Solomon in his wisdom understood this, for in Proverbs 23:7 he says: "For as a man thinketh in his heart, so is he." In other words, what a man believes, he will become. Conversely, what he is reveals what he believes. Words are acts, and teaching is life.

Right behaviour, governed by the characteristics of God, causes men and women to glorify God. No wonder we are termed in Peter's letter, "a royal priesthood" (1 Peter 2:9). Just as the priests were to manifest God to Israel, so now we are to do the same to the people of our day. We are to be representatives of God, showing the way to approach Him. This representation of God has to develop in our lives. It is a lifetime's process that is never completed, but we have to try our best. The virtues of God have to grow in our characters if we are to have the hope of eternal life.

"A people for his name"

Before Jesus was betrayed, he prayed that we may become one. Christ desires us to speak, do and think the will of God, a manifestation that causes others to believe. This oneness is achieved by the same motive of love, by which God gave His Son and His Son obeyed Him. We see the accomplishment of this in a people that will bear His name, for we know, "Simeon hath declared how God, at the first, did visit the Gentiles, to take out of them a people *for his name*".

So let us strive to overcome self and manifest the Lord, by looking to His only begotten Son, the Lord Jesus Christ; waiting in quiet confidence and anticipation for that age when we shall become part of the name of God:

> "Him that overcometh will I make a pillar in the temple of my God, and he shall go no more out: and I will write upon him the name of my God, and the name of the city of my God, which is new Jerusalem, which cometh down out of heaven from my God: and I will write upon him my new name."
>
> (Revelation 3:12)

3 |

Yahweh: the memorial name of God

(Graham Pearce)

In the Old Testament the phrase "the name of the LORD [Hebrew, *Yahweh*]" occurs nearly one hundred times, whilst the name Yahweh itself occurs well over six thousand times. Scripture tells us (among other things) to call upon the name of Yahweh, to remember it, to sing praise to it and to walk in it. To do these things fully requires us to have some understanding of what the name "Yahweh" means. In the October 1987 issue of *The Christadelphian* Brother Graham Pearce wrote an introduction to the "Yahweh" name, discussing its meaning, its institution as a memorial and its continuing relevance to believers in modern times.

IN Exodus we read of the mighty deeds by which God redeemed Israel by Moses. At the bush that burned with fire but was not consumed, Moses was instructed to go to Pharaoh and bring the children of Israel out of Egypt. Reluctant to undertake this awesome task, he protested that he would not readily be received by his people who would challenge his authority, asking who had sent him:

"They shall say to me, What is his name? what shall I say unto them?" (Exodus 3:13). The answer is given in verse 14:

> "And God said unto Moses, I AM THAT I AM [Hebrew, *Ehyeh asher Ehyeh*]: and he said, Thus shalt thou say unto the children of Israel, I AM hath sent me unto you."

In most other versions as well as the King James Version, the translation of 'Ehyeh' is I AM, though it is generally agreed that the tense is future and grammatically the phrase should read "I WILL BE WHO I WILL BE". No doubt the translators could not see much sense in God's name being "I will be who I will be"; and as in Hebrew the future tense at times is used for the present, we need not be surprised at this translation. To the translators I AM conveys the eternal existence of God and His continuing activity.

Brother John Thomas, in the middle of the nineteenth century, arrived at an understanding of the saving truth contained in the Abrahamic and Davidic promises. As he continued his studies of the word of God, he gave his attention to this important incident in Exodus 3, and with the knowledge of the Truth firmly established in his mind, he could see the significance of God describing Himself in the future tense, "I will be who I will be". This phrase picked up the content of the promises and covenants with Abraham; it could well be called "the covenant name". It conveyed the assurance, that what God had promised, He would fulfil. Not only is God ever existing, He is also a God of purpose, a purpose which is expressed in the promises. It was initiated in the birth of Isaac as the child of promise, and continued to unfold when Abraham's descendants were led out of a land of affliction and established in the land of promise. God would provide a special seed of Abraham – the "seed of the woman" of Genesis 3 who would suffer, but in suffering would conquer the serpent's seed. He would be mighty and possess the gate of his enemies; and finally, with Abraham, maintain an everlasting kingdom. The Davidic promises that came later made it clear that God would be the Father of this special seed of Abraham, so that he would be Emmanuel – God with us – God revealing Himself in a Son. In this Son the promise "I will be" would be fulfilled, though, as we shall see later, all the steps of the developing purpose are part of the "I will be", including the creation of His holy nation Israel at the Exodus.

After the announcement *Ehyeh asher Ehyeh* – "I WILL BE WHO I WILL BE" – God adds, "Thou shalt say unto the children of

Israel, I AM hath sent me unto you". The Hebrew here is the name *Yahweh* and should be translated "He who will be". Brother C. C. Walker commented on the two words *Ehyeh* and *Yahweh*:

> "Here, as a matter of truth and grammatical accuracy, the difference between Ehyeh and Yahweh should be noted once for all. Ehyeh, though but one word in the Hebrew, is in itself a complete sentence, and being translated into English is 'I will be', as sufficiently appears from Exodus 3:12. The Hebrew word Yahweh is not so, but is a 'singular verbal noun' meaning 'He who will be', as Dr. Thomas correctly puts it in *Phanerosis*, page 47."[1]

Accepted for over a century

This understanding of the memorial name has been maintained in our community for over a century. Brother J. W. Thirtle wrote a long article in *The Christadelphian* in 1881 (pages 206-215) supporting the future tense translation, and quoting various outside sources that accepted that the word conveyed a prophetic sense. Brother C. C. Walker in *Theophany* has an introductory chapter which opens with an extract from J. W. Thirtle, and further on he says:

> "In *Eureka* and *Phanerosis* Dr. Thomas wrote much about the name Yahweh. Though alone in grasping the interpretation of the word Yahweh, he is not alone in holding that the name is a prophetic one. Also, when he says that the words Ehyeh asher Ehyeh, found in Exodus 3:14, mean 'I will be who I will be' he only says something which no sober Hebraist, unbiased and unprejudiced, would like to be charged with questioning. Our present purpose is to show that in dealing with the interpretation of the Memorial Name of God, Dr. Thomas has, in several particulars, the support of the learned."[2]

Brother John Carter reprinted *Phanerosis* (together with other works of Brother Thomas) in 1954. In the preface he

---

1 *Theophany*, page 35.

2 *Ibid.*, page 2.

referred to the circumstances of the origin of *Phanerosis*, written some 100 years earlier, and added:

> "On one important point he [Brother Thomas] has been abundantly vindicated. His teaching on the Yahweh name, both in his adoption of the translation Yahweh and his exposition of the meaning of the name, stands firm. In many points scholars since his day have written what endorses his position. But his knowledge of the divine purpose of redemption which will reach its goal when 'God is all in all' and mortality swallowed up of life, enabled him to open up the fulness of the meaning which others have not reached."

The Yahweh name at the Exodus

The meaning of the Yahweh name may best be understood by considering the emphasis given to it at the Exodus. In chapter 3 the angel of God declared the Yahweh name; and in chapter 6 after Pharaoh had increased his oppression of the children of Israel, the angel spoke of the Yahweh name as a new development:

> "Then the LORD said unto Moses, Now shalt thou see what I will do to Pharaoh: for with a strong hand shall he let them go, and with a strong hand shall he drive them out ... And God spake unto Moses, and said unto him, I am the LORD [Yahweh]: and I appeared unto Abraham, unto Isaac, and unto Jacob, by the name of God Almighty, but by my name JEHOVAH [Yahweh] was I not known to them. And I have established my covenant with them, to give them the land of Canaan, the land of their pilgrimage, wherein they were strangers." (Exodus 6:1-4)

We note that the announcement of the name is closely associated with the promises and covenant with Abraham. The significance of this will appear as we proceed.

It is often thought that the reference to the two names "God Almighty" and "Jehovah" means that Abraham, Isaac and Jacob had never heard of the name Jehovah or Yahweh. But that is not the case. The words 'know' and 'not known' are used in a fuller sense than this. The Hebrew word *yada*, properly means, 'to ascertain by seeing' (Strong), and is variously translated in different contexts showing that the word carries the sense of full association and experience, rather than merely acquaintance. We can see how this applies to the name God Almighty, which the angel says Abraham, Isaac and Jacob had 'known'.

The Hebrew for 'God Almighty' is *El Shaddai*. *El* is a basic title for God describing His illimitable strength, as the source of all life and creation. Translating *Shaddai* as Mighty Ones (succourers), the title El Shaddai tells us that God is the power and authority behind the activity of the angels, His mighty ones, caring for His people. So the patriarchs knew God by the strength of the angels who carried out His wishes (see Psalm 103:20). These they knew in a very full sense. God's angels talked with Abraham and Jacob; they gave instructions to the patriarchs in the name of God; they cared for them, guiding them, making promises, and showing their power. Not surprisingly at the end of his life Jacob spoke of "the Angel which redeemed me from all evil". In a very real way the patriarchs 'knew' the title El Shaddai.

The name Yahweh linked with salvation

In this sense of acquaintance and experience the patriarchs did not 'know' the name Yahweh. But that they used the word is clear from various situations in the Genesis record. Four times we read that Abraham built altars to Yahweh and called upon the name of Yahweh (Genesis 12:8; 13:4,18; 21:33). It is not satisfactory to speculate that Moses in writing his record substituted the word Yahweh for some other name of God. It is only necessary to ask, Did Abraham call on the name of Yahweh or not? The record tells us that he did. Furthermore in Genesis 15 it is recorded that Abraham spoke directly to God using the words Lord GOD – *Adonai Yahweh* (verses 2,8).

Even more emphatic is Genesis 22:14. After Abraham had offered Isaac on Mount Moriah, we read:

> "And Abraham called the name of the place Jehovah-Jireh: as it is said to this day, In the mount of the LORD it shall be seen."

Did Abraham call the place Yahweh (Jehovah)-Jireh? The record says he did. Clearly in some sense Abraham, and also Isaac and Jacob, knew and used the name Yahweh.

It would appear that the name Yahweh was known in a limited sense long before the time of Abraham. We read at the end of Genesis 4:

> "And to Seth, to him also was born a son; and he called his name Enos: then began men to call on the name of the LORD [Yahweh]." (verse 26)

Seth and Enos were in the line of the covenant people, who understood the meaning of the promise of "the seed of the woman"; and in worship they recognised God's plan of redemption in the name of Yahweh.

Going back still earlier, it is surely significant that the word Yahweh is first used in Genesis 2 and 3 where the theme of sin and redemption through the promised seed is revealed.

From all this we conclude that the name of Yahweh is intended to be associated with God's purpose and promises. In line with this we find that as the detail of God's purpose is unfolded to Abraham in the several promises, the word Yahweh occurs, especially in the final occasion at the offering of Isaac:

> "By myself have I sworn, saith the LORD [Yahweh] ... that in blessing I will bless thee ... and thy seed shall possess the gate of his enemies." (Genesis 22:15-17)

Promises about to be fulfilled

We return to the passage in Exodus 6:3. Appreciating the full sense of the word 'know', we can understand that up to this point in time the name Yahweh, "He who will be", had only been a matter of promise. But now God's people were to know the name in a fuller sense. They were about to witness the beginning of the *fulfilment* of the promises. Note the active "I will ..." in verses 4-8 that follow. Israel were to see, experience and know, mighty deeds and wonders by which God was in part fulfilling His promises:

> "And I have established my covenant with them [the patriarchs] to give them the land of Canaan ... and I have remembered my covenant ... I am Yahweh, and *I will bring you* from under the burdens of the Egyptians, and *I will rid you* out of their bondage, and *I will redeem you* with a stretched out arm, and with great judgments: and *I will take you to me ... I will be to you a God ... I will bring you in unto the land*, concerning the which I did sware to give it to Abraham, to Isaac, and to Jacob; and *I will give it* you for an heritage." (Exodus 6:4-8)

This was the first time God was to manifest His power and judgements before the world in the fulfilment of His purpose in Israel. It was the beginning of a manifestation which would finally result in the earth being full of His glory.

The name emphasised

How understandable, then, that God should at this particular time give such emphasis to His memorial name:

1. God said to Moses, 'I will be who I will be'.
2. Moses was to say to Israel, Yahweh, 'He who will be', hath sent me unto you.
3. And again, Yahweh, God of Abraham, Isaac and Jacob, hath sent me unto you.
4. This is my name, my memorial to all generations.

From this point in Biblical history the divine purpose through Israel unfolds. It is taken out of Egypt and becomes the holy nation – *nationally* His son; it continues as His kingdom under His laws; in due time there is the great manifestation in a Son to sit upon the throne of Israel; and eventually through His Son God would manifest Himself in 'many sons', when Israel's new heavens and earth in which dwelleth righteousness (2 Peter 3:13) are established in the earth.

The memorial name

The titles of God gather up all this glorious purpose. Truly "Yahweh" is a memorial. It reminds us of this gracious purpose. This is *the* name of many names or titles of God, so precious to us because it expresses our redemption and sonship through God's Son. It is a memorial in another sense: it is a remembrancer to God, similar to the rainbow:

> "And it shall come to pass, when I bring a cloud over the earth, that the bow shall be seen in the cloud: and I will remember my covenant." (Genesis 9:14,15)

The memorial to God's active unchanging existence ("I am") is in the creation around us. The memorial to what He intends to do with this earth is enshrined in the name Yahweh.

The quality of the name was expressed to Moses:

> "The LORD, the LORD God, merciful and gracious, long-suffering, and abundant in goodness and truth, keeping mercy for thousands, forgiving iniquity and transgression and sin, and that will by no means clear the guilty." (Exodus 34:6,7)

It is these divine qualities that at the highest level are to be the fulfilment of the memorial name. First and essentially in His Son, "full of grace and truth", and then in His "many sons". This is how His glory will fill the earth.

To this name we have been called: high honour indeed, to be joined to the Israel of God; to be part of the gleanings from among the Gentiles. "Simeon hath declared how God did visit the Gentiles, to take out of them a people *for His name*" (Acts 15:14). The taking out must surely be nearly complete and then the name will be revealed in the manifestation of the sons of God and their King.

4 |

Examining the angels

(Jason Hensley, 2009)

Few Christian churches place the emphasis Christadelphians do on the fact that often in scripture when Yahweh is said to be speaking, His words were in fact being voiced by angels. At the beginning of his book on God Manifestation, *Unlocking the Mystery*, Brother Jason Hensley gives a useful modern day example of how the idea of 'name-bearing' works.

He asks the reader to imagine telephoning the customer service helpline of a company (he uses the example of the tech giant Apple). The customer service advisor, let's call him Fred, is a human being, not a multinational corporation. With regard to that phone call however, he becomes to us Apple itself. If we later relayed good advice Fred gave us, we would say that 'Apple told me to do this'. On the other hand, if Fred was rude to us we wouldn't tell our friends that Fred gave us bad service, we would say instead that Apple gave us bad service. In this way, we refer to Fred as Apple, as he is Apple's representative to us.

In a later chapter in his book, abridged below, Brother Jason discusses how the angels fulfil this representative role with regard to Yahweh Himself by means of a helpful list of worked examples.

THE angels are the messengers of God, going about to do His bidding. They speak His words, follow His will, and perform actions for Him. Angels are the representatives of God. Throughout this chapter, we will see how angels, just as Apple's employee, can carry the name of God and act on His behalf. We will do this by studying six different incidents in which angels were God's representatives, and even called "Yahweh". We will see that they could be called this because they were working for Him, because they were following His will and acting on His behalf. With this understanding, we will be able to see how certain "mysteries" of scripture become more apparent.

---

1 | The flight of Hagar

MANY promises had been made to Abram, which included a seed who would possess the land. Despite the fact that his wife Sarai had not yet been able to have children, Abram still believed what his God had told him. The years went by and still Sarai did not have a son. Her closed womb was troublesome, and thus Sarai came to Abram asking him to take Hagar, her Egyptian slave, as a wife and to try to have an heir through her. We all know the end of the story.

Because Hagar was able to have a son, she began to feel as though she were better than Sarai and despised her. As her master, Sarai treated her firmly for her behaviour, and Hagar ran away. While she was in the wilderness, one of God's angels appeared to her.

Take some time to examine Genesis 16:10-13 and then ask yourself "Who was it that spoke to Hagar?" It was an angel of the Lord – God's angel. Now, go through these four verses and note all of the phrases and words that would indicate to us that the angel was speaking God's words. After you have looked through the quotation, here are the things that I have noticed:

1. The angel actually said "I will surely multiply your offspring". This seems as though it would have been what God said to Hagar, speaking through the angel.
2. After the angel is finished speaking, the scripture tells us that Hagar "called the name of the LORD who spoke to her". Scripture tells us that "Yahweh" spoke to her.

You might have found some other indications as well, which just serve to reinforce this point. The angel who spoke to Hagar could come and speak God's words for Him. He was a representative of God, and so could speak the words of God to Hagar. Because he was God's representative, it was as though God had spoken the words, and so scripture writes, "she called the name of the LORD that spake unto her". It was Yahweh who had spoken to her through the angel. Angels are God's ambassadors, and we will see even further their ability to represent God by seeing them called by His name, "Yahweh".

2 | The destruction of Sodom and Gomorrah

A FEW chapters after the incident with Hagar, Abraham was then visited by Yahweh. This visit begins in Genesis 18:1,2.

We see there that Yahweh appeared to Abraham. If you read through the passage you will notice that "the LORD" is referred to often, so we can be sure that scripture wanted us to understand that it was Yahweh Himself who visited Abraham.

"The LORD" was there speaking to him. This is God's name, so it would make sense that it was He who was there speaking to Abraham. He was there. He appeared to Abraham, Abraham and Sarah prepared a meal for Him and He ate with Abraham, speaking to him about the promises. However, as we read through the chapter, God says something fairly striking, something that does not seem to fit with our understanding of God at all.

Look through Genesis 18:20,21. What is strange about these verses if it was literally Yahweh who had been speaking to Abraham?

> "I will go down now, and see whether they have done altogether according to the cry of it, which is come unto me; and if not, I will know."

If this is actually the Lord, then this saying seems very strange. It is written of our God that "there is no searching of

His understanding" (Isaiah 40:28). God knows everything that is taking place, for His understanding is limitless! Unless we understand this as speaking of representatives of God who were bearing His name, something seems very wrong. How could God not know what was going on in Sodom? Why would He have to go and see if things were as bad as He had heard? He would have known already! The way to reconcile the omniscience of God and this passage is to say that something was there representing Yahweh. Could they be angels? Let us continue to follow the story:

> "And the men turned their faces from thence, and went toward Sodom: but Abraham stood yet before the LORD."
> (Genesis 18:22)

Thus, one of these men stood before Abraham and spoke to him. From there comes the dialogue in which Abraham seeks to reason with God. He pleads to God to save Sodom if fifty righteous are found therein, then drops down to forty, then moves down to thirty, and so on. The other two men go down to Sodom as "the LORD" (remember that God had said that he would go to Sodom?). So, all three of the men represent God and are called by His name. The two men go down to Sodom as "the LORD" in order to fulfill what God had said in verses 20,21. Then, the other man stays before Abraham to speak to him and this man is called "Yahweh" as well (verse 22).

If the story just ended there, we would only be able to speculate about who these "men" were. All three of them were called "the LORD", and yet they were not omniscient. It is probably very tempting for many Trinitarians to look at this passage and try to squeeze the Trinity into it. However, the story does not end there; in fact, we can follow the two men who left for Sodom. When we do that, a very powerful revelation is opened up.

> "And there came two angels to Sodom at even; and Lot sat in the gate of Sodom: and Lot seeing them rose up to meet them; and he bowed himself with his face toward the ground."
> (Genesis 19:1)

Two angels! It is just as we had thought earlier when God had said "I will go down now and see whether they have done altogether according to the cry of it". In this passage, the ones called "Yahweh" were three angels bearing God's name. In Genesis 18:21, two men left to go to Sodom. In Genesis 19:1, two angels arrived at Sodom. Do we need a stronger connection? These three men that visited Abraham were angels who were called by God's name! They bore His name as His representatives. They were acting on His behalf.

A quick summary

We have now looked at two incidents in which angels were God's representatives, even being called "Yahweh" in the last example. I find God Manifestation through the angels to be a truly fascinating concept. The logic of the case is wonderful, and the scriptural proof is abundant. In addition, these are not things that you would notice just casually reading through the chapters. God hides the truths about Himself and wants us to dig deep to find them. It is like buried treasure that we have seek out.

Finding this treasure, we learn that as a messenger or ambassador of God, an angel can essentially speak God's words for Him, can act on His behalf, and can make decisions with His authority. It is important for us that we understand this concept, because it will be a powerful help in our understanding of Jesus' relationship with God. In order to understand God Manifestation with the angels better, we will look at four more examples of representative angels being called "the LORD".

3 | Jacob's angel

OUR next example begins with Jacob in Egypt. In Genesis 48:15,16 Jacob blesses the children of Joseph. If you examine the words that Jacob speaks here, you will notice a slight change in the way that he refers to the one who was watching over him. First, he begins by speaking of the God of his fathers, the God of

Abraham and Isaac. This is the word "elohim" that we had studied earlier, now applied to an angel! He is speaking of the God who fed him all of his life, and then suddenly, he calls that same God "the Angel which redeemed me from all evil". Here, Jacob is speaking of an angel who followed him, an angel who watched over him, an angel who provided for him throughout his life and he calls that angel "God" or "mighty one". When we see something referred to as "God" it does not have to mean that the thing referred to is part of the deity! Instead, as it is here, the word could be speaking of the being as one who is mighty. As we now take a trip back through the life of Jacob to examine this angel, we will see that Jacob's angel was called "God" many times, and also actually called "the LORD" or "Yahweh" throughout these experiences. The first experience that we will observe is based on an incident at Bethel.

You are probably familiar with the story, commonly known as Jacob's ladder. Jacob lay down in Bethel with a rock as his pillow. While he was sleeping, he dreamed about a ladder that reached forth from the earth, all the way up to heaven. On this ladder, he saw angels ascending and descending, going from heaven to earth and from earth to heaven. Above the ladder, Jacob saw Yahweh – he saw "the LORD" – who then spoke to him, saying "I am the LORD God of Abraham thy father, and the God of Isaac ..." Jacob saw the Lord and the Lord called Himself "Yahweh". This incident took place early in Jacob's life in the place called Bethel (Genesis 28:19). Let us then venture three chapters further, when Jacob called together his wives Rachel and Leah, telling them that it was time for them to leave their father's household.

If you read Genesis 31:11-13 you will notice that it was an angel that had spoken to Jacob. The angel called out his name, "Jacob", and then proceeded to speak to him about the animals of Laban. He then says, "I am the God of Bethel, where thou anointest the pillar, and where thou vowest a vow unto me". The angel just told Jacob that he was the God from Bethel! The *angel* was the one that Jacob saw above the ladder, the one that scripture called "the LORD"! He is the one that Jacob gazed upon during his dream! Is this not amazing? Again, this was probably the same angel that had followed Jacob throughout his life, a personal angel, who, as Jacob said, "redeemed me from all evil". This was the angel that had taken care of him, the same one that he referred to in Genesis 48. This angel was called Yahweh. This angel bore God's name and authority because he was God's representative. Let us follow the angel through another incident in Jacob's life.

Reading Genesis 32:28-30 we find Jacob wrestling, struggling with a man and Jacob would not let him go until the man had blessed him. Finally, the man blessed him by changing his name. Israel was his new name, and its meaning was 'Prince with God', hence, why the man told him "for as a prince hast thou power with God and with men, and hast prevailed". He had wrestled with the man, with "God", and had prevailed. In addition to this, Jacob also calls the man "God", "for I have seen God face to face, and my life is preserved". It sounds as though he believed that he had seen Yahweh face to face. Within this selection of verses, two references are made to the man being God. However, let us turn to the prophets and we will see the true identity of this man:

> "He took his brother by the heel in the womb, and by his strength he had power with God: yea, he had power over the angel, and prevailed: he wept, and made supplication unto him: he found him in Bethel, and there he spake with us."
>
> (Hosea 12:3,4)

These words in Hosea are looking back to the life of Jacob, speaking of his birth, when he grabbed Esau's heel in the womb (Genesis 25:26); then looking to the incident that we just read about in Genesis 32, wrestling with God. But now, Hosea adds something. "He had power with God: yea, he had power over the angel, and prevailed." Note the connection between the words spoken when Jacob is given his new name and the words said here. The man told Jacob that he had power with God and had prevailed. Hosea says that Jacob had power with the angel and had prevailed. Again, from looking at the context we can see that Hosea is talking about the same incident as Genesis. The man that Jacob had struggled with was an angel! And in Genesis the angel is called God!

When we bring all of these experiences together, we see that there was an angel that was taking care of Jacob all throughout his life. We saw the angel in Bethel, we saw him struggling with Jacob just before he met Esau, and we saw Jacob reference him in Egypt. This angel was called God multiple times, and even once referred to as "the LORD".

This was not because he was God, not by any means! But instead, the angel was a representative of God. He could do things for God, speak God's words, and be called by God's name.

---

4 | The burning bush

ONE of the strongest examples of God manifestation in the angels occurs at the burning bush. Many of us know the story very well. Moses was on Mount Horeb tending the flocks of his father-in-law, Jethro.

An angel of the Lord appeared to Moses (Exodus 3:2,3). The angel appeared as a fiery, glowing heat that was burning on a bush, but not actually destroying it. This was an amazing scene! Imagine what it would be like for you if you were working at your job and suddenly you saw something taking place that you knew was impossible. This would be something that would catch your attention and draw you towards it, just as it did to Moses. An angel had just appeared to him.

As the chapter progresses, God spoke to Moses out of the bush and charged him to bring the Israelites out of Egypt. But, after being rejected as their deliverer forty years previously (see Acts 7:25-30), Moses was still hesitant. He did not want to go back to the people who had cast him aside. He explained, "When I come to the elders of Israel and say 'the God of your fathers has sent me to you,' and they say 'what is His name?' What shall I say?"

It is here at the burning bush that God revealed His memorial name "Yahweh" to Moses, "I will be whom I will be", as we understand it. And then, hidden throughout this narrative, as is often the case with examples of God Manifestation, we see a connection that again calls an angel "Yahweh".

The angel had appeared to Moses in a flame of fire, Exodus 3:2. And now, speaking to him, God says, "Say unto them, 'The LORD God of your fathers, the God of Abraham, of Isaac, and of Jacob, appeared unto me'". Who was it that had appeared to Moses according to verse 2? Who was it that appeared to Moses according to verse 16? Moses had seen an angel. The angel was fiery, was burning a bush, and yet God told him to tell the people that "Yahweh" had appeared to him, in fact, the God of Abraham, that of Isaac, and that of Jacob. This angel was called by God's memorial name. And we can understand why! The angel was a representative of God. Yahweh was there, through the angel.

As we proceed through this entire experience, Moses is still reluctant to return to Egypt. At the beginning of chapter 4, he states, "They will say, The LORD hath not appeared unto thee". From there God even reinforces this fact – He had appeared to Moses through an angel (Exodus 4:1-5).

This time, Moses is actually given a sign to prove to people that Yahweh had appeared to him. For us, this is an emphasis that the angel who appeared to Moses could be called "the LORD". An angel appeared to Moses, told him to tell the elders that "Yahweh" had appeared to him, and then later gives him signs to prove to all of them that it was Yahweh that had actually appeared. This angel stood for God here because he was God to Moses. He was God's ambassador. Was he literally Yahweh? By no means, but he was His representative.

---

5 | The giving of the Law

WHEN the Law of Moses was given to Israel, another scene of God Manifestation with the angels opens up. As we look at the New Testament quotations about the giving of the law, make a note in your mind of who it was that gave the law.

> "This is that Moses, which said unto the children of Israel, A prophet shall the Lord your God raise up unto you of your brethren, like unto me; him shall ye hear. This is he, that was in the church in the wilderness with the angel which spake to him in the mount Sina, and with our fathers: who received the lively oracles to give unto us." (Acts 7:37,38)

Stephen defended the Truth before a restless body of Jews. Throughout this testimony, he gave a fairly extensive history of Israel, showing how they had been strangers and wanderers all throughout their lives as a nation. He showed how God could be worshipped without a temple, and what true worship was really about. In the midst of this defence, he brought the Jews' minds back to Moses and the giving of the law:

> "This is he, that was in the church in the wilderness with the angel which spake to him in the mount Sina, and with our fathers: who received the lively oracles to give unto us."

"Sina" is the same as "Sinai". The law was spoken both to Moses and to the people, or the "fathers" as Stephen specifically says. From mount Sinai the fiery and blasting voice of an angel pierced through the sky. The law was heard throughout the congregation. It was an angel who spoke to Israel, an angel who had spoken to Moses and given the law, "the angel which spake to him in the mount Sina, and with our fathers". This same conclusion is brought out if we read Hebrews 2:1-3.

In that passage the apostle is contrasting the law and the new covenant through Christ. The word spoken by angels (that is, the law) was steadfast, and every time it was broken a consequence was given. Therefore, since our calling (the new covenant) was given by Jesus himself, how much more will we be punished if we disobey our calling? The writer is proving the superiority of Jesus over the angels (see his arguments in Hebrews 1)! Notice also that the angels were the ones who gave the law. While this is not the point of these particular verses, this is the point on which we will focus. The law was given by angels.

As we understand that, let us turn our attention to the actual law itself and what it tells us about its presenter.

In Exodus 20 we see the giving of the Ten Commandments, a well-known part of the law. From what we looked at in the New Testament, we understand that the law was given and spoken by angels. Compare this to the first few words of Exodus 20:

> "And God spake all these words, saying, I am the LORD thy God, which have brought thee out of the land of Egypt, out of the house of bondage." (Exodus 20:1,2)

Exodus tells us that God was speaking these things, and in addition to that, God says, "I am the LORD thy God". This again is another example of God Manifestation through the angels that can only be discovered through careful study and comparing passages. The law was given by angels, and the angels who gave it were called "God" and said to the nation "I am the LORD thy God"! As you turn a few chapters forward, you see the same thing. More laws were given, and as we read earlier they were given by angels. But, in Exodus 25:1 we are told "the LORD spake unto Moses, saying ..."

It was "Yahweh" who spoke these words. And yet from comparing all four passages, we realise that it was angels who possessed God's name that were speaking. The angels could be called Yahweh. God Manifestation through the angels (and men as well) is found all throughout scripture; it occurs with the angel who meets Joshua just before the people pass into Jericho (Joshua 5:13–6:5). It takes place with the angel who led Israel through the wilderness as a cloud and pillar of fire (Exodus 14:19; Deuteronomy 1:32,33). As well, the Lord Jesus brings it up to the Jews when they want to stone him for calling himself the Son of God (John 10:34-36). We will examine one more example together – it is hidden in the story of Balaam.

6 | Balaam and Balak

WHEN we think of Balaam, we think of a talking donkey, or more so, a rebuking donkey. Balaam was a diviner, a prophet who worked for hire. He was hired by Balak, the king of Moab, to curse the people of Israel. Often as we read through these chapters, it may be almost painful to see Balaam trying to edge himself around God's boundaries, and then to see God pull him back in, even using such means as a talking donkey. The story begins with Balak's servants appearing to Balaam and asking him if he will go with them and curse Israel. Balaam responds by telling them to stay the night and he will see what the Lord speaks to him.

God's response was "no" (Numbers 22:8-12). Balaam was not to go with the messengers. He could not curse these people, they were blessed, they were the people of Yahweh, those who were called by His name. Thus, Balaam sent the people home. But Balak was not willing to hear a "no" from Balaam; again he sent his messengers, and this time – following the prophet's initial disobedience which merited a divine rebuke – he was told that he could go with them (verse 35).

He was allowed to go, yet whatever word God spoke to him, he had to speak. He was tied to speaking the words of the Lord. This will come up all throughout this story; Balak will want Balaam to say something different, because God only allows Balaam to bless Israel rather than curse them. But, Balaam constantly has to remind Balak that he can only speak Yahweh's words. Here are some more instances in which Balaam reiterates this point:

> "Have I now any power at all to say any thing? The word that God putteth in my mouth, that shall I speak." (verse 38)
>
> "And Balaam said unto Balak, Stand by thy burnt offering and I will go: peradventure the LORD will come to meet me: and whatsoever he sheweth me I will tell thee." (23:3,4)
>
> "And he answered and said, Must I not take heed to speak that which the LORD hath put in my mouth?" (verse 12)
>
> "And the LORD met Balaam, and put a word in his mouth, and said, Go again unto Balak, and say thus." (verse 16)

The Lord met Balaam. The Lord spoke to Balaam and He was in control. God was putting these words in Balaam's mouth.

But, as we will see, the one called “the LORD” is again an angel. By digging a little deeper, we can find some telling clues as to the angel’s identity. Let us look at the time just after Balaam’s donkey spoke to him – the angel of the Lord had stood in the donkey’s path and then revealed himself to Balaam. He was not pleased that Balaam had left to go curse the people of Israel, but still gave him permission to go.

Think back to what we had read about Balaam and his words. He was only allowed to speak the words of Yahweh! Now, bring that together with what the angel says in Numbers 22:35: “Only the word that I shall speak unto thee, that thou shalt speak.” Balaam could only speak the words that the angel had spoken to him. He could only speak those things that the angel put into his mouth. This angel was the one that was called “the LORD” when “the LORD” appeared to Balaam. He was the one who gave Balaam the words to say, and he spoke the words on behalf of God. He was God’s representative. He was the one who had been coming to Balaam since the beginning of the story; he was the one that had originally told Balaam, ‘you can only speak my words’. This angel was a direct ambassador for God, and so when he appeared before Balaam, it was as though God had appeared. When he spoke to Balaam, he was speaking God’s words.

Unlocked mysteries

Angels show us a beautiful example of God Manifestation. When we understand this, there are a number of difficult passages that begin to make sense, and there are a handful of passages that many look at as a “mystery” that are actually understandable. For example, we are told that no man has ever seen God (1 John 4:12), yet many have seen Him.

5 |

"The express image of his person"

(Allan Harvey, 2000)

The Epistle to the Hebrews begins with a kind of statement of faith about the Lord Jesus Christ – he is the heir to the kingdom, the atoning sacrifice, the end of Creation. For the purpose of that epistle the main emphasis is on Christ as the exact manifestation of his Father, "*the express image of his person*".

Exodus 34 is often taken as a key text with regard to Yahweh's self-declaration of His name and character, verses 5-7 listing some of the attributes that make up His moral glory. In this article, from *The Christadelphian* of September 2000, Brother Allan Harvey links Exodus and Hebrews by showing how the New Testament portrays Jesus as having the same virtues as his Father.

GOD said: "I will make all my goodness pass before thee, and I will proclaim the name of the LORD." This was in answer to the request of Moses, "I beseech thee, shew me thy glory" (Exodus 33:18,19). Moses, it must be remembered, had already seen the glory in the Mount (24:15-18); but this was to be something different – the declaration of His name and character – *all* His goodness would now be revealed before Moses. So great would this manifestation be, that Moses could not behold it without a "vail" between him and the glory.

> "Behold ... thou shalt stand upon a rock: and ... while my glory passeth by, I will put thee in a cleft of the rock, and cover thee

> with my hand ... and thou shalt see my back parts: but my face shall not be seen." (33:22,23)

And so it came to pass. Early next morning he went up Mount Sinai and presented himself before the Lord who passed by before him and proclaimed:

> "The LORD, The LORD God, merciful and gracious, longsuffering, and abundant in goodness and truth, keeping mercy for thousands, forgiving iniquity and transgression and sin, and that will by no means clear the guilty." (Exodus 34:5-7)

Here, then, the revealed glory was seen in His character – just as "the heavens declare the glory of God", so the very way He worked among His people declared the same message. How many times was the mercy of God extended toward them when they murmured, or rebelled or turned aside to Baal? Their sin then required the faithful intercession of Moses, "Forgive this people". To this the Almighty responded, and forgave their iniquity, transgression and sin. Their very existence testified to the longsuffering and goodness of their Lord.

The glory in Israel

His purpose with Israel revolved around their manifesting this character in their lives, both individually and nationally: "Be ye holy, as I the LORD your God am holy" was the injunction placed upon them; and the Law was so designed to lead them, if they would be obedient, in the path of holiness. The purpose was declared in the words, "I will dwell among the children of Israel, and will be their God" (Exodus 29:45). The word "dwell" really means to stay permanently in or inhabit, while the word "among" carries the idea of bisection; so the overall thought is that the Lord would enter into this nation, the entrance of His word giving light, and would permanently manifest His power and majesty in them. The true figure of Deity would thereby be stamped upon His people – they would be true "images of the invisible God". Paul expresses the thought in 2 Corinthians 6:16, "I will *dwell* in them and I will *walk* in them".

Sadly this never came to fruition for there was "none that doeth good, no not one". Of the best of them, some spake inadvisedly with their lips; others sinned in the matter of Uriah, or similar. Generations came and generations went and not one individual in all those generations could truly say, "I delight to do thy will" – until, at long last, God's own arm brought forth salvation and –

"God was manifest in the flesh"

In Jesus was seen the perfect reflection of the divine character; so perfect indeed that the writer to the Hebrews declares him to be "the *express image* of his person", and that Greek word, meaning 'engraving' or 'a figure stamped' is the word from which we derive our word 'character'. Jesus manifested the character so clearly that he could say, "He that hath seen me hath seen the Father". The word so entered and permanently "dwelt" in him – so stamped upon him was the figure of his Father – that he is called by John "The Word made flesh"; and this Word "dwelt [tabernacled] among us" (John 1:14). The tabernacle, in the day it was dedicated, was *filled* with the glory of God – no room for Moses or Aaron, they were excluded – and the glory was seen *over* the tabernacle, as though the majesty overflowed God's dwelling place. So John says, "We beheld his glory, the glory as of the only begotten of the Father, *full* of (literally 'covered over, overflowing with') grace and truth ... and of his fulness have all we received" (1:14-16). John then draws a contrast between Jesus and Moses: "No man hath seen God at any time; the only begotten Son, which is *in the bosom* of the Father, he hath *declared* him" (verse 18). Moses was hidden in the cleft of a rock, seeing but the back parts; whereas Jesus was enfolded by the Father and openly revealed Him. All the goodness of God was seen to pass by before the people, if they had but eyes to see and ears to hear, as he "preached righteousness in the great congregation ... I have *declared* thy faithfulness and thy salvation" (Psalm 40:8-10). Yet as he did so, the elders had the audacity to say, "Thou hast a devil".

He did not hide God's righteousness nor refrain his lips; but in all his words and in all his actions he unfolded his Father, to the end that as he approached his final hour he could say in the prayer recorded in John 17, "I have *manifested thy name* unto the men thou gavest me".

The character declared

Throughout his ministry Jesus was seen to be:

- "**Merciful**": the Hebrew speaks of compassion – and how many times do we read of his compassion extended to those in need? A leper came to him: "Lord, if thou wilt thou canst make me clean" (Mark 1:40). This man had no doubt of the Master's ability to cleanse him of his leprosy; to him the big question was, Would he? We then read, "Jesus, moved with *compassion* ... touched him ... I will; be thou clean". The Widow of Nain, following the funeral procession of her only son, must have presented an unhappy picture as our Lord entered that city, so "when the Lord saw her, he had *compassion* on her ... and said, Weep not" and raised the lad (Luke 7:11-15). When, in Matthew 14:14, he saw a great multitude he was again "moved with *compassion* toward them and healed their sick". On all these occasions the Master declared his Father, for of Him it is written, "The LORD is gracious and full of compassion" (Psalm 145:8).
- "**Gracious**": the original word speaks of 'bending in kindness to an inferior' or 'to favour'. Psalm 45 speaks eloquently of him and verse 2 says, "Grace is poured into thy lips". Little wonder therefore that in the synagogue in Nazareth "they marvelled at the gracious words" he spake; words taken from Isaiah, of release, deliverance and liberty – the ultimate Jubilee – as he preached the acceptable year of the Lord. Or the words of our Lord as he hung on the cross, "Father, forgive them; they know not what they do". Whether he there prayed for the soldiers or for the people who, goaded by their leaders, had called for his death is

not absolutely clear: if for Israel, then there is a passage in Jeremiah that is so applicable in its Messianic context: "Pray not thou for this people, neither lift up cry nor prayer for them, neither make intercession to me: for I will not hear thee" (7:16). Yet we suggest that is precisely what he did; he interceded, as Moses had done so many times in the wilderness when he stood between the Lord and the people.

- "**Longsuffering**": just as the longsuffering of God waited in the days of Noah, when the divine patience recognised, and responded to, the needs of a faithful man, so Jesus reacted to others. Paul says: "I obtained mercy, that in me first Jesus Christ might shew forth all longsuffering" (1 Timothy 1:16). Philip, after three years close association with his Lord, failed to appreciate that Christ was "declaring" his Father, so the request he made of Jesus, "Shew us the Father", could have been a source of irritation to the Master; nevertheless the patience of Jesus shines through in his reply: "He that hath seen me hath seen the Father."
- "Abundant in **Goodness** and Truth": the word *chesed* (goodness) speaks of lovingkindness, a divine characteristic extended to the rebellious house of Israel: "Let him that glorieth glory in this, that he understandeth and knoweth me, that I am the LORD which exercise lovingkindness, judgement, and righteousness in the earth: for in these things I delight, saith the LORD" (Jeremiah 9:24). So the Lord Jesus manifested the same character. His invitation to "Come unto me" was heeded by many. One came, but was unable to measure up to the requirements of the Master; yet we read, "Then Jesus beholding him loved him" (Mark 10:21). Others responded and became "his own": "When Jesus knew that his hour was come ... having loved his own ... he loved them unto the end" (John 13:1). Therefore it was written of him, "I have not concealed thy lovingkindness and thy truth from the great congregation" (Psalm 40).

- "Abundant in Goodness and **Truth**": the word *emeth* suggests not so much a statement of faith but rather faithfulness, certainty, stability and trustworthiness. Here it describes one who is the fountain of all these; the source of all truth and reliability, who revealed Himself in His only begotten Son. Therefore "grace and *truth* came by Jesus Christ"; and he said to those Jews who believed on him, "If ye continue in my word ... ye shall know the truth, and the truth shall make you free". How sad that he found it necessary to say later, "Ye seek to kill me, a man that hath told you the truth, which I have heard of God". To us he remains, and ever remains, "the Way, the Truth and the Life".
- "**Keeping mercy for thousands**": again the word is *chesed* – lovingkindness, here associated with thousands, the 144,000 who are redeemed because he first loved us, and gave himself for us.
- "**Forgiving iniquity, transgression and sin**": a woman taken in adultery was brought to him (what happened to the man?): "Master, Moses commanded that such should be stoned: but what sayest thou?" He bent down and wrote in the ground (cf. Jeremiah 17:13). He then said to the woman, "Neither do I condemn thee: go and sin no more" (John 8:3-11). Again, a paralysed man, brought for a cure for his physical illness; Jesus first cured his 'character illness': "Son, thy sins be forgiven thee."
- "**By no means clearing the guilty**": here is the righteous judge of Isaiah 11, before whom no repentant person could ever be condemned; yet no evil doer be justified. Therefore he said, "Woe unto you scribes and Pharisees, hypocrites ... blind guides ... whited sepulchres". They claimed to serve God, but he revealed their true state. One example, quoted above, suggests he wrote the names of the woman's accusers "in the earth" – because they had "departed from the fountain of living waters" (Jeremiah 17). Their names

were never to be written in heaven; so beginning at the eldest they left him.

The true image seen

So we see that in every word, in every action, he revealed his Father's character; truly he was the express image of the Father. As the divine glory shone in and upon the tabernacle to an overflowing capacity (Exodus 38:34), so did the divine majesty shine in the character of Jesus: an awe-inspiring sight for those who could behold it; howbeit some perhaps not realising just what they saw.

- Soldiers, sent to take him, returned empty-handed: "Never man spake like this man."
- Nicodemus added his testimony: "No man doeth the miracles that thou doest except God be with him."
- Bartimaeus, in his blindness, saw the glory pass by and, following, received his sight.
- Zacchaeus saw the glory and climbed a tree to obtain a better view – and received the Master into his home.
- Another saw the glory, came running – and went away sorrowing, because he had great possessions.
- Others saw it – and went away plotting his death: "This is the heir, come, let us kill him."

The exhortation

By God's grace we too have seen the glory of God in the face of Jesus Christ – so what is our response?

> "If then ye be risen with Christ, seek those things that are above ... Set your affection on things above ... For ye are dead, and your life is hid with Christ in God [not in the cleft of a rock in Horeb, but in the ultimate Rock of our salvation]. When Christ, who is our life, shall appear, then shall ye also appear with him in glory." (Colossians 3:1-4)

But this is conditional on our response in the days of our probation:

> "Mortify therefore your members which are upon earth; fornication, uncleanness, covetousness ... also *put off* all these; anger, wrath, malice, blasphemy, filthy communication out of your mouth. Lie not one to another, seeing ye have *put off* the old man ... and have *put on* the new man." (verses 5-10)

A character change is therefore expected, or rather demanded, of the disciple of the Lord; we are no longer our own, for we have been bought with a price – the Blood of Christ. However, if we do succeed in putting off these works of the flesh to a greater or lesser extent, we must not leave a void in our way of life. So Paul continues –

> "*Put on* therefore, as the elect of God, holy and beloved, bowels of *mercies*, *kindness*, humbleness of mind, meekness, *longsuffering*: forbearing one another, *forgiving* one another." (verses 12,13)

This is the character revealed in Exodus 33, and manifested by Jesus, which must now be cultivated in us. The "image" will thus be stamped upon us, so that in a measure the goodness of God will be seen – though we have this treasure in earthen vessels, and never rise to the high standard of our Lord.

> "And above all these things *put on* love, which is the bond of perfectness. And let the peace of God rule in your hearts ... Let the word of Christ dwell in you richly ..." (verses 14-16)

He was the Word made flesh; in him dwelt the fulness of the Godhead bodily; now we must follow his example. Without him we could never gain salvation; but through him we shall become sons and daughters of the Living God.

"We shall be like him ... what greater could our Father's love prepare?"

6 |

The Man of the One

(John Thomas, 1869)

In Daniel 10, the prophet is given a vision of a blindingly glorious human figure, a sight so powerful that it left him physically trembling on the ground. In the following extract from his pamphlet *Phanerosis* (see pages 79-103, *Phanerosis and Other Writings*, The Christadelphian, 1954), Brother Thomas interprets this symbolic man to be the "multitudinous Christ", representing in one figure Christ and the immortalized saints as the ultimate manifestation of God. He goes on to explain the significance of the details of the description given in the passage. To differing degrees, elements of the vision can be found in a number of other passages, such as Daniel 7, Ezekiel 1, Zechariah 14, Revelation 1 and Revelation 10.

IN this chapter he records a vision of very remarkable character, which he saw while in company with certain persons on the banks of Hiddekel or Tigris. The basis of what he saw was *ish-echahd*, **the Man of the One**, rendered in the English version, "a certain man". It was not a real man, but "the appearance of a man" (Daniel 10:18), or "like the similitude of the sons of Adam" (verse 16). Hence, it was a symbolical representation.[1] It was the shadowy representation of "*the Man*

1 A *symbol* is a form of comprehending divers parts. As a whole it is a compendious abstract of something else than itself – much in a condensed form. A *symbolical*

of the One" **Eternal Spirit**. It was, therefore, truly "a certain man," not an uncertain one. The son of the old age of Zacharias and Elisabeth "*saw the Spirit* descending from heaven *like a Dove*" (John 1:32); and Daniel saw the same Spirit, "like the *similitude* of the sons of Adam". Now, the description he gives us of this **Spirit-Form** is, that he was clothed in linen, having also his *loins* girded with fine gold of Uphaz; his *body* was like the beryl, and his *face* as the appearance of lightning, and his *eyes* as lamps of fire, and his *arms* and his *feet* like in colour to polished brass, and the *voice* of his words like the *voice* of a multitude." He saw this in Eden, by "the third" of its rivers, "the Hiddekel", where "the Cherubim and the devouring fire" were originally located (Genesis 2:14; 3:24). This that he saw there was the same that Moses and the Israelites beheld on Sinai's top; and the effect of the sight on Daniel and his companions was the same as upon them – "all the people in the camp trembled" – so also, though Daniel only saw the vision, "a great quaking fell upon them that were with him, so that they fled to hide themselves"; and as for Daniel when left alone, he says, "there remained no strength in me, for my brightness was changed within me into corruption, and I retained no strength ... Neither was there breath left in me" (Daniel 10:8,18).

Here then was a symbolic man blazing in glory and power: and representative of the Eternal Spirit hereafter to be manifested in a **new order of elohim** – aggregately **One Man** – the One Man of the One Spirit, whom the true believers shall all come unto – "**a perfect man**" – into the measure of the full age of the fulness of the Christ: who is **the Head**, from whom the whole Body, fitly joined together and compacted by that which every joint [heir] supplieth, according to the effectual working in the measure of every part, maketh increase of the Body unto the edifying of itself in love" (Ephesians 4:3,4,13,15,16). Daniel saw the "perfect man" – the Eternal manifested in the glorified flesh of a multitude – symbolically represented in the measure of his full age.

---

representation is the act of showing by forms or types the real thing intended – it is the shadowy form of a true substance; and in the chapter before us that substance so potentially foreshadowed is Christ personal and corporate.

The "thing" that was revealed to the prophet at the Tigris was also seen of John in Patmos. "I saw", saith he, "in the midst of the Seven Lampstands a thing like [*homoion*] to a Son of Man, having been clothed to the foot, and girt around the breast with a golden girdle; also his head and the hairs white, as it were wool white as snow, and his eyes as a flame of fire; and his feet resembled transparent brass, as if they had been burning in a furnace; and his voice as the sound of many waters: and having in his right hand Seven Stars; and proceeding forth out of his mouth a two-edged broadsword; and his face as the sun shines in his strength." This represents the One Body, of which Jesus is the head, prepared "to execute the judgment written". It is that One Body in its post-resurrectional development invested with omnipotence – the apocalyptic Spirit-Form, symbolical of the saints glorified in power.

"Clothed in linen"

Daniel informs us that the Spirit-Man he beheld was "clothed with linen"; while John tells us only that he was "clothed to the feet". Now this clothing is significant of the character and office of the persons represented by the symbol. The holy garments of Aaron and his sons were of linen, "to cover their nakedness", that when they ministered in the holy places "they bear not iniquity and die" (Exodus 28:42,43). Nakedness and iniquity are convertible terms in scripture; as also are "clothed" and righteous or holy. Hence, in Revelation 19:8, it is said of the Lamb's Wife, that "to her it was given that she should be arrayed in fine linen, pure and bright". Now they that constitute the bride "are called, and chosen, and faithful" (Revelation 17:14); "they follow the Lamb withersoever he goeth" (14:4); as his horse guards, "clothed in fine linen, white and pure", which is declared to be the righteousness of the saints" (Revelation 19:14,8); who are "redeemed from among men"; and made for God "kings and priests to reign on earth". Hence their clothing, which is sacerdotal and royal. The reader will understand, then, that the clothing peculiar to a symbol indicates the class of persons to which it refers. Thus in Revelation 15:6, "the Seven Angels", or messengers of the Spirit, who consummate the wrath of "the seven last plagues", are symbolical of the saints, including Jesus as their Head or Chief; for they are described as "clothed in pure and bright linen, and girded about the breasts with golden girdles".

"Girded with fine gold of Uphaz"

The linen and the gold are associated both by Daniel and John. The Spirit-Man symbolised to Daniel was "girded with fine gold of Uphaz". This Uphaz is the Ophir of other passages. In the times of the prophets it was the gold region of the earth, whence the most abundant supplies of the finest gold were obtained. The fitting up of the temple, which in its places and furniture was "the patterns of things in the heavens" – figures of the true heavenly things themselves – were all of gold, or of precious woods overlaid with gold; to wit, the Cherubim, the Ark of the Testimony, the Mercy-Seat, the Altar of Incense, the Seven-Branched Lampstand, the Table of Shew Bread, spoons, tongs, censers, hinges, staves, and so forth. And besides all this, the "holy garments for glory and beauty", worn by the High Priest, who officiated in this golden temple, were brilliant with gold and precious stones; such as, the breastplate of righteousness, the ephod, the mitre, or "helmet of salvation", etc. This was chosen as the most precious of all known metals, to represent the most precious of "heavenly things" before the Eternal Spirit – **faith perfected by trial**, which is "much more precious than of gold that perisheth, though it be refined by fire", and "without which it is impossible to please God" (Hebrews 11:6; James 2:22; 1 Peter 1:7; 2 Peter 1:1). It is the basis of righteousness unto life eternal; for "we are justified by faith" – the fine linen of righteousness is girded about the saints by the golden girdle of a tried faith. "When God hath tried me", saith Job, "I shall come forth as gold." Thus David, in celebrating the future glory of the New Order of Elohim, consisting of the King and his Brethren, styles the latter "the Queen" in Psalm 45:10, saying to his Majesty, "the Queen hath been placed at thy right hand in fine gold of Ophir". He then addresses the Consort of the Great King, who being the Eternal Spirit manifested in David's son, is both Father and Husband to the Bride ("thy Maker is thine Husband; Yahweh Tz'vaoth is His name; the Elohim of the whole earth shall be called" Isaiah 54:5) saying:

> "Hear, O Daughter and consider, and incline thine ear; and forget thy nation, and the house of thy father; and the King shall greatly desire thy beauty; for he is thy Lord, therefore do thou homage unto him. So the Daughter of Tyre with tribute, the rich of the people, shall supplicate thy favour. The Daughter of the King is all glorious within; her clothing is of interweavings of gold; in embroideries shall she be conducted to thee; the Virgins her companions, following her, shall be brought to thee. They shall be conducted with joyous shouts and exultation; they shall enter into the palace of the King."
> (Psalm 45:10-15)

Thus David sings of "the Spirit and the Bride", clothed in the holy garments of righteousness and faith, for glory and for beauty. They are apocalyptically represented as "a Great City", styled "the Holy City, New Jerusalem, having been prepared as a Bride adorned for her husband" – "a city of pure gold like to transparent crystal"; "the precious sons of Zion", saith the prophet, "are comparable to fine gold", for in their glory they are the spirit-incarnations of a tried and precious faith.

"His body was like the beryl"

Daniel next informs us concerning the Spirit-man – "the Man of the One" – that "His body was like the beryl". The "body" here is the "One Body" of which Paul speaks in his epistles; as, "the Ecclesia which is His body, the fulness of Him [the Spirit] who perfects all things in all [saints]". When the fulness is brought in the body will be complete (Romans 11:25; Ephesians 1:23); and it will then be "like a beryl". The original word in Daniel for this precious stone is *Tarshish*. It is said to have been so called because it was brought from Tarshish; but the learned are not agreed as to what particular gem is meant. The Greeks called it *beryllos*;

hence the word in the English version *beryl*; and Pliny says, it was rarely found elsewhere than in India, the Tarshish of the Bible. The prevailing opinion is that its colour is a bluish or sea-green. But the interpretation of the original depends upon the teaching in connection with the word, not upon the colour of the gem.

"His body was like a Tarshish." This word occurs in six other places in the original. In the first two it designates one of the three precious stones in the fourth row of the Aaronic breast-plate of righteousness, and answers to the tribe of *Dan* which signifies '*judge*'; and of Dan's career in the latter days, Jacob prophesied, saying:

> "Dan, as one of the tribes of Israel, shall avenge his nation. There shall be a Judge, a serpent in the way, an adder in the path, biting the heels of the horse, so that its rider shall fall backward. I have laid in wait for thy salvation, O Yahweh!"
>
> (Genesis 49:16-18; Hebrews 2:7)

That is, Jacob, who was about to die when he uttered these words, foresaw that he would sleep in the dust until Dan, as a lion's whelp, should leap from Bashan (Deuteronomy 33:22); that then, "in the latter days", would be the era of deliverance, when he would himself be saved, and all the tribes would do valiantly, and the Judge of Israel would avenge his nation, to the overthrow of their oppressors (Deuteronomy 32:29-43).

Here then is a destroying and conquering power associated with the *tarshish* or beryl in the breastplate of judgement. It is similarly associated by Ezekiel with the wheels of the Cherubic chariot. He says, "the appearance of the wheels and their work was as the aspect of the *tarshish*"; and their felloes were full of eyes, and so lofty, "that they were dreadful". And "the Spirit of the Living One was in the wheels". Hence they are styled, in Daniel 7:9, "The wheels of the Ancient of Days", whose description identifies him with "the Man of the One", and the apocalyptic "Son of Man": "His garment white as snow, and the hair of his head as pure wool; his throne flames of fire, *his wheels a consuming fire*." The eighth foundation gem (answering to the priestly tribe of Levi) of the wall of the golden city on which the name of an apostle is engraved, is a *tarshish* or beryl. We conclude then, from these premisses, that the tarshish-like body of the Spirit-Man seen by Daniel, is a priestly body or community, in which is incarnated the spirit of the Eternal; and that in the latter days, it will eventuate the great salvation in concert with the tribes of Israel, as a destroying and conquering power. This God-manifestation "is a consuming fire".

Such is the doctrinal interpretation of *tarshish* as a representative precious stone. The root from which it is derived, is also in harmony with the exposition; for *tarshish* is derived from *rahshash*, 'to break in pieces to destroy', which is the mission of the **Stone** *Power*, when the time comes to smite the Babylonian Image upon the feet (Daniel 2:34,35,44,45).

His face as the appearance of lightning

Literally "his *faces*" as the appearance of lightning; that is, the Faces of the Spirit through which the Eternal expresses His favour or indignation towards the posterity of Adam in the age to come. Every individual element of the heavenly Adam is a face of Daniel's symbolic man by synecdoche; a figure by which a part is taken for the whole, and is of general occurrence in the construction of symbols. It is by the expression of the face that the workings of the brain of one man are manifested to others. It is so, also, with the Eternal Spirit Yahweh. But as He hath said, "no man can see His face, and live"; His face then, when seen, is not His face peculiar to His person, but to certain other persons, the expression of whose faces is the exact representation of the workings of the Eternal Mind. During the times preceding Messiah's, the Elohim who appeared to Abraham, Job, Jacob, Moses, and the seventy, Manoah, Daniel, Zechariah, Mary, Jesus, and the apostles (of whom the only ones named are Gabriel and Michael), are the faces of Yahweh, with respect to man; but when Messiah's times arrive, new faces will flash upon the world, and give expression to the pent-up fires that burn in the Eternal Mind against the kings, the clerical orders, and the intoxicated peoples of the earth. All these faces of Yahweh, both old and new, are "against them that do evil"; but "shine upon" the heirs of salvation. The faces of the Eternal Spirit are symbolized by the faces of the Cherubim in Ezekiel 1:10, 10:14 and Revelation 4:7. But as we are not now engaged upon these passages, we shall not enter further upon their exposition at present.

When Yahweh is angry (and "He is angry with the wicked" and therefore with the clergy "every day"), and when the time arrives for the manifestation of His wrath, His anger flashes up into "His Faces", and they become "as the appearance of lightning". Now lightnings shooting forth from a divine countenance are not indications of favour and kind affection. They express the contrary. They represent great fury and consuming indignation against them "that know not God, and obey not the gospel of the Lord, the Anointed Jesus"; the *Aion-Destruction* – from the face (Hebrew *faces*) of the Lord, and from the glory of His might, when He is apocalypsed from heaven, with the messengers of His power (the other faces associated with Him) in devouring fire (2 Thessalonians 1:7-9).

The nature of symbolical *lightning* may be readily deduced from the use of the word in scripture. Thus, in that grand description of Messiah's advent to punish the sons of Belial with *aion-destruction*, David in spirit says:

> "The earth shall shake and tremble; and the foundations of the mountains shall be troubled and shaken, because there was wrath with him. In his anger, a smoke ascended, and fire from his mouth shall devour; *lightnings* kindled from it. And he shall bow the heavens and descend, and darkness under his feet. And he shall ride upon the cherub and fly; and he shall soar on the wings of the spirit. He will make darkness his hiding place: the circuits of his pavilion the darkness of waters, thick clouds of the skies. Because of the brightness before him, his thick clouds passed away; hail *and lightnings of the fire*. Yahweh also will thunder in the heavens, and the Most High will give forth his voice; hail and *lightnings of the fire*. Yea,

> he will shoot his arrows and scatter them; yea, he flashed forth *lightnings* and will put them to the rout. Then the channels of the waters shall be seen; and the foundation of the habitable shall be laid bare, because of thy rebuke, O Yahweh, because of the blast of the spirit of thy nostrils." (Psalm 18:8-16)

The reader will have no difficulty in perceiving that this passage is descriptive of a great breaking-up of the foundation of the political organization of the world; for the wrath of Yahweh expends itself, not upon inanimate and unoffending nature, but upon the unrighteous and rebellious. These are "the earth", and its civil and ecclesiastical organization, "the mountains", "the heavens", "the channels", and "foundations of the habitable"; while that which is to overthrow, destroy, lay bare, and abolish, is the smoking fire of His indignation, flashing forth its lightnings and crashing thunders through Israel and their kings – the lightning-faced Elohim of all the earth.

"The lightnings of the fire" are flashings kindled by the avenging wrath of Yahweh. The fiery abyss from which they shoot forth is said to be "*His mouth*", because it is by His command His mighty ones go forth against the enemy as a storm of lightning, thunder and hail. The fire typifies the Eternal Spirit in wrath. "Our God", saith Paul, "is a consuming fire." Hence, the flashing fires are "the lightnings of the fire".

"Bow Thine heavens", saith David in another place, "and come down, O Yahweh, touch upon the mountains, and they shall smoke; flash forth lightning, and thou shalt scatter them; shoot thine arrows, and thou shalt put them to the rout" (Psalm 144:6). Isaiah puts an interpretation upon this in the exclamation:

> "Oh, that thou wouldest rend the heavens, that thou wouldest come down, that the mountains [or kingdoms] might flow down before Thy faces as the burning of liquid fire – the fire shall cause the waters to boil – to make known thy Name to thine adversaries: Before thy Faces the nations shall tremble. At thy doing of terrible deeds we shall not confide in, thou descendest; before thy Faces the mountains were poured out,

> and from the age [*u-mai-olahm*, from the beginning of the Mosaic Economy] *men* have not heard, they have not given ear to, the eye hath not seen *besides thee, O Elohim* [mighty ones] *what* he shall prepare for him that is waiting diligently for him." (Isaiah 64:1-4)

Paul quotes this in 1 Corinthians 2:9, in such a way as to show that the "*Elohim*" apostrophised by Isaiah, as the *many in one* who alone hath given ear to the things that shall be prepared, are the saints in Christ; for he saith to this class of persons –

> "God hath revealed them to *us* by his Spirit ... that we might know the things that are freely given to *us* of God. For all things are *ours* and for *our* sakes." (3:21; 2 Corinthians 4:15)

The Elohim only have heard and given ear to, and seen by the eye of faith, the all things to be inherited. Thus saith Isaiah. But Paul also saith, that he and his brethren discerned them; therefore, admitting Paul to be a competent witness in the premisses, "the saints in Christ Jesus" who are finally approved, and the Elohim of Isaiah in the text before us, are the same.

The "lightnings" and "arrows" of the Eternal Spirit are to scatter and put the armies of the nations to the rout. "Yahweh's arrows shall go forth as the lightning" (Zechariah 9:14). An arrow is an instrument of death, and requires *a bow* for its projection, strong and well strung, to give the arrow the velocity and deadliness of lightning. Now, the prophets tell us that Judah, Ephraim, and the resurrected Sons of Zion, are Yahweh's bow and arrow, battle-axe and sword. But before they are developed in this character, they are "prisoners of hope in the pit where no water is" of life, physical or national. They must, therefore, become the subject of a personal and political resurrection; those who are dead in the grave, of a personal; and Judah and Ephraim dispersed among the nations, politically dead and buried there, of a national resurrection, "standing upon their feet an exceedingly great army" ready for action, as the result (Ezekiel 37:10).

With reference to this crisis the Spirit of Christ in the prophet saith –

"Fear not thou worm Jacob, ye men of Israel: I will help thee, saith Yahweh, even thy near kinsman, [2] the Holy One of Israel. Behold I will make thee a new sharp threshing instrument, having teeth; thou shalt thresh the mountains, and beat them small, and shalt make the hills as chaff. Thou shalt fan them and the wind shall carry them away, and the whirlwind shall scatter them; and thou shalt rejoice in **Yahweh** [He who shall be], and shalt glory in the Holy One of Israel – i.e., Jesus of Nazareth, the King of the Jews." (Isaiah 41:14-16)

Again, the spirit in another prophet, in addressing Israel, the rod of Yahweh's inheritance, saith –

"Thou art my battle-axe and weapons of war; for by thee will I break in pieces the nations, and by thee will I destroy kingdoms; and by thee will I break in pieces the horse and

---

2 The word is *Goel* from *gahal* to redeem. Now the interpretation of Goel, rendered in the English version, redeemer, must be sought for in the Mosaic law of redemption. According to this, all the firstborns of man and beast in Israel are Yahweh's, and were all to be sacrificed to Him, except the firstborn of an ass, and the firstborn children, being males (Exodus 13:1,13-15; 34:20); fields, houses, cities and servants (Leviticus 25:25-34); all these, when sold were returnable to their original owners, because these, as Yahweh's representatives, had the *fee simple* right in them, and could therefore not convey an unlimited right. The absolute fee simple right was in Yahweh; first, because He brought Israel's firstborn out of Egypt, while he slew those of the Egyptians (Exodus 13:14); and secondly, because He claimed the Holy Land as absolutely His, the Israelites being only strangers and sojourners with Him (Leviticus 25:23). The firstling of a cow, of a sheep and of a goat, were not redeemable from death; they were to be sacrificed to Yahweh, being typical of Messiah the prince in his cutting off (Numbers 18:17). The redemption of redeemable things was to be effected by a blood relation of the nearest kin. Hence, *Goel* stands for the nearest relative, a blood relation, the next of kin or a redeemer in this sense. It was his duty in redeeming to pay a stipulated price, so that the near kinsman became a purchaser, and the firstborns and so forth, a purchased people, and purchased things. Under the law, the price was blood and money. Now all this was a pattern of heavenly things. It was an illustration of the substance expressed in the text words: "Yahweh, Goel of Israel"; that is, "He shall be the nearest kinsman of Israel". This necessitates that the Effluence of the Eternal should become an Israelite, or as Paul expresses it, "He", the Spirit, "took upon himself of the nature of Abraham; for in all things it behoved him to be made like his brethren". The Spirit becoming thus a blood relation, and by resurrection Son of Power and firstborn, he is the one of right to redeem the Holy Land and Israel by a blood-price out of the hand of strangers, who desolate and oppress them. They are the Eternal's, and His near kinsman is Jesus the Holy One of Israel.

> his rider ... and by thee will I break in pieces captains and rulers. And I will render unto Babylon, and all the inhabitants of Chaldea, all their evil that they have done in Zion, in your sight, saith Yahweh." (Jeremiah 51:20)

But Israel has never been the conquering power indicated in this testimony since it was delivered. From that time to this they have been oppressed, and in a state of punishment. Therefore, as Jesus truly taught, seeing that "the scripture cannot be broken", it yet remains to be accomplished when the Faces of the Spirit shall shine upon them, and scatter their enemies with the lightnings of His fury.

Again also the Spirit of Christ in yet another prophet, predicts that the king of Zion and Jerusalem, who, at one period of his history, was to come to them in humility, "riding upon an ass, even upon a colt, the foal of an ass", "should speak peace to the nations", and have universal dominion. Having declared this, the Spirit, addressing the just and lowly Monarch of Israel, saith, "As to thee, *through the blood of thy cutting off*, I will call forth thy captives out of the pit wherein are no waters". Then apostrophizing the captives, He saith "return to the stronghold [Zion] ye prisoners of the hope; this day itself he causes to announce that I will cause to restore double unto thee". Having announced this redemption at the price of the king's blood, the Spirit characterises the day of redemption, or "year of his redeemed", as a "day of vengeance" –

> "when I have bent Judah for Me, have filled the bow with Ephraim, and raised up thy Sons, O Zion, against thy sons, O Greece, and made thee as the Sword of the Mighty One. And Yahweh shall be seen over them, and His arrow shall go forth as the lightning, and the Adonai Yahweh [the Faces of the Spirit] shall blow with the trumpet, and go with whirlwinds of Teman. And Yahweh Tz'vaoth shall protect them, and they shall devour and conquer the slingers of stones ... And in that day Yahweh Elohim shall save them as the flock of his people; for **the gems of the diadem** are exalting themselves upon His land." (Zechariah 9:9-16)

And, illustrative of these last words, the testimony may be added, that in that day shall Yahweh Tz'vaoth be –

> "for *a crown of glory* and for a *diadem of beauty* unto the residue of his people, and for a spirit of judgment to him that sitteth in judgment, and for strength to them who turn the battle to the gate." (Isaiah 28:5,6)

> "Thou, O Zion, shalt be *a crown of glory* in the hands of Yahweh, and a royal diadem in the palm of thine Elohim." (62:3)

From these premisses we learn, that on the day of the manifestation of Daniel's great vision of the Spirit-man, Judah will be the battle-bow; that Ephraim, or the Ten Tribes of Israel, will be His arrow; and that with the Judah-bow in one hand, and the Ephraim arrow in the other, strung to the utmost bent, the tribes will shoot forth from His faces with the velocity and destructiveness of lightning against the nations. The Man of the One Spirit is Yahweh, Goel and Holy One of Israel; styled in many passages Yahweh-Tz'vaoth, which signifies 'He shall be hosts': that is 'He shall be Captain of the armies of Israel'; for Moses says: "Yahweh is a man of war" (Exodus 15:3). Thus, in "the great day of the war of the Almighty Power" (Revelation 16:14) upon the kingdoms of the world, wherever there is a section of the Jewish captivity – prisoners in their Gentile houses of death – there will be an army of the Yahweh-Man, styled by Paul, "the man, the anointed Jesus"; the Man of Multitude, "in whom" are all the saints – a constituency attained through the blood of his covenant or cutting off. In the day of approaching vengeance, the sons of Zion, according to the flesh, will be a sharp two-edged broadsword, proceeding forth from the mouth of this mighty Man of War, the Sons of Zion according to the Spirit. Thus com manded, their armies shall be among the Gentiles as a lion among the beasts of the forest, and as a young lion among flocks of goats, who, going through, treads down and tears in pieces, and none can deliver (Micah 5:8). "The slingers of stones", or as we term them in modern technique, the gunners, cannoniers, or artillerists, whose ordinance is the glory and strength of the armies of the world –

the fire and brimstone of their warfare shall be conquered; "they shall conquer the slingers of stones" (Zechariah 9:15), and scatter their hosts as chaff before the whirlwinds of Teman.

Having said enough in illustration of the facial similitude of the Yahweh Man, we proceed to the contemplation of –

"His eyes as lamps of fire"

The eye is the symbol of intelligence: for, "the light of the body is the eye". The extent, and, perhaps, the degree of intelligence, is indicated by the number, and its character by the expression of the symbol. Daniel does not record the number of the eyes of the glorious Man of Multitude: but tells us that their appearance was "as lamps of fire", which would give them a flaming, and therefore, terrible expression to those whom they will neither spare nor pity (Ezekiel 5:11).

The symbolical number of these flaming orbs is revealed in Zechariah. In chapter 3, the Eternal saith, "Behold, I will bring forth my servant, the Branch"; or Messiah. "For, behold, the stone which I have placed before the Faces of Joshua [or Jesus, in Greek], upon the same stone shall be **seven eyes**" (verses 8,9): and "they shall rejoice and see the stone of separation in the hands of Zerubbabel, *even* those Seven. They are the eyes of **Yahweh**, *scourging* in all the earth" (Zechariah 4:10). In this testimony and its context, the Eternal Spirit sets before us several representative men – Joshua and his brethren, and Zerubbabel; the former, the High Priest and his household at the time of the restoration from Babylon, and the latter, governor of Judah and of the house of David at the same crisis. They were constituted a symbolical group, and were so regarded by their contemporaries in Jerusalem; as it is written, "they are men wondered at", or *anshai mophaith*, "Men of Sign", that is, men representing others besides themselves.

But as the things to be represented by them required other symbols than those furnished by the human form, priests, and governors, the deficiencies are supplied from other sources. Joshua and his brethren represented Messiah and his brethren in name and office; as did also Zerubbabel as a governor of the house of David; and as a group of sign-men, they symbolised the kings and priests of the Eternal Power of the house of David, occupying their places over Israel in Messiah's times, commonly styled "the millennium". But it was required also to represent that the Spirit's servant, "the man whose name is the Branch", styled in the New Testament "Jesus Christ", was the same who had been styled by Jacob, David, Isaiah and Daniel, "the Stone"; that the precious gem in its brightness and splendour was to blaze forth in the glory of the Spirit; that, as a consuming fire, he and his companions were to scourge the wicked; in short, that Israel was not to expect redemption by their own prowess, apart from the Man of the Eternal Power, according to "the word of Yahweh to Zerubbabel, saying, Not by multitude nor by strength, but rather by my Spirit, saith Yahweh Tz'vaoth" (Zechariah 4:6).

To represent these requirements, a stone was placed before Joshua, by which action a relation between them was established. It is afterwards seen in the hand of Zerubbabel, by which also he becomes identified with it. Hence the stone comes to represent at once the High Priest and Governor of Judah – "a Priest upon the throne" of the house of David, which indicated a change in the kingdom of Israel. In the hand of Zerubbabel it is styled the "Stone of Separation", by which we are taught that "the Shepherd, the Stone of Israel" will be a purifier of his nation from all alloy; for –

> "He is like a refiner's fire, and like fullers' soap. And he shall sit as a refiner and purifier of silver; and He shall purify the sons of Levi, and purge them as gold and silver, that they may offer unto Yahweh an offering in righteousness. Afterwards shall the offering of Judah and Jerusalem be pleasant unto Yahweh, as in the days of old, and as in ancient years." (Malachi 3:2-4)

But the nature of the case demanded that intelligence and multitudinousness should be symbolized in the Stone. To answer this, "Seven Eyes" are placed upon it with the inscription "I will remove the iniquity of that land in one day." These eyes, we are told, are "the Eyes of Yahweh"; that is, the eyes of the spirit, self-styled Yahweh.

Now, John in Patmos saw the same vision; and in his description of what he saw, uses the words of Daniel and Zechariah, which he blends together. He says there were "Seven lamps of fire burning before the throne". He then tells what they represent, saying, "which are the Seven Spirits of power", or of God. "Grace and peace" were sent through John to the Seven Ecclesias from these Seven Spirits in concert with Jesus Anointed (Revelation 1:4,5); who, in chapter 5:6, is symbolized "by a lamb that had been slain". Now, the description of this lamb identifies it with the Stone of Joshua and Zerubbabel; and with the Eyes of Daniel's Man of the One Spirit. The slain lamb had "seven horns and seven eyes, which [Horns and eyes] are", or represent, "the Seven Spirits of Power, sent forth into all the earth" (Revelation 5:6).

The symbolical number is "seven". This is a *sign*-number, *signifying* more or less. That it does not signify less than seven, is evident from other symbols of the Spirit. The Four living Ones of Ezekiel and John are symbols of the Spirit, multitudinously manifested; for "whither the Spirit was to go, they went", "as the appearance of a flash of lightning" (Ezekiel 1:14,20; Revelation 4:6). Their actions are identical; therefore the Spirit and the Living Ones are the same – "that which is born of the Spirit is spirit". Ezekiel tells us that what he describes was "the appearance of the likeness of the glory of Yahweh", or of the Eternal Spirit. It was not the thing itself, but its similitude: the reality pertaining to the New Order of Elohim, to Jesus and his brethren. Now, Paul teaches that we are invited to the glory of God through the gospel; and Peter, that "He hath called us to his eternal glory". Hence, the Four Living Ones that John saw are represented as celebrating in song their redemption by the Lamb, that they might reign as God's kings and priests upon the earth. The Living Ones are, therefore, spirit symbols of the Sons of God in glorious manifestation. Their Eyes, however, are not limited to "seven", but are numberless; for "their whole body, their backs, and their hands, and their wings, and their wheels were full of eyes round about" (Ezekiel 10:12). This is also John's testimony, who says "the Four Living Ones were full of eyes before and behind ... and within; and they had six wings", which identifies them with Isaiah's Seraphim.

We conclude, then, that the symbolical number "seven" in the case before us, is representative of a great and innumerable multitude – "a multitude which *no man* can number", because its amount is not revealed. The eyes of Daniel's symbol are identical with the eyes of the cherubim: each eye being the representative of an individual saint. In the aggregate they are "as lamps of fire", whose mission is to slay the beast, and to destroy his body, and to give it to the burning flame (Daniel 7:11); and to take away the dominion of the rest of the beasts (verse 12): or as John expresses it, to burn Babylon utterly with fire; to torment her adherents and the kings of the earth with fire and brimstone, and the sword; to bind the Dragon, and take possession of the kingdoms of the nations in all the earth (Revelation 18:8; 14:8-11; 17:14; 20:2; 11:15): all of which is implied in the words of Zechariah, that the Seven Eyes as lamps of fire, "are the Eyes of Yahweh *scourging* in all the earth".

The Man of the One Spirit: "his arms"

> "Who among the sons of the mighty can be likened to Yahweh? O, Yahweh Elohim of Hosts, who is a strong Yah like to thee? Thou hast a mighty arm; strong is thy hand, and high is thy right hand." (Psalm 89)

> "Behold Adonai Yahweh with strong hand shall come, and his arm be ruler for him: behold his reward is with him, and his work before him." (Isaiah 40:10)

> "Yahweh has sworn by the arm of His strength: I will gather you, O Israel, with a stretched out arm, and fury poured out." (Ezekiel 20:33,34)

> "There is none like the El of Yeshurun who rides upon the heavens in thy help, and in his excellency upon the skies. The Mighty Ones of the East thy refuge, and underneath the arms

> of the Olahm; and he shall thrust out the enemy from before thee; and shall say, Destroy. Israel then shall dwell in safety alone." (Deuteronomy 33:27).

From these passages and many others that might be produced, it is evident that "arms", in a symbolical use of the word, signifies power, forces, sovereign authority; and when *outstretched*, power in energetic and furious operation. "The arms of the Olahm", referred to by Moses in his song, and termed "the everlasting arms" in the English version, are in the highest sense, the armies of Israel, of which the Eternal Spirit our Messiah and his Brethren is, in that manifestation, Yahweh. Hence the name of that spirit-incorporated community, *Yahweh Tz'vaoth*: an enigmatical title, signifying **He shall be Commanders of the armies** *of Israel*. These Spirit Commanders are each focalisations of the One Eternal Power. Hence the ungrammatical expression, **He** *the Commanders*. These are the Arms of the Olahm – the arms to be outstretched in "the Hour of Judgment"; and which are to break the Bow of Brass (Psalm 18:34). Moses styles these *Arms* in his song *Elohai kedem*, "Mighty Ones of the East", in the English version rendered "the Eternal God". But John, in Revelation 16:12, justifies our translation. He there styles them *hai basileiai hai apo anatolōn hēliou*, "the Kings from risings of a Sun"; but in the English version "the Kings of the East". The *kedem* of Moses is the *apo anatolōn hēliou*, of John. John paraphrases Moses. The *Hēlios* or Sun, is the "Sun of Righteousness" spoken of in Malachi 4:2, who is to heal, and afterwards to send forth the sparkling gems of the Eternal, to tread down the wicked as ashes under the soles of their feet, in the day that Yahweh shall do it. The *Jewels* of Malachi, and the *Elohim* of Moses are *the Kings* of John, and the *Arms* of Daniel's vision. Each individual King is a *rising* of the healing Sun, in the sense of being brought from the grave and quickened by his vitalising beams. Collectively, the Kings of Power or of God, are the "risings of a Sun"; and that Sun is He who proclaimed himself "the Resurrection and the Life", even the Eternal Father, who raises up the dead by the anointed Son of Mary (2 Corinthians 4:14); styled by her royal ancestor, "the

Handmaid of Yahweh" (Psalm 86:16; 116:16); and so recognised by Gabriel, Zacharias, Elisabeth, Simeon and Anna, all instructed and proficients in the law. When their mission is accomplished, they also will sing the song of Moses, "and of the Lamb", the prophet like to him (Exodus 15; Revelation 15).

These "Arms" of Daniel's vision, are represented by John in battle array in the train of their Commander-in-Chief, "the King of the Jews" (Revelation 19:14; Isaiah 55:4). John styles them "the forces of the heaven, following the Faithful and True One upon white horses, arrayed in fine linen, white and clean". Collectively, they are the Four Chariots of the heavens seen by Zechariah emerging from between the Two Mountains of Brass, which it is their mission to reduce to a molten furnace, glowing with intense heat. In the symbol of "the Lamb slain", the "Arms" are equivalent to the "Seven Horns", or Spirit Powers, which are as innumerable, but equal in number, whatever its amount may be, to the "Seven Eyes".

And at his feet as the aspect of glowing brass

Joshua called for all the men of Israel, and said to the captains of the warriors who went with him: "Come near; put your feet upon the necks of these kings." And they did so. Then Joshua said to them, "Fear not, nor be dismayed, be strong and of good courage; for thus shall Yahweh do to all your enemies against whom you fight". He then slew them, and hanged the five kings on as many trees, until evening (Joshua 10:25,26).

The history of Israel is not only as strictly literal as any other histories, and truer too than those of the nations contemporary with their prophetic times, but it *is also allegorical*, which theirs are not. Joshua and his Captains were like Joshua, the High Priest, and his companions, "men of sign"; and represented Messiah and his Captains in their future wars with "the Kings of the Earth, and of the whole Habitable (Revelation 16) – whom they are to tread down as ashes under the soles of their feet.

In Psalm 18:31, the Spirit inquires:

"Who is *Eloah* beside *Yahweh*? And who a Rock except our *Elohim* – the El girding me with might? Even he will make my way complete. He causes *my feet to be like hinds*, and he will make me to stand upon my high places. He is training my hands for the war; *so that the Bow of Brass might be broken by my arms* ... Thou wilt cause my going to extend under me; and my ankle joints have not wavered. *I will pursue my enemies*, and shall overtake them, and I will not return till they be destroyed; I will wound them so that they shall not be able to rise; *they shall fall under my feet*. Thou wilt gird me with might for the war. Thou wilt subdue under me those who rise up against me. And thou hast given to me *the neck* of my enemies; and those who hate me, I will cut them off. They will cry for help, but there is none to save them – unto Yahweh, but he answered them not. Then will I grind them fine as dust before the Faces of the Spirit; as the mire of the streets will I pour them out. Thou wilt deliver me from the contentions of the nations; thou hast appointed me for prince of the nations. A nation which I know not shall serve me. At the hearing of the ear they shall obey; the sons of the foreigner shall submit to me; and the sons of the foreigner shall fall, and tremble from their strongholds."

46. – "Yahweh lives, and blessed be my rock; and he shall raise the Elohim of my salvation. The **El** that giveth avengements to me, even he will subdue the nations under me."

48. – "Thou wilt exalt me: from the Man of Violence (Paul's 'Man of Sin', the Lawless One) thou wilt deliver me. Therefore, O Yahweh, I will give Thee thanks among the Gentiles, and sing psalms unto thy name, magnifying the deliverances of **His King**, and performing the promise to **His Messiah**, to David, and to his seed for the Olahm."

In this passage, the Eternal Spirit through his prophet, speaks of Messiah in the crisis of his controversy for Zion, in which, as the representative and chief of Daniel's "Man of the One Spirit", he puts his feet upon the necks of the kings of the earth, scatters their armies like dust before the wind, and becomes Prince or Head of the nations in their stead. But this is true also of all the individual members of this **New Man** (Ephesians 2:15; 4:24; 2 Corinthians 5:17; Galatians 6:15). If the New Adam himself thus make war upon, and trample in the mire the kings and armies of the Old Adam nature, He has promised that all true believers "in Him" – all who are Abraham's seed by being Christ's – that is, all the Saints, shall do the same; and shall share with Him in the fruits of his and their victory.

In proof of this we refer the reader to the following passages:

> "The righteous shall rejoice when he sees the vengeance; he shall wash *his feet* in the blood of the wicked. So that a man shall say, Verily, there is a reward for the righteous: verily, there are Elohim ruling in the earth." (Psalm 58:10,11)

"All the horns of the wicked I will cut off; but the horns of the righteous shall be exalted" (Psalm 75:10). "He shall put off the spirit of princes; He is terrible to the kings of the earth" (Psalm 76:12). "Arise, O Elohim, judge the earth; for thou shalt acquire possession in all the nations" (Psalm 82:8). "He will exalt the horn of his nation; the glory of all his saints; of the sons of Israel, a people near to him" (Psalm 148:14). "Israel shall rejoice in him that made him; the sons of Zion shall exult in their king ... The saints shall exult in glory; they shall shout with joy upon their couches. The high things of **El** shall be in their mouths; and a two-edged sword in their hands, to execute vengeance upon the nations and punishment upon the peoples; to bind their kings with chains, and their honoured ones with fetters of iron, to execute upon them the judgment written; *this honour have* **all his saints**" (Psalm 149).

Now the phrase *all his saints* is comprehensive of Messiah and his brethren, who collectively form "the Man of the one Spirit", or Paul's "New Man". Hence, the same things are affirmed of them that are predicated concerning Him. Their feet will be like hinds – swift in the pursuit of their enemies, whom they will overtake and destroy. These will fall before their power; and as Malachi says, they will trample them as ashes under the soles of their feet; and, when they have got the victory, they will rule with Messiah as "princes in all the earth" (Psalm 45:16): the resurrected "Elohim ruling in the earth", the Elohim of "Messiah's salvation".

This is the teaching of the Old Testament, with which the New Testament is in exact conformity; for they harmonise upon every subject, as might be expected from the declaration of its writers, that they taught none other things than Moses and other prophets had already predicted.

Now the apostles have proved beyond all confutation that Jesus is the Messiah or Christ of Yahweh promised to Abraham, David and Judah. Hence, all that is said about the Christ in the Old Testament must, sooner or later, be fulfilled in Jesus. But the prophets exhibit the Christ, not as a solitary man only, but also as a man of Multitude, as we have abundantly shown. Therefore, Jesus and his apostles preached the Christ in the same form – *as One Person, and a Multitude in that One, in and through all of whom the Eternal Spirit would dwell and manifest His power.* "I and the Father", said Jesus, "are One" **One Yahweh**; and concerning his apostles, and all Jews and Gentiles believing into him through the apostles' testimony, he also said, "I pray that they all may be one; **as** *thou Father art in me and I in thee*, that they also may be **one in us** – that they may be one *even as we* are one; *I in them and thou in me*, that they may be made *perfect in one*" (John 17:21) – in One **Yahweh**; that is, in the one perfect Man of the Spirit, styled Jehovah, Yahweh, or Yah, because **He Shall Be**. "Hear, O Israel, Yahweh, our Mighty Ones is One Yahweh." This is the "incommunicable name" as ye term it – a Name of Multitude, which Isaiah saith, "is coming from afar, His anger burning, and the violence of a conflagration; His lips are full of indignation, and His tongue as a devouring fire, and His breath as an overflowing stream shall reach to the neck for the scattering of the nations with the fan of destruction" (Isaiah 30:27). It is the Name of Multitude expressed in the formula or symbol, into which the believers are baptized – "The Name of the Father, and of the Son, and of the Holy Spirit"; every such believer when so immersed, being a constituent of that name; and therefore addressed by Paul as "in God the Father, and the Lord Jesus Anointed". This is that "glorious and fearful Name – Yahweh *Elohaikha*", O Israel, which your fathers would not enter into by obeying; and on account of which, as Moses forewarned you in Deuteronomy 28:58, the Eternal Power has made thy plagues wonderful to this day.

Daniel's "great vision" was of this consuming Name – the mystical or multitudinous Christ – to every accepted member of which "One Body" it is said by the Spirit, "that which ye have, hold fast till I come. And he that overcometh and keepeth my works to the end, to him will I give dominion over the nations; and he shall rule them with a rod of iron; as the earthen vessels they shall be broken to pieces; even as I also received of my Father" (Revelation 2:25). And again –

> "He that overcometh, I will make him a pillar in the temple of my God, and he shall go no more out; and I will write upon him the name of my God, and the name of the city of my God, the New Jerusalem descending out of the heaven from my God, even my new name." (Revelation 3:12)

> "He that overcometh, I will give to him *to sit with me* on my throne, even as I also overcame, and sit with my Father on his throne." (verse 21)

To write upon one who has gained a victory over himself and the world, the name of Deity, and the name of the city of Deity, is to declare him a constituent of the name inscribed upon him. Messiah and his brethren are "joint heirs" – the eyes, and ears, and arms, and feet of Daniel's Spirit-Man, whose name is **Yahweh-Elohim**.

John says that the feet of this Man, whom he also saw in vision, are "like unto incandescent brass, as if they had been glowing in a furnace" (Revelation 1:15). The arms and the feet are symbolized in brass to connect them with the temple-pattern of heavenly things. The altar of burnt-offering and the laver, and the two pillars of the temple-porch, and many other things pertaining to the Court of the Priests, were all of brass, or overlaid therewith.

The brass pertaining to the temple was all holy. The Brazen Altar was "most holy", so that whoever touched it was holy; no Israelite, however, was permitted to touch it, unless he belonged to the Seed of Aaron; and even they were not permitted to approach the altar till they had first washed their hands and feet in the Brazen Sea.

The Altar of Burnt-Offering prefigured the Messiah's Body in sacrificial manifestation. The idea of an altar of sacrifice representing a personal and divine plurality is frequent in scripture. Thus, Jacob erected an altar at Shalem, in the land of Canaan, and called it **El-Elohai Yisrael**, that is, the "*Strength of the Mighty Ones of Israel*" (Genesis 33:20); and Moses, before the law was given, and in memory of the victory of Joshua over Amalek, "built an altar, and called the name of it **Yahweh-Nissi**"; that is, *He shall be my Ensign* – He who was symbolised by the altar (Exodus 17:15; Isaiah 11:10,12; 18:3; 31:9; Zechariah 9:16).

This Yahweh-nissi-altar was superseded by an altar overlaid with plates of brass. These plates represented "the flesh of sin" purified by fiery trial. "Gold, silver, brass, iron, tin and lead, everything", said Moses, "that may abide the fire, ye shall make go through the fire, *and it shall be clean*; nevertheless, it shall be purified with the water of separation; and all that abideth not the fire, ye shall make go through the water" (Numbers 31:22,23). The connection of the plates with sin's flesh, is established by their history. They were the "censers of those sinners against their own souls", Korah, Dathan, Abiram and their company, two hundred and fifty of them, who rebelled against the Strength of Israel. He commanded Eleazar, Aaron's son, to melt them, and roll them into broad plates, for "a covering of the altar", and "a sign to the children of Israel" (Numbers 16:37,38). The Brazen Altar, which was four-square, had four horns of brass, one at each corner; and in sacrifice the blood was applied to the horns by the Priest's fingers; and the rest was all poured beside the bottom of the altar (Exodus 29:12). These horns represent the same things as the Four Cherubim, the Four Carpenters, and the Four Living Ones, of Ezekiel, Zechariah, and John; only in the Brazen State which precedes the Golden Olahm, or Millennium. As horns of brass, they "execute the judgment written" as a consuming fire; for brass and offering by fire are the association of things in the type.

The Brazen Altar and its horns of brass, then, are symbolical of **El**, the Eternal power in *Elohal*, or sacrificial and judicial manifestation in flesh. "*Eloah* will come from Teman", saith the prophet, "the Holy One from Mount Paran: consider! His glory covers the heavens, and his praise fills the earth; and the splendour shall be as the light; he has *horns* out of his hand; and there is the *covering of his Strong Ones*. Before his faces shall go pestilence, and from his feet lightnings shall proceed. He stood, and measured the earth; he beheld and caused the nations to tremble; and the mountains of antiquity were dispersed; and the hills of the Olahm did bow; the goings of the Olahm are his" (Habakkuk 3:3-6).

The Horns of the Brazen and Golden Altars are His Eternal Spirit's strong ones, who disperse the empires of antiquity, and subjugate the kingdoms of the latter days to Him and His Anointed; so that the current of the world's affairs will be directed by His *Elohim*, in the ensuing thousand years, or Daniel's "season and a time".

The saints, then, are the brazen arms and feet of the Man of the One Spirit, who have all passed through the fire, and the water of separation, and been consecrated by the blood of the covenant; and "are partakers with the Altar", even Jesus (1 Corinthians 9:13; 10:18; Hebrews 13:10,12); and those of them who have been slain have been poured out "beside the bottom", or "under the altar", from whence the cry ascends to the Father, "How long, O Lord, holy and true, dost Thou not judge and avenge our blood on them that dwell upon the earth?" (Revelation 6:10; 11:1). Hence, those who dwell upon the earth, being like Israel of old, grievous revolters, *brass and iron*, corrupters all (Jeremiah 6:28), are to be cast into a furnace glowing with the heat of Yahweh's indignation. Israel has been passing through the process for ages. They have been trampled under foot of the Gentiles in a great furnace of affliction; for punishment was to begin first at the Jew; and afterwards to be visited upon the brass and iron of the Gentiles. Ezekiel's description of Israel's punishment by Gentile agency will illustrate that of the Gentiles by the agency of Israel, under the direction of the men "whose feet are like incandescent brass, glowing in a furnace"; and will furnish an obvious interpretation of the text. "The word of Yahweh", says the prophet, "came unto me, saying, Son of Man, the house of Israel is to me become dross; they are all *brass*, and tin, and iron, and lead, *in the midst of the furnace*; they are the dross of silver. Therefore, thus saith Yahweh Elohim, because ye are all become dross, behold, therefore, I will gather you *into the midst of Jerusalem*. As they gather silver, and *brass*, and iron, and lead, and tin, into the midst of the furnace, to blow the fire upon it to melt it, so will I gather you in my anger and in my fury; and I will leave you, and blow upon you *in the fire of my wrath*, and ye shall be melted in the midst thereof. As silver is melted in the midst of the furnace, so shall ye be melted in the midst thereof; and ye shall know that I, Yahweh, have poured out my fury upon you" (Ezekiel 22:18-20). Israel in the flesh are here compared to brass and other metals, *full of dross*. This drossy nature of the brass is the characteristic by which they are distinguished from "the fine" or "incandescent brass" of the Man of the One Spirit, or Israel in the Spirit, in glowing or burning operation upon the subjects of Yahweh's fiery indignation.

Israel as dross is exemplified in the denunciations of the prophets. Their drossiness is seen in the abominations they practised in burning incense to reptiles and filthy beasts, and idols of every sort; in their women weeping for Tammuz, the Adonis of the Greeks; and in their worshipping the sun between the porch and the altar with their backs toward the temple of Yahweh (Ezekiel 8:7,8). They are still in the drossy state with the curse of Moses on them. With the exception of circumcision (which, however, was not from Moses, but from Abraham) they do nothing he commanded them to do; and, therefore, disregarding him, they necessarily reject Jesus, of whom he wrote. "Cursed is every one", says Moses, "that continueth not in all things which are written in the book of the law to do them". Israel lives in the perpetual violation of the law, and yet seeks justification by that law, which only thunders the curses of mount Ebal in their ears. "Cursed be he", saith Moses, "that taketh reward to slay an innocent person". This Israel did in paying Judas thirty pieces of silver for the betraying of Jesus, and in their priests taking the price of blood returned to them, and purchasing therewith the Potter's Field. The Pagan judge pronounced him faultless; and in this declaration convicts the Jewish nation of the crime of "**taking the reward of treachery paid to effect the death of an innocent person**". And the crime being committed, the people shouted the "Amen", saying: "Let his blood be upon us, and upon our children!" These children, or posterity, are with us at this day – "the dross of silver in the midst of the furnace of affliction, '*left*' of Yahweh, and '*melted*'".

But, if Israel be the dross of silver, the Gentiles are the dross of brass, iron, lead, and tin. The Gentile dross is no purer than Israel's. Israel boasts in Moses, and pays no regard to what he prescribes; and the Gentiles bepraise Jesus while their eyes are closed and their hearts steeled against his doctrine and commands; so that Jews and Gentiles are all guilty before God – they only excepted who believe the Gospel of the kingdom and obey it. They have all, therefore, to be gathered into a furnace glowing with intense combustion, before they attain to the blessedness that is to come upon all nations through Abraham and his seed. Jews and Gentiles must he "melted in the fire of Yahweh's wrath", which fire will burn through the operations of the arms and feet of the Man of the One – "the saints executing the judgment written", and "treading the wicked as ashes under the soles of their feet".

The furnace in which Israel will become molten brass is "*the wilderness of the peoples*", where Yahweh saith He will plead with them face to face; rule over them with fury poured out, and purge out from among them the rebellious, whom He will not permit to enter into the Holy Land to live there in His sight under the government of His King – the Christ (Ezekiel 20:33-44). When thus purged, the Jewish nation will be brass and silver well refined (Malachi 3:2,3). The rebellious dross will be cleaned out, and Anti-Mosaic-Judaism, by which they are now caused to wander out of the way, will have been destroyed from the earth. The refining furnace is the "time of Jacob's trouble", out of which he is to be delivered (Jeremiah 30:7); and though they are now "prostrate among the cattle pens", they will be "the wings of the *Dove* covered with silver and her feathers with the brightness of fine gold" (Psalm 68:13).

But the Gentiles are to become molten brass as well as Israel. Their brass, therefore, is also to be gathered into the furnace, that it may be melted and refined in the fire of Yahweh's wrath, The place of the furnace is also "the wilderness of the peoples", that wilderness inhabited by the peoples, multitudes, nations, and tongues – the "many waters upon which the Great Harlot sitteth", that John of Patmos refers to in Revelation 17:1,15 – Portugal, Spain, France, Germany, Italy, Greece, Egypt; and, in short, all the Mediterranean and Euphratean countries, being the territories of the four beasts of Daniel, constitute the furnace in which the Nebuchadnezzar-gold, silver and brass, and iron, and clay are made to glow with torrid heat of seven-fold intensity; and in which the four men of God – the Cherubim – walk to and fro, without hurt, "the fire having no power upon their bodies"; as symbolized by Nebuchadnezzar's furnace, and by John's mystical Son of Man, in Revelation 1:15; Daniel 3:19-27. The melting and refining the Gentile brass in this Babylonian furnace, incandescent with the wrath of Deity, is Daniel's "time of trouble, such as never was, since there was a nation to that same time" (Daniel 12:1). It is "the day that shall burn as an oven" (or furnace) which shall consume the proud and all that do wickedness, with their anti-Christian Gentilism, by which the peoples are deceived; but which shall have no power for evil against the people represented by Shadrach, Meshach, Abednego, and the one like the Son of God; they shall come forth unharmed, unsinged, unchanged and inodorous of the fire. For these are the daughters of Zion, to whom the Spirit saith:

> "Arise and thresh: for I will make thine horn iron, and I will make thy *hoofs brass*: and thou shalt beat in pieces many

> peoples; and I will consecrate their spoil to Yahweh, and their wealth to the Adon of the whole earth." (Micah 4:13)

So that while Israel is passing through the furnace under the conduct of the saints, and are themselves being purged from dross, they are also made use of by the commanders as a torch of fire among the sheaves, or a lion among flocks of goats (Micah 5:8; Zechariah 12:6), to destroy the power and kingdoms of the world, after the allegorical example of their transit out of Egypt into the land of their inheritance; for though passing under the rod themselves, they became also a rod of iron in the hand of Yahweh for the destruction of the nations, whose iniquity was full.

"And the voice of his words as the voice of a multitude"

This is the last characteristic of the symbolic Man of the One Spirit, noted by the prophet Daniel. In John's vision of the Mystic Christ, it is testified that "His voice was as the sound of many waters". These "many waters" are Daniel's "multitude"; for "many waters" signify, as apocalyptically explained, a multitude of people. In Ezekiel's "*visions of Elohim*", the voice of Daniel's and John's symbolic man comes from the wings of the cherubim. "I heard", saith he, "the noise of their wings, like the noise of *many waters*, as the voice of *Shaddai* [Mighty Ones] in their going, the voice of *speech*, as the noise of a *camp*: in standing, they let down their wings" (Ezekiel 1:24). The meaning of this is, that Ezekiel heard the voice of a multitude of Mighty Ones, speaking as the warriors of a camp in motion against an enemy; and that when they were not in progress, their voice was not heard – "in standing they let down their wings", and, consequently, there was no sound of war. But the voice of Daniel's and John's symbolic man was heard as the roar of a multitude – the roaring of many waters; by which we are to understand that their Man of Multitude was in progress, leading on the body and wings of his brazen-footed battalions against the Fourth Beast, or the Apocalyptic Beast and False Prophet, and the kings of the earth and their armies; the former consumed *in the furnace*, or "lake of fire, burning with sulphur"; and the kings and their armies slain with the sword of the resurrected and glorified Mystic Man" (Revelation 19:19,20).

Now, Daniel, as the representative of his people, saw the Spirit Man, while those who are no constituent part thereof see him not, but tremble before him, and flee, as the Old Adam did, "to hide themselves".

7 |

The Cherubim

(John Thomas, 1848)

The subject of the Cherubim is one that can be studied at length. They appear in a number of passages throughout scripture, from Genesis to Revelation. Sometimes they are described in detail, sometimes hardly at all. The short passage below, from *Elpis Israel* (pages 159-162, fifteenth edition), gives an introduction to the topic. At the same time, it demonstrates the abiding interest in the Cherubim among the Christadelphian community, from the time of Brother Thomas to the present day. Accompanying the text are two footnotes by Brother C. C. Walker, written for the edition of *Elpis Israel* he published in 1903.

LITTLE is said about the *Cherubim* in the Mosaic narrative. The word is a plural noun, and represents therefore more objects than one. But, in what did this plurality consist? I should say, judging from a text in the next chapter, that it had especial regard to a plurality of *faces*; for when the Lord God sentenced Cain to a fugitive and vagabond life, the fratricide answered, "Behold, then, from **thy faces** [*plural in the Hebrew*] [1] shall I be hid" (Genesis 4:14); that is, "I shall no more be permitted to come before the Cherubic faces, which thou hast placed at the east of the garden, to present an offering for my sin." As he truly

1 The word is plural *only* in the Hebrew; even in the case of Jacob and the angel (Genesis 32:30; compare also Ezekiel 10:14).

observed, "Mine iniquity is greater than that it may be forgiven". He was exiled from the Faces of God still further to the east, as a murderer doomed to eternal death (1 John 3:15) as the end of his career.

That the faces were connected with the Cherubim seems unquestionable from other passages of scripture where Cherubim are described. The Lord spoke of them to Moses in the mount. Having commanded him to make an ark, or open chest, overlaid with gold, with a crown along its upper margin, he said, "Thou shalt make a *mercy-seat* of pure gold. And thou shalt make *two cherubim* of beaten gold in the two ends of the mercy-seat". In another place, it is explained that "Out of the mercy-seat made he the cherubim on the two ends thereof". Then it is continued, "And the cherubim shall stretch forth *wings* on high, covering the mercy-seat with their wings, and their *faces* one to another, toward the mercy-seat shall the faces of the cherubim be. And thou shalt put the mercy-seat *above upon* the ark, and *in the ark thou shalt put the testimony* that I shall give thee" (Exodus 25:10-21).

It is probable, that the reason why Moses gave no description of them in Genesis was, because he intended to speak more particularly when he came to record their introduction into the most holy place of the tabernacle. In the text above recited, they are described as having wings and faces; and being made out of the same piece of gold as the mercy-seat, upon which they looked down, beholding, as it were, the blood sprinkled upon it; it is evident, they were symbols connected with the institution of atonement for sin through the shedding of blood. But they were still more significative. They were God's throne in Israel. Hence, the psalmist saith, "The Lord reigneth; he *sitteth* between the cherubim". This throne was erected upon mercy; and for this reason it was, that the covering of the ark containing the testimony, the manna (Exodus 16:33; John 6:33), and the resurrected rod (Numbers 17:8; Isaiah 11:1), was styled the Mercy-seat, or throne, where the Lord covered the sins of the people. It was also the Oracle, or place from which God communed with Israel through Moses. "There", said the Lord, "will I meet with thee, and I will commune with thee from above the mercy seat, from between the two cherubim which are upon the Ark of Testimony, of all things which I will give thee in commandment unto the children of Israel."

But, though Moses informs us of two cherubim with a plurality of faces and wings each, [2] he does not tell us what kind of faces, or how many wings they had. This deficiency, however, seems to be supplied by Ezekiel. Those he saw had each of them *four faces* and *four wings*; a human body with feet like a calf's, and the hands of a man under their wings. Of their faces, one was like a man's; a second, like a lion's; a third, like that of an ox; and a fourth, like an eagle's. The things of his first chapter taken collectively evidently represent *the Messiah upon his throne, surrounded by his saints, and all energized and made glorious by the Spirit of God*. The rings of Ezekiel's wheels were full of eyes; but in the cherubim which John saw, the wheels were not introduced, but two more wings were added, and the eyes were transferred to the six wings (Revelation 4:8). In this place, the cherubim are styled "beasts", more properly *living creatures*; and are associated with "twenty-four elders".

Now, by attending to what is affirmed of them in another place, we shall see who are represented by the four cherubim of Ezekiel with four faces each, and their wheels; and the four of John with one different face each, and twenty-four typical elders. It is written, that "they fell down before the Lamb, having every one of them harps, and golden vials full of odours, which are [or represent] the prayers of the saints. And *they* sung a new song, saying, Thou art worthy to take the book, and to open the seals thereof: for thou wast slain, and hast redeemed *us* to God by thy blood out of every kindred, and tongue, and people, and nation;

2 They would of necessity have two wings each; but the scripture does not here specify a plurality of faces *each* (Exodus 25:37). We read of "the face of a cherub" (Ezekiel 10). "*The* cherubim of Eden (Genesis 3:24, RV) appear to be the angels (compare the incident of Balaam, Numbers 22:31); those of Moses and Solomon were manufactured figures of divine specification, that ritually represented men of God made one in Christ and "equal unto the angels". The cherubim and living creatures of Ezekiel and John represent this "one body" in the relations here graphically described by Dr. Thomas.

and hast made *us* unto our God kings and priests; and **we** *shall reign on earth*" (Revelation 5:8-10). *From this it is evident, that the cherubim, etc., represent the aggregate of those redeemed from the nations, in their resurrection state.* The Lamb, the four cherubs, and the twenty-four elders, are a symbolical representation of what is expressed by the phrase, "them that are sanctified *in* Christ Jesus, called *saints*"; that is, those who have been constituted the righteousness of God in Christ *in a glorified state*.

The Cherubim are the *federal* symbol; and *the eyes*, representative of the *individuals* constituted *in him* who is signified by the Cherubim. The Lamb is introduced to represent the relationship between the holy eyes, or saints, and the Cherubic Faces; that is, between them and the Lord Jesus; while "*the twenty-four elders*" are indicative of their constitution as "the Israel of God". There are *twenty-four*, because the kingdom of God, being an Israelitish Commonwealth, is arranged with the *twelve sons of Jacob* as its gates (Revelation 21:12); and with *the twelve apostles of the Lamb* as its foundations (verse 14; Ephesians 2:20); the former being the entrance into present life of the *fleshly* tribes, or *subjects*; and the latter, the foundations of the *adopted* tribes, or **heirs** of the kingdom; so that twenty-four is the representative constitutional number of the spiritual Israel of God; for without the natural the spiritual could not be; any more than there could be adopted Americans, if there was no American nation.

But, the Mosaic Cherubim were deficient of several of the characteristics which distinguish those of Ezekiel and John. They had simply the wings and the faces. His Cherubim were not only of beaten gold continuous with the substance of the mercy seat; but they were embroidered into the Veil, made of blue, purple, and scarlet, and fine twined linen, which divided the holy and the holiest places of the tabernacle. Now, when "Jesus cried with a loud voice, he expired; and *the Veil of the Temple was rent in twain from top to bottom*" (Mark 15:37,38). Thus, we see the breaking of the body of Jesus identified with the rending of the Cherubic Veil; thereby indicating that the latter was representative of the Lord.

We have arrived then at this, that the Mosaic Cherubim were symbolical of "*God manifest in the flesh*". We wish now to ascertain upon what principles His incarnate manifestation was represented by the Cherubim? First, then, in the solution of this interesting problem, I remark, that the scriptures speak of God after the following manner: "God is *light*, and in him is no darkness at all" (1 John 1:5); again, "God is a *Spirit*; and they that worship him, must worship him in spirit and in truth" (1 John 4:24); and thirdly, "Our God is a consuming *fire*" (Deuteronomy 4:24). In these three texts, which are only a sample of many others, we perceive that God is represented by *light*, *spirit*, and *fire*; when, therefore, He is symbolized as manifest in *flesh*, it becomes necessary to select certain signs representative of light, spirit, and fire, derived from the *animal* kingdom. Now, the ancients selected the *lion*, the *ox*, and the *eagle* for this purpose, probably from tradition of the signification of these animals, or the faces of them, in the original Cherubim. They are called God's Faces because His omniscience, purity, and jealousy are expressed in them. But the omniscient, jealous, and incorruptible God was to be manifested in a particular kind of flesh. Hence, it was necessary to add *a fourth face* to show in what *nature* He would show Himself. For this reason, the *human* face was associated with the lion, the ox, and the eagle.

These four faces united in one human shape, formed out of beaten gold; and two such, not separate and distinct symbols, but standing one on each end of the mercy-seat, and the same in continuity and substance with it; – taken as a whole, represented Jesus, the true blood-sprinkled mercy-seat, or propitiatory, "in whom dwelleth the fulness of the Godhead bodily" (Romans 3:25; Colossians 2:3,9). All four faces were to look upon the mercy-seat, so as to behold the sprinkled blood of the yearly sacrifice. To accomplish this, two cherubs were necessary; so that the lion and the ox faces of the one; and the man and the eagle faces of the other, should all be "mercy-seat-ward".

It will be seen from this view of things, how important a place the Cherubim occupied in the worship of God connected with "*the representation of the truth*". They were not objects of adoration; but symbols representing to the mind of an intelligent believer the Seed of the woman as God manifested in the likeness of sinful flesh. This I take it was the significance of the Cherubim which the Lord God placed at the east of the garden; and which became the germ, as it were, of the shadowy observances of the patriarchal and Mosaic institutions; whose substance was of Christ.

8 |

The seraphim

(C. C. Walker, 1926)

Although the seraphim appear less often than the cherubim, they are to be found in one of the most exalted visions of all scripture (Isaiah 6). In this article from *The Christadelphian* of October 1926, Brother C. C. Walker briefly looks at the seraphim and a key occurrence of the Hebrew root word *saraph*. The article was part of a series on God Manifestation that were later published in book form under the title *Theophany*.

THE manifestations of God are often set forth in the scriptures in visions of cherubim and seraphim. These words are Hebrew plural forms, the singular in each case being cherub and seraph. In the English Bible the singular cherub is found frequently; but the singular seraph is not found. In the Hebrew Bible the singular seraph (*saraph*) is found in what at first sight appears to be a strange connection. Moses was commanded by God saying –

> "Make thee a fiery serpent [*saraph*] and set it upon a pole; and it shall come to pass that everyone that is bitten, when he looketh upon it shall live. And Moses made a serpent of brass [*nechash nechosheth*] and put it upon a pole, and it came to pass that if a serpent had bitten any man when he beheld the serpent of brass he lived." (Numbers 21:8,9)

From the words of Jesus to Nicodemus there is no mistaking the theophany represented by this serpent (*saraph*). He said:

> "As Moses lifted up the serpent in the wilderness, even so must the Son of Man be lifted up; that whosoever believeth in him should not perish, but have eternal life." (John 3:14,15)

The *saraph* on the pole then is "Jesus Christ and him crucified", on whom Paul, for example, "looked" so earnestly that he told the Corinthians that he was "determined to know nothing else among them" (1 Corinthians 2:2).

The only enquiry necessary then is, why these serpents of the wilderness should be called "fiery serpents" (*hannachashim hasseraphim*), and why brass (or copper) should be divinely specified as the metal for the manufacture of the symbolic serpent. Gesenius tells us that the secondary meaning of the verb *saraph* is "to burn, to consume", and hence supposes the word as applied to the serpents in the wilderness to refer to the poisonous bite. "The sting of death is sin" (1 Corinthians 15:56). And God "hath made Jesus to be sin for us who knew no sin; that we might be made the righteousness of God in him" (2 Corinthians 5:21). But he was "a brand plucked out of the fire" (Zechariah 3:2).

Brass or copper is made by the fiery treatment of the ore, and there may perhaps be some reference to the natural colour of the serpents (compare the "copperheads" of the USA). Gesenius gives as the primary meaning of the word *nachash* "to hiss", but suggests as a secondary meaning "to shine"; and Bullinger, in *The Companion Bible*, has applied this to the supernatural "Devil" of Christendom. This we cannot receive; but there appears to be the alternate "shining" of copper and brass, which is superficially so much like that of the more precious metal gold and actually so far removed from it in chemical nature and value. Metaphorically, the "grievous revolters" of Israel were "brass and iron ... corrupters". "Reprobate silver shall men call them because the Lord hath rejected them" (Jeremiah 6:28-30). When the Israelites in Hezekiah's day had made a god of the brazen serpent, he broke it up and called it "Nehushtan", a piece of brass

(2 Kings 18:4). And it would almost seem that the Hebrew word for brass (*nechosheth*) was always associated with the idea of the serpent (*nechash*) in the wilderness.

In Isaiah, chapter six, the plural *seraphim* (RV) is found (verses 2,6) in connection with a vision of the glory of Christ. This we are told by John (12:41): "These things said Esaias when he saw his glory and spake of him." What the prophet saw was a vision of the temple-throne of God in Jerusalem when the whole earth is filled with the glory of the Lord. "Then shall the righteous shine forth as the Sun in the Kingdom of their Father" (Matthew 13:43; Ezekiel 43:1-9). If Jesus be the central manifestation of the glory that the Father has given him (John 17:22), the Seraph by pre-eminence, who are the seraphim but those whom the Father has given him, as he says, "The glory which thou gavest me I have given them; that they may be one, even as we are one. I in them, and thou in me, that they may be made perfect in one; and that the world may know that thou hast sent me, and hast loved them as thou hast loved me".

This does not exclude the idea that the *seraphim* of Isaiah may also represent other immortal sons of God (angels) who actually ministered to the prophet, and afterwards to Jesus, in the days of the flesh; for Jesus promises that the "worthy" shall be "equal unto the angels, and the children of God, being the children of the resurrection" (Luke 20:36). The prophet was made the subject of a purification by "one of the seraphim", who touched his lips with a live coal taken from off the altar, saying, "Lo, this hath touched thy lips; and thine iniquity is taken away, and thy sin is purged" (Isaiah 6:7).

Thus prepared he was sent against the house of Israel to proclaim a hardening and blinding "until the cities should be wasted without inhabitant, and the houses without man and the land be utterly desolate". "But yet", said the word of the Lord, "there shall be a tenth that shall return ... the holy seed shall be the substance thereof." "I will come again", said Jesus, "and receive you unto myself, that where I am, there ye may be also"

(John 14:3). This he spoke concerning the many "abiding places" in "the Father's house". This is the substance of Isaiah's vision of the seraphim.

9 |

Difficulties for solution

(John Thomas, 1858)

From 1851 until 1861, Brother Thomas edited the magazine *The Herald of the Kingdom and Age to Come*, initially from his base in Richmond, Virginia (USA) and later from New York City. Often he would field questions from readers. In the April 1858 issue, questions were put to the Doctor from a Brother George Dean Wilson. Brother Wilson had moved to the USA from Halifax (UK) in 1856, and was an energetic force in both preaching the Gospel and in sharpening the internal organisation of the growing ecclesias of the Midwest. The second of his questions gave Brother Thomas opportunity to comment on God Manifestation, in the course of which he made one of his most well-known statements on the subject, highlighted by the current publishers in bold.

DEAR BROTHER, – Again I beg to trespass a little upon your valuable time and space, but as I know that your pages are always open to the investigation of Bible truths, I wish to lay some important questions before you, a few at a time. Many of them will be rather "deep", but as we have great confidence in your ability to solve them, I do not think they will be too difficult for you. I ask them, too, more for the sake of some of the dear brethren, to whom they have been more or less perplexing, than for my own sake. I will reserve a few of the most difficult to the last.

1. Would Jesus have established his kingdom at his first advent if the Jews had received him, as Luke 13:34, and others like it, seem to prove? Or what would this gathering have been? And how would it have affected the destinies of our race? Have they not lost a chance of being delivered from their miseries long ago?
2. Why are the people of one age more favoured than those of another, in hearing the Gospel and being saved? For instance, see what numbers were converted during the apostolic age, whilst whole nations and generations of men had gone down to the dust without ever having heard a message of warning, or testimony of mercy and righteousness. And, again, in millennial times, what multitudes will be blessed and saved under divine knowledge and government, whilst millions have perished in their intervening ages. I know that in those two favoured ages – apostolic and millennial – it is the *direct working* of the Spirit's power, in a more visible and potent manner, which is the cause of such eminent success, but why does God put it forth more signally in one age than another, seeing that one generation needs the blessings of salvation as much as another? And it is said that "God will have all men to be saved" (1 Timothy 2:4); that "he is not willing that any should perish" (2 Peter 3:9). Some would be ready to accuse Him of partiality and injustice, but I would not entertain such a wicked thought of my Heavenly Father for one moment, but rather attribute the fault to men. Still, if you can give the *scriptural philosophy* of this matter, it will help many of us to expound the things of salvation more clearly on such points, when laying them before our dying fellow men.
3. Why are we commanded to baptize into the name of the Holy Spirit if he be not a distinct personality, like the Father and the Son (Matthew 28:19)? If the Spirit be nothing more than a substance, a power, or an attribute of God, or of Christ, and not a third person, it seems strange to

> command men to be immersed in the name of the Father, and the Son (who are both distinct persons or beings), and then into the Holy Spirit, which you seem to make out to be only another name for the Father, or something of that sort, and not a third personality. This text alone has held my mind from embracing the idea of the *non-personality* of the Spirit, although I admit that in most places in the Bible the "Spirit of the Lord", etc., seems to denote a *power*, *divine strength*, or energy, both physical and spiritual, rather than a person. But there are difficulties in the way. In John 15:16 and many similar passages, proper person or *being* and *action* are ascribed to him.

I will not trouble you with any more at present, though there are some questions remaining yet on my list.

May the Lord give you health, joy and happiness, and spare your valuable labours long to us, and keep you blameless till the day of Christ. Amen.

Yours, in hope of the coming kingdom,

GEO. D. WILSON.

Geneva, Ill., Aug. 15, 1856.

The difficulties considered

1. *Would Jesus have established his kingdom at his first advent if the Jews had received him?*

In the absence of all testimony in regard to such an eventuality, it is impossible to say what would have been done. This is certain, that a testament, covenant, or will, is of no force while the testator lives. The right of Jesus and his brethren to the Holy Land and to the kingdom proper to it, rests upon the covenants made with Abraham and David. These covenants were ordained in the hands of a Mediator, who was to be the Eternal Spirit manifested in their seed, who was to be, also, Son of God. If the mediator of the new covenant had appeared and been received by the Jews, he would have had no right to attempt the establishment of the kingdom. It was absolutely necessary that he should die by violence of the Serpent-power,

1. That sin might be condemned in sin's flesh;
2. That the sins of his brethren might be borne by him on the cross; and,
3. That the covenants might come into force, etc.

If the Jews had received him, they would not have put him to death, how, then, could the saving be fulfilled, "They shall look upon Me, whom they have pierced"? It should have read, in that case, "They shall look on Me, whom they received". But if the Jews had received him the Romans would not, and had he then, in the days of his weakness (and he was crucified through weakness), aided by the Jews, attempted to establish the kingdom, the force of the Roman Empire would have been brought against him, and would certainly have prevailed; for it had been before predicted in Daniel that "the Little Horn should make war upon the saints, and prevail against them". Daniel and Isaiah would have been turned into false prophets, and God would have been filled with darkness. In short, the question may be said to propound an impossible supposition, impossible in view of the testimony.

2. *Why are the people of one age more favoured than those of another, in hearing the Gospel and being saved?*

Because one generation of flesh and blood happens to live contemporary with the times appointed in the original plan, while other generations do not. No injustice is done to the nations and generations that never heard the Gospel. Before they were born into the world they were nothing; after they died they went to nothing, so they became as though they had never been. They had no hopes, and now they have no regrets; why, then, need we burden ourselves with sorrowings for them that know nothing and care for nothing? "The dead know not anything."

Men were not ushered into being for the purpose of being saved or lost. God-manifestation, not human

salvation, was the grand purpose of the Eternal Spirit. The salvation of a multitude is incidental to the manifestation, but it was not the end proposed. The Eternal Spirit intended to enthrone Himself on the earth, and, in so doing, to develop a Divine Family from among men, every one of whom shall be spirit because born of the Spirit, and that this family shall be large enough to fill the earth, when perfected, to the entire exclusion of flesh and blood. In elaborating this purpose, upon the principles revealed in the Bible, a far greater production of human kind occurs than is necessary. Hence vast multitudes are swept off by disease, war, and so forth, and the multitude left are of but little more use than to keep the world going until the Divine Family shall become complete. God will take out from the human race as many for His name as His purpose requires. If He chose to make apostolic demonstrations every two hundred years, He could, doubtless, obtain a hundred fold more for the kingdom than upon the present system; but He does not so operate. It is fair, then, to conclude that His purpose does not demand so many, and that, therefore, He only employs means adequate to what He desires.

True, "one generation *needs* the blessings of salvation as much as another", but it is not God's pleasure to respond to all their needs, for the plain reason that He does not. The more light the more responsibility; hence, there will be, no doubt, more raised to Aion judgment who have previously lived in the apostolic age than of those who live in this generation of ours. It is, therefore, a merciful dispensation to leave "the Veil of the Covering" over the intoxicated nations until the appointed time to teach them righteousness by the only means that can effect it – by the argument of Divine force, as introductory to the force of Divine argument. "When thy judgments, O Jehovah, are in the earth the inhabitants of the world will learn righteousness" (Isaiah 26:9). This is the only remedy for our rebellious race.

God has given light enough and ample means enough for the taking out all needed for His name. The light is strong enough for an honest and good heart to see by, but it is not strong enough to bring men to obedience of a contrary description. Men who do not think and dare not reason or act, lest they should jeopardise their social position or be wounded in the vested interests, can never see the kingdom of God. The light is not strong enough for them, and their constant exclamation is, "I do not see it in that light", "I cannot so understand it". It is never convenient for them to see anything by which "*the idols of the den*" are made to follow the lead of Dagon:

"The household gods must be preserved,
Whatever else betide!"

God does not "*will* all men to be saved and come to the knowledge of the truth", in the sense of *compelling* such a result. That He does not is clear, from the fact that very few of mankind in each generation arrive at that knowledge, and the salvation is scrupulously predicated upon the knowledge and obedience of the truth. The original words of Paul to Timothy do not sanction such a supposition. Speaking of God, he says, "who is willing that all men be saved and come to the exact knowledge of truth; for there is one God and one Mediator of God and men, Jesus, a man anointed, who gave himself a ransom for all; the testimony in its proper times" (1 Timothy 2:4-6). The proof of God's willingness is seen in His sending an invitation to all men, offering them the kingdom, power, and glory, of which the Gospel treats, with eternal life at the resurrection; and the extent of the salvation or amplitude of the "*all*" is also seen in accompanying the invitation in the history of its proclamation; so that when his willingness shall have found its full development, and the fruits shall be gathered in, they will sing, "Thou hast purchased us for God with thy blood **out of every** kindred, and tongue, and people, and nation" (Revelation 5:9). He is willing that any man, Jew, Turk, Protestant, Pagan, or Papist should be saved on the terms He has appointed, for "he is no respecter of persons", but He will not force men to be saved, nor will He permit them to be saved if they will not believe His promises and do His commands.

In 2 Peter 3:9, the word rendered "*willing*" is not the same as used by Paul above. Peter said, "Not desiring or wishing that any perish". The "any" are related to the "*toward*", in the sentence immediately before. He is willing that the incorrigible perish, but He does not desire or wish that any of the saints should perish. There were certain before Peter's mind who had obeyed the truth, but "had forsaken the right way" (2:15), and who were about to fall into that furnace of fire that was shortly to devour Judah. It was the Lord's long-suffering towards such errorists of the circumcision that caused the seeming delay with which the apostles were taunted. He did not wish any of them to perish, but that they might all come to a change of mind.

In relation to the name of the Holy Spirit, let the reader turn to what we have already written upon it, in our article of this number, on the *Mosaic and Nazarene Teaching Concerning God*, which, for the present, will suffice.

EDITOR.

Feb. 26, 1858

Section 2

The God of truth

(John Morris)

In section 1 we considered God Manifestation as the relationship between the Father, who alone has immortality, and His *elohim* of all classes. We also considered what might be considered the more technical elements of the subject, for instance the Yahweh name or the symbol of the Cherubim. These things are all vital to a correct understanding of this important Bible doctrine.

There is however, another important side to the matter. For any true disciple, the name Yahweh Elohim is a challenge as well as a promise. For in the Bible, we do not have a detailed description of the physical person of the Father. Instead we have Him as a character, and it is this character that is to be manifest in the life of a saint. The outworking of God Manifestation can therefore only be identified using knowledge of the personality of the Father. It was this personality, declared most clearly in the life of the Lord Jesus, that Brother John Morris gives an initial introduction to in the fifteen articles that follow. They first appeared in *The Christadelphian* over consecutive months from January 1994 to March 1995, under the heading "The God of truth".

---

1 |

Names, titles and attributes of the Almighty

FROM the scriptures we learn the great truths of God's revelation of Himself and His purpose. Early on in the Old Testament we are introduced to His Names and Titles – El, Elohim, El Shaddai, Adonai and others; we are taught His covenant Name, Yahweh, the Name by which especially He was to be known among His people:

> "The LORD, the LORD God, merciful and gracious, longsuffering, and abundant in goodness and truth, keeping mercy for thousands, forgiving iniquity and transgression and sin, and that will by no means clear the guilty ..."
>
> (Exodus 34:6,7)

Then, as we move from the Old to the New Testament, we meet him who was foreshadowed not only in type and prophecy but also in the very names of God Himself: the one to whom was given "a name that is above every name" – the Lord Jesus Christ, embodiment in human form of the nature and characteristics of the Father:

> "For the law was given by Moses, but grace and truth came by Jesus Christ." (John 1:17)

God Manifestation

Christadelphian writings on the subject of God's Names, from passages in *Elpis Israel* onwards, are readily available; and their study has led to rewarding expositions of God-manifestation. What we wish to attempt in this series is something supplementary to the necessary study of God's Names: to look at attributes of God which, though closely associated with His Memorial Name, or other names, are worthy of consideration in their own right – such qualities as Holiness, Mercy, Goodness, Love, Salvation, Truth and Judgement.

Every attribute that one can name, every quality and virtue, finds its full expression in the Almighty: "Righteousness and judgement are the foundation of thy throne: mercy and truth go before thy face" (Psalm 89:14, RV). "With him is plenteous redemption" (130:7). "Thou art holy, thou that inhabitest the praises of Israel" (22:3). The wonder of the Hebrew language, particularly, is that it speaks always in concrete terms. God is not merely merciful: He is mercy – the embodiment and essence of all that mercy means. He is not just a Saviour: He is salvation. Typically, it is in a Jewish commentary that this feature of Bible idiom in relation to God is brought out:

> "This noble language [in Deuteronomy] gives utterance to truths which are always and everywhere sovereign – that God is one ... that *God is Righteousness and Faithfulness, Mercy and Love*." (Introduction to Deuteronomy, in *The Pentateuch and Haftorahs*)

The aim of these articles will be to draw from scripture itself a deeper understanding of qualities which are God's own, but which He seeks to manifest in His servants – and which were fully and wonderfully portrayed in His Son. Our study will of course take us into both Old and New Testaments, for although the divine characteristics are taught first in the Old Testament, they are revealed afresh in the New, and in particular in the person and character of the Lord Jesus Christ himself. Indeed, in a style very reminiscent of that used to describe the attributes of the Lord God in the Old Testament, Paul speaks of the Son – "who of God is *made unto us wisdom, and righteousness, and sanctification, and redemption*" (1 Corinthians 1:30).

Divine qualities

The purpose of the series is to explore a little of this vast subject. Often words will fail us in trying to describe the character of God, and we shall be humbled in our contemplation. For those, however, who are attuned by the reading of the word, these truths shine forth; and today as never before they need to be proclaimed. In a world which has forgotten God, which rejects divine standards, which knows no absolutes (save that of evil) we need to have our understanding of God refreshed, confirmed and deepened; to be reminded of God's perfection and the promise that, through our faltering attempts to imitate His qualities, we may at last be partakers of the divine nature ourselves:

> "Beloved, now are we the sons of God, and it doth not yet appear what we shall be: but we know that, when he shall appear, we shall be like him; for we shall see him as he is."
>
> (1 John 3:2)

2 |

"Holy, Holy, Holy"

THE Bible introduces God without defining His character: "In the beginning God created the heaven and the earth." There is no description of His nature, no account of His attributes: indeed, we are well on into the Old Testament before most of the characteristics we take for granted are actually named. Yet many of those attributes are evident from the earliest pages of Genesis – implicit in what God says and does.

In the very first chapter of Genesis, although no attribute is specified, certain important characteristics are manifest. He is a God who "created", "said", "divided", "made", "called", "set", "blessed", "ended", and "rested" (1:1-2:2). Such actions speak of God's creative power, His omnipotence, purpose and care for creation. In chapter 3, God's holiness is not mentioned, yet the fact that Adam and Eve hid themselves, having eaten of the forbidden tree, is proof that the knowledge of good and evil had taught them the holiness of God, one who is "of purer eyes than to behold evil" (Habakkuk 1:13). The events leading up to the Flood speak eloquently of God's love for mankind, His grief at man's wickedness, His mercy towards Noah, who "found grace in the eyes of the LORD" (Genesis 6:8). And after the Flood we learn of God's lovingkindness shown in His covenant "no more ... to destroy all flesh" (9:15). Paradoxically, Noah's righteousness is mentioned before that of God Himself (6:9) – though, even if God's righteousness has not been spoken of, it shines clearly enough through His dealings with unrighteous Cain and the world which perished in the Flood, and with the men of Babel. Abraham was commanded: "Walk before me, and be thou perfect [upright, or sincere]", with the implication that these are divine qualities which man must imitate.

Perhaps enough has been said to show that the Bible does not commence with a 'Glossary of terms' to describe our Maker; there is no list of attributes, by which God's character is defined. Instead the pages of the Bible introduce us to a God who, initially at least, reveals His attributes by His actions.

Of all the many characteristics of God, which one should be considered first? His glory? His mercy? His righteousness? His love? Do the scriptures suggest which one is paramount? In a sense, no characteristic of the Almighty is less, or more, significant than another. We suggest, however, that one aspect of His nature does stand out as altogether special – His holiness. Holiness is the watershed from which so many other qualities spring. Holiness stems from God's uniqueness, His 'other-ness'; it is that quality which distinguishes Him from His creation, the attribute that engenders contrition in those who would be godly, and that requires judgement to be visited on the ungodly. Holiness leads on to righteousness, grace, mercy, truth and love, to fear and judgement: it justifies consideration first.

'Separated', 'set apart'

The concordance tells us that (in the Old Testament) "holiness" is a translation of the Hebrew word *qodesh*, which describes a place or person 'set apart', 'separated' for an exalted purpose. The adjective "holy" and the verb "to hallow" are translations of closely related words. In God is seen absolute holiness, for He is the One totally set apart, separate from His humbler creation, exalted in the heavens, of ultimate purity and perfection. The first occurrence of "holiness" is in Exodus: "Who is like unto thee, O LORD, among the gods? Who is like thee, glorious in holiness, fearful in praises, doing wonders?" (15:11).

But while God represents absolute holiness, He is able to endue with holiness those objects and persons who may to some imperfect degree represent that holiness on earth. Touched by God's holiness, they are 'set apart', consecrated to the service of God. On a golden plate worn on the High Priest's forehead was to be inscribed "HOLINESS TO THE LORD" (Exodus 28:36; 39:30). Everything about the Law of Moses spoke of the holiness of God: sacrifices, washings, the arrangements of the tabernacle, the attire of the priests, the holy anointing oil – each aspect was designed to educate the worshipper in holiness. They were, after all, called to be "an holy people unto the LORD thy God ... a special people unto himself" (Deuteronomy 7:6). "Ye shall be holy: for I the LORD your God am holy" (Leviticus 19:2). Like all men and women, they were in fact unholy, unworthy because of sin to come into God's holy presence, but the Law provided a means whereby the people, by bringing their offerings to the *sanctuary* ('holy place'), might be *sanctified* ('declared holy'); they could become *saints* ('holy ones', *qadosh*). Holiness could even (contrary to normal expectations) be transmitted from holy objects to those who touched them: "And thou shalt sanctify them [the altar, laver, vessels, etc.] that they may be most holy: whatsoever toucheth them shall be holy" (Exodus 30:26-29; see Haggai 2:12-14).

In fact, of course, the people never achieved true holiness: "The law having a shadow of the good things to come, and not the very image of the things, can never with those sacrifices which they offered year by year continually, make the comers thereunto perfect" (Hebrews 10:1). In Christ, on the other hand, by virtue of the personal holiness which he manifested, we have "boldness to enter into the holiest by the blood of Jesus" (verse 19); "We are sanctified through the offering of the body of Jesus Christ once for all" (verse 10).

The Law was holy (Romans 7:12). Yet it failed to make man holy; and though it should have taught the holiness of God, even in this it did not fully achieve its object. Mercifully, God also revealed His holiness at other times and in other ways. At the burning bush, Moses learned that "the place whereon thou standest is holy ground" (Exodus 3:5 – the first occurrence of *qodesh*, 'holy'). Joshua, standing before the captain of the LORD's host at Jericho, heard almost the same words (Joshua 5:15). David had a deep appreciation of the holiness of God and His piercing gaze: "The LORD is in his holy temple, the LORD's throne is in heaven: his eyes behold, his eyelids try, the children of men" (Psalm 11:4; cf. Habakkuk 2:20).

God the Holy One

More than any other man of God, Isaiah was granted an intimate understanding of the holiness of God: "The LORD of hosts is exalted in judgement, and God *the Holy One* is sanctified in righteousness" (5:16, RV). "For thus saith the high and lofty One that inhabiteth eternity, whose name is Holy; I dwell in the high and holy place ..." (57:15). In both of these quotations, the idea of God's holiness is coupled with His exaltedness. But especially in the vision of chapter 6 is this association impressed upon us, for the prophet "saw the Lord sitting upon a throne, high and lifted up ... And one cried unto another, and said, Holy, holy, holy, is the LORD of Hosts: the whole earth is full of his glory" (6:1-3).

Few mortals have been granted such a vision. Moses, Aaron, Nadab and Abihu, and seventy of the elders of Israel went up into the mountain of God and "saw the God of Israel: and there was under his feet as it were a paved work of sapphire stone, and as it were the very heaven for clearness" (Exodus 24:10, RV). The disciples had a glimpse of heavenly things in the mount of transfiguration. John had a vision very similar to that of Isaiah – "a throne set in heaven, and one sitting upon the throne ... And the four living creatures ... have no rest day and night, saying, Holy, holy, holy, is the Lord God, the Almighty, which was and which is and which is to come" (Revelation 4:1,2,8, RV).

The most High God

What these visions have in common is the fact that the Lord God is "lifted up", a feature that takes our minds to one of the divine names, El Elyon, "the most high God". This was the name used by Melchizedek, who "blessed Abram and said, Blessed be Abram of the most high God, possessor of heaven and earth" (Genesis 14:19). Balaam, in his visions, refers to "the most High" (Numbers 24:16). In the Song of Moses, God is "the most High" and "the Rock" – one to whom man looks up, in whose shadow one can feel secure (Deuteronomy 32:4,8). In David's Song, imagery appropriate to an exalted God is again employed: "The LORD is my rock, and my fortress ... my high tower, and my refuge ... The LORD thundered from heaven, and the most High uttered his voice" (2 Samuel 22:2-14). And similar language is to be found in the Psalms – for example, 57:2,5,10,11; 91:1,2,14.

We need today to enter a little more into the Hebrew mind, which sees God always "on high", "lifted up", and man correspondingly lowly. Yet if man will learn to be contrite, repentant, then he will himself be lifted up. As David goes on to say:

> "He setteth me upon my high places ... Thou also hast lifted me up on high above them that rose up against me."
>
> (2 Samuel 22:34,49)

Returning now to Isaiah 6, we observe the prophet overawed at the vision he had seen. The reason he gives for his distress is that "mine eyes have seen the King": the contrast between God's holiness and his own uncleanness provokes the cry, "Woe is me! for I am undone" (verse 5). But the prophet's contrite and humble reaction to the vision leads to him being cleansed and lifted up. James may well have had Isaiah in mind when he wrote: "Humble yourselves in the sight of the Lord, and he shall lift you up" (4:10).

Before we leave Isaiah 6, one feature of the incident is worthy of note, namely, the "live coal" with which the prophet's lips were purged. God's holiness is frequently associated with fire – for example, at the burning bush (Exodus 3:2); and when God answered Moses through thunder and lightning on Mount Sinai, "and the smoke thereof ascended as the smoke of a furnace" (19:18; Deuteronomy 4:12, etc.). The significance is plain enough, for fire represents judgement: it purges and destroys, and if man is to come within the holiness of God, then purging is both necessary and good. We shall return to the subject of divine judgement in a later chapter.

"Holy, harmless, undefiled"

These thoughts prepare us for a consideration of the One who, in close communion with his Father, had an infinitely greater comprehension of God's holiness and exaltedness than any who had lived before. As the Spirit of God had moved upon the face of the waters in the first creation, so God's Spirit – the *Holy* Spirit – now brought about the miracle of the new creation in the birth of Jesus:

> "The Holy Spirit shall come upon thee, and the power of the Most High shall overshadow thee: wherefore also that which is to be born shall be called holy [*hagion*, 'separate', 'set apart'], the Son of God." (Luke 1:32-35)

And how often is his coming seen as an expression of God's *holy* will. Mary said: "He that is mighty hath done to me great things; and *holy* is his name" (verse 49). Zacharias (in connection with the coming of the forerunner, John the Baptist) prophesied:

> "God hath visited and redeemed his people ... as he spake by the mouth of his *holy* prophets ... to remember his *holy* covenant ... that we ... might serve him without fear, in *holiness* and righteousness before him." (verses 68-75)

The Lord Jesus Christ did, of course, fulfil all that was foretold of him: he was "*holy*, harmless, undefiled, *separate* from sinners, *and made higher than the heavens*" (Hebrews 7:26 – note once more the association of holiness and exaltedness). He was described to the angel of the church in Philadelphia as "he that is true, *he that is holy*, he that hath the key of David ..." (Revelation 3:7; cf. 6:10).

"Hallowed be thy name"

By manifesting true holiness, Jesus acknowledged the source and inspiration of all holiness – the Father Himself. "*Hallowed* be thy name" was for our Lord not merely part of a prayer but a way of life, seeking in every action to proclaim the holiness of God. John's Gospel, curiously, hardly mentions the attribute of holiness, but in the intimacy of his "high-priestly" prayer Jesus addresses the Lord God once as "Holy Father" (John 17:11). When he prays, "*Sanctify* them through thy truth ... that they also might be *sanctified* through the truth" (verses 17,19), the Lord is, moreover, using a verb (*hagiazō*, 'set apart') corresponding with the word holy and showing that in him we can be accounted holy.

How we, as sinners, may be accounted holy is a subject in itself – outside the remit of this series (though it will be touched upon as we consider God's mercy, grace and lovingkindness). Suffice it here to remind ourselves that the God of holiness has provided the means whereby we can be "holy and without blame before him in love" (Ephesians 1:4).

"Be ye holy"

We are "called to be saints" (1 Corinthians 1:2); "He hath saved us, and called us with a holy calling" (2 Timothy 1:9). In the Epistles of Peter, we encounter phrases which take us back to Old Testament passages we have already quoted:

> "As he which hath called you is holy, so be ye holy in all manner of conversation; because it is written, Be ye holy; for I am holy." (1 Peter 1:15,16; Leviticus 11:44)

We have no open vision of the holiness of God. In "the holy one of God", however, that holiness was fully revealed; and with his example before us we are called upon to walk in holiness ourselves: "Seeing then that all these things shall be dissolved, what manner of persons ought ye to be in all holy conversation and godliness?" (2 Peter 3:11).

"Having therefore these promises, dearly beloved, let us cleanse ourselves from all filthiness of the flesh and spirit, *perfecting holiness in the fear of God*." (2 Corinthians 7:1)

3 |

"The glory of the LORD"

THE consideration of God's attributes makes the highest demands on our faculties. True, we are made in God's image, wonderfully endowed with the capacity to think godly thoughts; supplied in scripture with the vocabulary by which we can talk of spiritual matters. Yet here we are, earthbound creatures, hampered by our finite comprehension, limited by the misshapen language of our mother tongue – how can we speak adequately of things divine, things absolute and infinite?

In fact, we must acknowledge with gratitude that the English language, having been moulded by scriptural ideas, is among the best for conveying spiritual concepts. These are much harder to communicate in many other languages. Even so, a declining acquaintance with the Bible means that we need to redefine or explain words which, though in our dictionaries, have lost the special significance they formerly had. On the one hand, a word like "sin" is no longer so dark (in men's eyes) as once it was; on the other hand, concepts such as "holiness" (our topic in the last chapter) or "glory" (which we shall now examine) are no longer so exalted in meaning. "Love", "honour", "power", "truth", "fear" – each of them an aspect of the character of God – have become trivialised; while the divine sense of other words such as "grace", "redemption", "jealousy" has been lost.

Excellency, honour, majesty

If, then, we would discover the meaning of "glory", we must look behind the superficiality of today's meaning. A dictionary will suggest 'splendour', 'fame', 'renown': these, certainly, are *part* of the quality as it applies to God, but how much more exalted is that divine attribute in its fulness! In the Old Testament, *kabod* is the Hebrew word most often translated "glory", and also sometimes rendered "honour". Less frequently employed are *hod* and *hadar*, translated "beauty", "comeliness", "excellency", "glory", "honour", "majesty"; and also *tipharah*, rendered "beauty", "bravery", "glory", "honour", "comely", "excellent", "fair". In the New Testament, *doxa* is the principal Greek word: usually translated "glory", it is also rendered "dignity", "honour", "praise", "worship".

Surveying *all* these meanings we begin to see the compass of the Biblical idea of "glory". The first occurrence of *kabod* in relation to God is in Exodus 16 when, at Elim, in response to the murmurings of the Israelites, God provided the manna and the quails:

> "They looked toward the wilderness, and, behold, the glory of the LORD appeared in the cloud. And the LORD spake unto Moses, saying, I have heard the murmurings of the children of Israel: speak unto them, saying, At even ye shall eat flesh, and in the morning ye shall be filled with bread ..."
>
> (Exodus 16:10-12)

What the people saw was, presumably, some display of brilliant light identifying the presence of God. Yet glory is more than just a display of light: that can be seen in a sunset, an example of "glory" at its most immediate level. When God reveals His glory to the full, it has an awe-inspiring effect: it commands reverence; it warns, moreover, of indignation against those who would turn away or treat it lightly. On this occasion the people were losing faith in Moses and in God – "Would that we had died in the land of Egypt" (verse 3) – and, far from merely indulging their appetite, God expresses in this chapter both His goodness and His severity (cf. Romans 11:22). When Israel obstinately tried to preserve the manna, or go out in search of it on the sabbath, God shows His anger: "How long refuse ye to keep my commandments?" (Exodus 16:28).

As with holiness, so with glory, the manifestation of the divine attribute always carries overtones of judgement if man decides to ignore it. Only a few chapters further on in Exodus (an incident referred to in the last chapter), Moses and Joshua went up into Sinai, into the cloud which covered the mount.

> "And the glory of the Lord abode upon mount Sinai, and the cloud covered it six days: and the seventh day he called unto Moses out of the midst of the cloud. And the sight of the glory of the LORD was like *devouring fire* on the top of the mount in the eyes of the children of Israel." (24:16,17)

"Splendour", "excellency", "majesty": such words may describe the outward appearance of the glory of God, but "glory" must also include some hint of the dread and fear of the Lord, which cause men to bow in awe and worship. This, at the very least, is "glory" in its Biblical sense.

The principle is the same when we turn to the New Testament and observe the reactions of the disciples to the transfiguration of the Lord Jesus Christ. Peter recounts that they "were eyewitnesses of his majesty. For he received from God the Father honour and glory, when there came such a voice to him from the excellent glory ..." (2 Peter 1:17). The Gospel record, however, touches on the element of fear: "When the disciples heard it, they fell on their face, and were sore afraid" (Matthew 17:6). Though Jesus himself then said, "Be not afraid", they were right in their response to the appearance of Christ in his glory. Ezekiel's response to his indescribable vision of glory (1:28) and John's reaction to "one like unto the Son of man", whose "countenance was as the sun shineth in his strength" were similar: they fell down in obeisance.

"For glory and for beauty"

But let us return to the Exodus, and to the developing revelation of God's glory. In chapter 28 instructions are given concerning the garments to be made for Aaron and his sons: "And thou shalt make holy garments for Aaron thy brother, for glory [*kabod*]and for beauty [*tipharah*]" (verses 2,40). For whose glory and beauty were such garments made? Certainly they would enhance the splendour and dignity of the High Priest, and show forth his honour among the people of God. Aaron, however, was but God's representative and it was *God's* glory that was here being proclaimed. The materials used for the robes and every aspect of their design spoke of their Designer: as we see from repeated references in this chapter, much use was made of "the gold, and the blue, and the purple, and the scarlet, and the fine twined linen" – all of which in their way, and especially the gold and the blue, reflected a heavenly origin.

And if "glory and beauty" were seen in the High Priesthood of Aaron's line, how much more were those attributes to be discerned in that greater High Priest, the Son of God himself, "the brightness of his glory, and the express image of his person ... Thou crownest him with glory and honour ... The Apostle and High Priest of our profession ... was counted worthy of more glory than Moses" (Hebrews 1:3; 2:7; 3:1,3).

There is, in Exodus 29, a verse of profound significance to our subject. Following on from chapter 28, it is concerned with the consecration of the priests, the altar and the tabernacle generally; it records the various offerings to be brought, whereby all that had to do with divine worship might be sanctified and hallowed. Yet there is a statement towards the end of the chapter which reminds us that, in the end, holiness is not achieved merely by the sacrifices, but by God, and God alone. And by what means? "And there [in the tabernacle of the congregation] I will meet with the children of Israel, and the tabernacle shall be sanctified *by my glory*." How wonderfully do God's holiness and His glory thus come together! In this instance, at least, it is the manifestation of God's glory, His very presence in pillar of cloud and fire, that brings about sanctification.

Holiness and glory are found together in other passages too: the one that immediately comes to mind is Isaiah 6, where the cry of the seraphim, "Holy, holy, holy, is the LORD of hosts" is immediately followed by "the whole earth is full of his glory" (verse 3) – not merely the tabernacle but the earth in its entirety is now seen to be sanctified by the glory of the Lord.

"Shew me thy glory"

And still there is more to learn from Exodus. We go now to chapter 33, and to the request of Moses, the man of God, "I beseech thee, shew me thy glory" (verse 18). God did not chide Moses for his wish: he knew that Moses needed reassurance, and He did not deny him a vision that would strengthen him for the tasks that lay ahead. Isaiah, Jeremiah, Ezekiel, the Lord Jesus Christ himself, and Saul of Tarsus were each granted special visions of God's glory to strengthen them at critical times in their lives.

Moses too had this privilege – yet what, in fact, did he see? The Lord promised that, "while my glory passeth by, I will put thee in a cleft of the rock ... and thou shalt see my back, but my face shall not be seen" (Exodus 33:22, RV). As the Lord passed by, however, it was not the visible splendour of God that was emphasised but aspects of His covenant Name: "The LORD, a God full of compassion, and gracious, slow to anger, and plenteous in mercy and truth ..." (34:6, RV). Once again, here and in so many places in scripture, we are taught that God's attributes are indivisible: we may, for the purpose of human understanding, choose to examine "holiness", then "glory", and study in turn each of the countless qualities of God. In truth, the characteristics of the Almighty defy human analysis.

We leave Exodus with the glory of God filling the tabernacle, as later it would fill the temple of Solomon, and (in vision) the temple of Ezekiel's prophecy (40:34-38; 2 Chronicles 7:1-3; Ezekiel 43:4,5). But before we pass on we note a principle that emerges on each occasion, namely, that sinful man cannot approach into the presence of God's glory: "Moses was *not able to enter* into the tent of the congregation, because the cloud abode thereon, and the glory of the LORD filled the tabernacle" (Exodus

40:35; cf. 2 Chronicles 7:2). Why? The impression given is that mortal man was forced back by the blinding splendour, and that was doubtless the case; but the principle behind this was that man, unholy, unredeemed, in spite of sacrifice and offering, still had no proper access into the presence of God. Only by the work of the Son would that way finally be opened:

> "For it became him, for whom are all things, and by whom are all things, *in bringing many sons unto glory*, to make the captain of their salvation perfect through sufferings." (Hebrews 2:10)

"We beheld his glory ..."

And so, passing over countless references to God's glory in the psalms and prophets, we move to the New Testament. Isaiah had promised that "the glory of the LORD shall be revealed, and all flesh shall see it together" (40:5). The Gentiles too would see it and be glad: "Arise, shine; for thy light is come, and the glory of the LORD is risen upon thee" (60:1). And when he came, the faithful were not disappointed: "We beheld his glory, glory as of the only begotten from the Father, full of grace and truth" (John 1:14). The Father's glory was manifested through the Son to those, like us, who had "come short of the glory of God" (Romans 3:23). More than that, something of the same divine glory was imparted to them – "I have glorified thee on the earth ... And the glory which thou gavest me I have given them" (John 17:1-5,22-24).

Who is sufficient for these things? Our minds go to Paul's magnificent exposition of the glory of God in 2 Corinthians, and we marvel that in an epistle full of so much heart-searching, even recrimination, the apostle can rise to this exalted theme. His thoughts go back to Sinai, as ours have done, and he reflects on the manifestation of the glory of God in the giving of the law:

> "But if the ministration of death, written and engraven on stones, came with glory, so that the children of Israel could not look stedfastly upon the face of Moses for the glory of his face; which glory was passing away: how shall not rather the ministration of the spirit be with glory? For if the ministration

> of death is glory, much rather doth the ministration of righteousness exceed in glory." (2 Corinthians 3:7-9, RV)

Paul's point is that the hardness of heart shown by Israel necessitated a veil being put over the transfigured face of Moses, a veil which, changing the application of the metaphor, obscured for them a true appreciation of God's purpose. For those in Christ, on the other hand, the veil is removed, and "we all, with unveiled face reflecting as a mirror the glory of the Lord, are transformed into the same image from glory to glory" (verse 18).

The dissertation does not end in chapter 3, however, for now in chapter 4 the apostle goes on to refer to those of his own day whose vision of God's glory was still obscured, "in whom the god of this world hath blinded the minds of the unbelieving, that the light of the gospel of the glory of Christ, who is the image of God, should not dawn upon them ... Seeing it is God who said, Light shall shine out of darkness, who shined in our hearts, to give the light of the knowledge of the glory of God in the face of Jesus Christ" (2 Corinthians 4:4-6, RV).

In Revelation we have visions of the final manifestation of the glory of God: the consummation and fulfilment of all those partial manifestations that have gone before. Ascriptions of glory, honour and power ascend time and again to the throne of God and to the Lamb (4:11; 5:12,13; 7:12; 19:1; etc.); and as the new Jerusalem descended out of heaven from God it shone with light divine: "The city had no need of the sun, neither of the moon, to shine in it: for the glory of God did lighten it, and the Lamb is the light thereof" (21:10,11,23-26). "The earth shall be filled with the knowledge of the glory of the LORD, as the waters cover the sea" (Habakkuk 2:14).

"Thine, O Lord, is the glory"

'Doxology' is a word used to describe a prayer or hymn giving glory to God. We shall conclude with an example from the richly endowed mind of David the psalmist:

"Thine, O Lord, is the greatness, and the power, and the glory, and the victory, and the majesty: for all that is in the heaven and in the earth is thine; thine is the kingdom, O Lord, and thou art exalted as head over all ... we thank thee, and praise thy glorious name." (1 Chronicles 29:11-13)

4 |

"Righteous art Thou, O LORD"

THE first positive quality referred to in the Bible is "good": "God saw the light, that it was good" (Genesis 1:4). All too quickly we are introduced to the idea of "evil" as we encounter in the midst of Eden the "tree of the knowledge of good and evil" (2:9), and there follow, sadly, a number of words which accompany the loss of that pristine state of goodness and purity with which the world began. Words such as "subtil", "beguiled", "cursed", "enmity", "bruise", "sorrow" appear in rapid succession in Genesis 3, as the man and woman discover their free will and succumb to temptation. Chapter 4 widens scripture vocabulary with yet harsher words as we encounter "wrath", "slew", "vengeance" etc.

What a relief and reassurance it is, then, to come to Genesis 6 and to meet (albeit alongside words such as "wickedness", "corrupt" and "violence") the description "just" (RV, "righteous") (6:9). The one thus described is Noah, and he was not only "a *righteous* man", but also "*perfect* in his generations, and Noah *walked with God*". We acknowledge, of course, that no man, other than the Lord Jesus Christ, was truly righteous: "Shall mortal man be just before God? Shall a man be pure before his Maker?" (Job 4:17, with margin). God, however, by His grace, may *account* a person righteous. As God prepares Noah for the Flood that is to rid the earth of its wickedness, He says: "Come thou and all thy house into the ark; for thee have I *seen righteous before me* in this generation" (Genesis 7:1). It was not merely that by earthly standards Noah was upright in his behaviour, but that he was *seen* and *accounted* righteous by God.

"His faith is counted for righteousness"

All men and women come short of the righteousness of God, but God can account them righteous – imputing, reckoning righteousness unto them, imperfect though their works may be. "To him that worketh not, but believeth on him that justifieth the ungodly, his faith is counted for righteousness" (Romans 4:3). Faith is the virtue that counts when God imputes righteousness to one of His servants:

> "By faith, Noah ... moved with godly fear, prepared an ark to the saving of his house; through which he condemned the world, and became heir of *the righteousness which is according to faith.*" (Hebrews 11:7, RV)

The use of the word "heir" in this context is interesting: it could be taken to imply no more than the fact that Noah, like Abraham after him, had righteousness reckoned to him. There is, however, a fuller meaning which can be discovered from a remarkably similar verse in Romans 4. Here, in connection with Abraham, the three words "heir", "righteousness" and "faith" again come together: "For the promise, that he should be the heir of the world, was not to Abraham, or to his seed, through the law, but through *the righteousness of faith*" (Romans 4:13). Comparing the verse in Romans with that in Hebrews the implication is clearly that both Abraham and Noah were worthy not only to be accounted righteous, but to be "heir of the world".

God's righteousness

We have, in this article, looked first at *man's* righteousness because, paradoxically perhaps, it is mentioned in scripture before the righteousness of God Himself. Approaching our subject in this way does, however, have the advantage that when we now turn to contemplate God's righteousness we see it in marvellous contrast to man's limited attainment.

One chapter that is indispensable in helping to set the scene is Genesis 18. The Lord was about to visit upon Sodom the judgements which the cities of the plain deserved; but, knowing that Abraham had a nephew there, God said:

> "Shall I hide from Abraham that thing which I do? ... For I know him, that he will command his children and his household after him, and they shall keep the way of the LORD, to do *justice* and *judgment* ..." (verses 17-19)

This generous testimonial to Abraham's standing before God introduces us to two vital words: "justice" is the word *tsedaqah*; while "judgement" is the word *mishpat*.

Let us look more closely at the first of these: *tsedaqah* is fifteen times translated "justice" but it is well over one hundred times rendered "righteousness" – in fact, all the occurrences of "righteousness" in the KJV are translations of *tsedaqah* or another closely related Hebrew word, *tsedeq*. The word "righteous" has a similar root: in the passages in Genesis 6 and 7 which we quoted earlier, "just" in 6:9 and "righteous" in 7:1 are both translations of *tsaddiq*. We shall, moreover, recognise the same root in the name Melchi*sedek*, which, as Hebrews 7:2 tells us, means "king of righteousness".

Righteousness and judgement

Turning now to the second of the two words introduced in Genesis 18:19, we can say of *mishpat* that, although it is nearly three hundred times translated "judgement", it is eighteen times translated "right" and very often occurs in the context of righteousness. One could go so far as to say that, certainly in connection with God, "judgement" and "righteousness" are facets of the same quality: God's absolute righteousness demands the exercise of His judgement.

So far, however, in examining Genesis 18, we have still only seen these vital words applied to man, and not yet to God.

As Abraham begins to realise what God has in store for Sodom, and starts to plead for those who may be righteous in that city, the attributes of God Himself are at last touched upon:

> "That be far from thee to do after this manner, to slay the righteous [*tsaddiq*] with the wicked ... *shall not the Judge of all the earth do right* [*mishpat*]?" (verse 25)

This is as close as we get in Genesis to a mention of God's righteousness and, except for the words of Elihu in Job 36:3 (which must be contemporary with Genesis) – "I will ascribe righteousness to my Maker" – it is not until Exodus 9:27 that we finally discover the word *tsaddiq* applied to the Almighty Himself – and then by an alien!

> "And Pharaoh sent, and called for Moses and Aaron, and said unto them, I have sinned this time: *the LORD is righteous*, and I and my people are wicked."

If we wish to see God's righteousness more fully acknowledged and extolled, then we need to turn the pages of our Old Testament to the Psalms. Here there are ascriptions of God's righteousness in abundance: "I will praise the LORD according to his righteousness" (7:17); "My tongue shall speak of thy righteousness and of thy praise all the day long" (35:28). For David the sinner, the contemplation of God's righteousness leads him to deep repentance: in Psalm 51 he asks for mercy; he pleads for his transgressions to be blotted out; for a clean heart, and a right spirit. But he does not ask to be justified; rather, he desires "that *thou* [God] mightest be justified when thou speakest, and be clear when thou judgest" (verse 4). As David says in a later Psalm, "In thy sight shall no man living be justified" (143:2).

But there would be a way of justification, a means whereby man could be made righteous before his Maker; and there is in the psalms a foreshadowing of the character of that Son of righteousness who would come:

> "Thou lovest righteousness, and hatest wickedness: therefore God, thy God, hath anointed thee with the oil of gladness above thy fellows"; "Give the king thy judgments [*mishpat*],

O God, and thy righteousness [*tsedaqah*] unto the king's son. He shall judge thy people with righteousness [*tsedeq*], and thy poor with judgment [*mishpat*]." (72:1,2)

All the attributes of God pour forth from the pen of Isaiah, as he tells of divine holiness, righteousness, justice, peace, strength, lovingkindness and salvation. Again, *mishpat* and *tsedaqah* often come together (see, for example 5:7 and 59:15,16). In chapter 45, which has so much to tell of God's character and purpose, the prophet also expounds His righteousness:

"I the LORD speak righteousness [*tsedeq*] ... There is no God beside me; a just [*tsaddiq*] God and a Saviour; there is none beside me ... The word is gone out of my mouth in righteousness [*tsedaqah*] ... Surely, shall one say, in the LORD have I righteousness [*tsedaqah*] and strength ... In the LORD shall all the seed of Israel be justified [*tsadaq*]." (verses 19-25)

There is of course more than a hint here of the principle that the only true righteousness to which man can attain is that which God Himself imputes. Isaiah brings this out even more strongly in chapter 54: "All thy children shall be taught of the LORD; and great shall be the peace of thy children. In righteousness shalt thou be established ... This is the heritage of the servants of the LORD, and their righteousness *which is of me*, saith the LORD" (verses 13,14,17, RV – and note the occurrence of "heritage", echoing the use of "heir" we explored earlier).

"The LORD our righteousness"

And it is Jeremiah who, in worship and gratitude, cries, "Righteous [*tsaddiq*] art thou, O LORD, when I plead with thee: yet let me talk with thee of thy judgments [*mishpat*]" (12:1). Later he introduces us to "the Branch of righteousness", who "shall execute judgment and righteousness in the land. In those days shall Judah be saved, and Jerusalem shall dwell safely: and this is the name wherewith she shall be called, The LORD our righteousness" (33:15,16).

The Old Testament concludes with the assurance of the coming of "the Lord, whom ye seek ... the messenger of the covenant, whom ye delight in". Judgement and righteousness are brought together once more as Malachi portrays the refining and purifying that must be accomplished before the people can be presented to God in righteousness. "But unto you that fear my name shall the Sun of righteousness arise with healing in his wings" (Malachi 3:1-3; 4:2).

With the coming of the Lord Jesus Christ, the inspired words of the prophets came to pass, and the hopes of the faithful were fulfilled. None understood more intimately than he the righteousness of God, whom he addressed, "O righteous Father" (John 17:25). Having a mind steeped in the Hebrew scriptures, the Lord naturally resorted to the language of the patriarchs and prophets, as he brought judgement and righteousness once again into juxtaposition: "When he [the Comforter] is come, he will reprove the world of sin, and of righteousness, and of judgment" (John 16:8; see also 5:30). Jesus was proclaimed by Peter as "the Holy One and the Just" (Acts 3:14); by Stephen and James as "the Just [RV, Righteous] One" (7:52; James 5:6). He was described by Paul as having been "made unto us wisdom, and righteousness, and sanctification, and redemption" (1 Corinthians 1:30); by John as "Jesus Christ the righteous" (1 John 2:1).

Here at last was God's "righteous servant" who came to make many righteous, "for he shall bear their iniquities" (Isaiah 53:11). In the gospel of Christ, as Paul expounds so eloquently to the Romans, "the righteousness of God without the law is manifested, being witnessed by the law and the prophets; even the righteousness of God which is by faith of Jesus Christ" (3:21,22). But Christ came to do more than manifest in himself the righteousness of God – wondrous though that revelation was. He came so that, as types and prophecies foreshadowed, God's righteousness might be imputed to those who had faith in God through him. God's righteousness, far from being a distant, abstract quality, infinitely removed from man's situation, is in fact an active, purposeful righteousness seeking to save man from his situation.

"To declare his righteousness"

Translators have difficulty in conveying in the English language the elegance of Paul's argument in Romans 3. Where the original has single words, English versions have to compromise with a mixture of words and phrases based on the word *righteous* – "righteousness", "righteous", "make righteous", and "one who makes righteous". The alternative, which some versions employ, is to use a family of words based on *just* – "justice", "just", "justify", and "justifier". The Twentieth Century New Testament is one which adopts the former style:

> "It is a righteousness which comes from God through faith in Jesus Christ ... For all have sinned, and all fall short of God's glorious ideal, but, in his mercy, are being set right with him through the deliverance which is in Christ Jesus ... God did this, in order to prove his righteousness ... in order that he might be righteous, and make those who have faith in Jesus stand right with himself." (3:22-26)

By the grace of God, working with our faith and true repentance, God accounts His children righteous through His Son. Of ourselves we have nothing in which to boast, but by association with Christ we can be "found in him, not having a righteousness of my own that comes from the law, but that which is through faith in Christ – the righteousness that comes from God and is by faith" (Philippians 3:9, NIV). "If ye know that he is righteous, ye know that every one that doeth righteousness is born of him" (1 John 2:29).

"Then shall the righteous shine forth"

From the days of the apostles until now, the world has been awaiting the further and final revelations of the righteous judgements of God. When the third angel poured out his vial, John heard the words:

> "Thou art righteous, O Lord, which art, and wast, and shalt be, because thou hast judged thus ... And I heard another out of

> the altar say, Even so, Lord God Almighty, true and righteous are thy judgments." (Revelation 16:4-7)

With longing and wonder, if tinged with awe and expectation, we await the day when God will fill the earth with His righteousness:

> "Then shall the righteous shine forth as the sun in the kingdom of their Father." (Matthew 13:43; cf. Daniel 12:3)

> "Then judgment shall dwell in the wilderness, and righteousness remain in the fruitful field. And the work of righteousness shall be peace; and the effect of righteousness quietness and assurance for ever." (Isaiah 32:16,17)

5 |

"He will be very gracious"

THE holiness, glory and righteousness of God are among those qualities which set Him apart from His creation. They are attributes which we have referred to as the 'absolutes' of His nature – characteristics infinitely above and beyond those of mankind. Yet the Lord our God is not a God who places Himself out of the reach of man: He is a God who seeks to communicate, to manifest Himself in the men and women He has created in His image, that they in turn might show forth something of the same qualities and reflect honour to their Creator.

Yet how can God, infinite in holiness, have dealings with fallen mankind? The answer to this question, reduced to a single word, is "grace". The whole of God's purpose with the earth could well have terminated in the time of Noah:

> "And the LORD God said, I will destroy ... man, and beast, and the creeping thing, and the fowls of the air; for it repenteth me that I have made them." (Genesis 6:7)

Viewed in terms of God's holiness, glory, or righteousness, man had shown himself unworthy of His Maker and merited only destruction. Yet the God who is holy is also gracious, and resolved to show that grace to one, Noah, who (as we saw previously) was "a just man and perfect in his generations" (verse 9).

The Hebrew word *chen* is translated (in the KJV) most often by "grace" and somewhat less frequently by "favour".

When God, represented by the three men, appeared to Abraham with the promise of a child for Sarah, Abraham extended his hospitality with the words: "My Lord, if now I have found favour in thy sight ..." (18:3). Man can communicate with God only by virtue of the fact that he has "found favour" or "found grace" in His sight.

Grace is *undeserved* favour. From a superficial reading of Genesis 6 one might conclude that, in Noah's case, the divine grace was actually deserved. Noah was in no way so wicked as those of his generation; the thoughts of *his* heart were not "evil continually" – yet in the sense in which God's standards demand, he was not faultless; he cannot be said to have *merited* God's grace. Neither Noah, nor Abraham, nor any since apart from the Lord Jesus, could claim the grace of God as of merit: "For by grace are ye saved through faith; and that not of yourselves: it is the gift of God" (Ephesians 2:8).

"That I may find grace in thy sight"

We turn on to Exodus 33 (another chapter that has figured already in our study) and it is now Moses who, after the Eastern manner, prefaces his request to God, "If I have found grace in thy sight ..." (verse 13). And his request goes on, rather quaintly in our ears perhaps, "shew me now thy ways, that I may know thee, *to the end that I may find grace in thy sight*: and consider that this nation is thy people" (verse 13). How meek was Moses: how wonderfully humble in the presence of his God, not presuming on His grace, and while claiming that grace yet asking for it too! Sometimes, today, it seems as if our freedom of access to God through Christ encourages a little too much familiarity and even a presumption in God's presence: let us learn from the meekness of Moses. Moses' request was answered by a vision of the Almighty God and the proclamation of His Name:

> "And the LORD passed by before him and proclaimed, The LORD, the LORD, a God full of compassion and *gracious*, slow to anger, and plenteous in mercy and truth; keeping mercy for

thousands, forgiving iniquity and transgression and sin ..." (34:6,7, RV)

In a way, we are in danger of diminishing the nature of our God by analysing His attributes one by one; His characteristics belong together – the quotation from Exodus 34 is proof enough of this. Grace belongs with compassion, truth and mercy; grace is manifested in God's willingness to forgive iniquity, transgression and sin. And because Moses understood these things, he "bowed his head toward the earth and worshipped. And he said, If now I have found grace in thy sight, O Lord, let the Lord, I pray thee, go among us ... and pardon our iniquity and our sin, and take us for thine inheritance" (verses 8,9). Even at this stage, there is no question of Moses presuming upon God's grace – the "If now I have found ..." is repeated yet again – but Moses is clearly reassured, while God, for His part, then confirms the covenant with which His Name is associated:

"And he said, Behold, I make a covenant ... with thee and with Israel ... And he wrote upon the tables the words of the covenant, the ten commandments." (verses 10,27,28)

So Israel grew to understand their special covenant relationship with God. The high-priestly blessing focused upon God's graciousness to His people:

"On this wise ye shall bless the children of Israel; ye shall say unto them, The LORD bless thee, and keep thee: the LORD make his face to shine upon thee, and be *gracious* unto thee: the LORD lift up his countenance upon thee, and give thee peace. So shall they put my name upon the children of Israel; and I will bless them." (Numbers 6:22-27)

As is so often the case, the Psalms pick up the truths first introduced in the Pentateuch. There is a very troubled psalm in which for a moment the man of God seems to doubt the terms of the covenant:

"Will the Lord cast off for ever? and will he be favourable no more? Is his mercy clean gone for ever? doth his promise fail

> for evermore? Hath God forgotten to be gracious? hath he in anger shut up his tender mercies?" (77:7-9)

Immediately, however, the psalmist pulls himself together, and pours out his confidence in God: "I will remember thy wonders of old ..." And the prophets too confirm that there is no cause to doubt the eternal qualities of Israel's God:

> "Therefore the LORD longs to be gracious to you, and therefore He waits on high to have compassion on you. For the LORD is a God of justice; how blessed are all those who long for Him." (Isaiah 30:18, NASB)

And it is from the following verse that our chapter title is taken: "He will be very gracious unto thee at the voice of thy cry; when he shall hear it, he will answer thee."

But we return to the psalms, and in the obviously Messianic Psalm 45, we meet "the king", who is "fairer than the children of men: grace is poured into thy lips: therefore God hath blessed thee for ever" (verses 1,2). But we cannot fail to notice also how this psalm speaks of grace, as did Exodus, always in the context of the other divine qualities, "... with thy glory and thy majesty ... because of truth and meekness and righteousness", for the King, the Son of God, bears the attributes of the Father:

> "Thy throne is the throne of God (RV margin) for ever and ever ... Thou hast loved righteousness, and hated wickedness: therefore God, thy God, hath anointed thee with the oil of gladness above thy fellows." (verses 3-7)

"Full of grace and truth"

When he appeared, the faithful in Israel had no difficulty in recognising the one who bore all these divine attributes:

> "And the Word was made flesh, and dwelt among us ... full of grace [*charis*] and truth ... For the law was given by Moses, but grace and truth came by Jesus Christ. No man hath seen God at any time; the only begotten Son, which is in the bosom of the Father, he hath declared him." (John 1:14-18)

God's favour (*charis*) came upon Mary, the handmaid of the Lord:

> "Hail, thou that art highly *favoured*, the Lord is with thee ... And the angel said unto her, Fear not, Mary: for thou hast found *favour* with God. And, behold, thou shalt ... bring forth a son, and shalt call his name JESUS." (Luke 1:28-31)

> "And the child grew ... and the *grace* of God was upon him ... And Jesus increased in wisdom and stature, and in *favour* with God and man." (2:52)

Through the Lord Jesus Christ, then, God's grace was revealed anew, and more fully, and finally. Amazingly, Jesus did not himself use or explain the word "grace" – but he did not need to, for he was its very embodiment. After his death and resurrection, he sent forth the apostles to proclaim the Gospel of saving grace: "We believe that through the grace of the Lord Jesus Christ we shall be saved" (Acts 15:11); and, in fact, the Gospel itself came to be referred to as "the grace of God" – see and compare Acts 11:23; 13:43; 14:3,26; 20:24,32.

It is when we come to the epistles that we find the topic of God expounded in detail. Romans, especially, elaborates the doctrine of salvation by grace; for those to whom Paul wrote were "justified freely by his grace through the redemption that is in Christ Jesus" and "have access by faith into this grace wherein we stand", "that as sin hath reigned unto death, even so might grace reign through righteousness unto eternal life by Jesus Christ our Lord" (3:24; 5:2,21).

While Romans represents the pinnacle of Paul's exposition of grace, there is another most remarkable New Testament book where other facets of the word *charis* are explored – where it is applied not only to the work of God in Christ, but to the service of every believer: it is the Second Epistle to Corinth, and especially chapter 8. The context is the great collection for the saints at Jerusalem. Paul refers to "the *grace* that God has given the Macedonian churches"; he goes on to say how "we urged Titus ... to bring to completion this act of *grace* on your part"; and he challenges them to "excel in this *grace* of giving" (verses

1,6,7, NIV). And how could they fail to respond when the apostle sets before them the example of the Lord himself:

> "For you know the grace of our Lord Jesus Christ, that though he was rich, yet for your sakes he became poor, so that you through his poverty might become rich." (verses 9)

Each time Paul uses the word *charis*, he reveals yet another facet of its meaning. And there is one further usage, obscured in English versions, where – perhaps to our astonishment – *charis* is translated "thanks": "*Thanks* be to God" (8:16; 9:15; see also Romans 6:17). The spectrum of meaning takes us from "favour", to "gift", and finally – full circle as it were – to the "thanks" we offer in response to God's grace. Profound though it is, the grace of God expounded in 2 Corinthians 8 may be defined very simply: God gave the Lord Jesus Christ; Jesus gave himself, a living sacrifice; we are called upon to minister grace to others; and to give thanks – gratitude – back to God.

> "The God of all grace, who hath called us unto his eternal glory by Christ Jesus, after that ye have suffered a while, make you perfect, stablish, strengthen, settle you. To him be glory and dominion for ever and ever. Amen." (2 Peter 5:10)

6 |

"His merciful kindness is great toward us"

SO far in this series, we have contemplated the holiness, glory, righteousness, and grace of God. What divine attribute should come next in sequence? Actually, it becomes increasingly difficult to consider God's characteristics singly, for they are so inter-connected. Often in scripture we find divine qualities referred to in pairs or in parallelisms – in the Old Testament, "righteousness and judgment", "mercy and truth", "goodness and mercy"; in the New Testament, "grace and truth", "grace, mercy, and peace" – and, of course, many other combinations.

The choice of an attribute to follow "grace" is especially difficult: truly, once we have introduced "grace" we have opened up the whole sphere of God's plan of redemption for mankind, a plan in which His righteousness, justice, grace, compassion, love, goodness, mercy, lovingkindness, forgiveness, each separately, and together, have a place. If we look at each attribute strictly in isolation we are in danger of missing the fuller perspective; yet how can one realistically expound all these qualities at once? The compromise we shall adopt is to give brief consideration to several from the above list, then continue our closer study of each one – some, in fact we have already explored.

Man's salvation has its origin, its source, its impulse, in the *holiness* of God: it is God's holiness, His separateness, which demands from man a commitment to be set apart, sanctified to God's will (see chapter 2, page 99). The study of God's *glory* (chapter 3, page 107) pointed the way to man's ultimate attainment of glory by Christ's redeeming work. God's *righteousness* (or justice) and *judgement*, considered in chapter 4 (page 115), reminded us of the absolute standards which God sets, the condemnation deserved by those who do not live up to such standards, and – in spite of this – the wonder that God can account men and women righteous if they come to Him in faith through Christ. This inevitably led us, in chapter 5 (page 123), to *grace*, God's undeserved favour by which, in Christ, we can be forgiven.

Justice and grace lead on in turn to *mercy*, which, though one word in English, opens up at least two words in Hebrew: *racham* and *chesed*. The second of these will occupy our attention as the article proceeds, but first we shall consider *racham*. This appears in our Bibles as "compassion", "mercy", or "pity": "He is gracious, and *full of compassion* and righteous" (Psalm 112:4). It expresses the tender feelings of a parent for a child, especially God's deep feelings for His children: "Like as a father *pitieth* his children, so the LORD *pitieth* them that fear Him" (Psalm 103:13). A related word, *rachamim*, is translated "tender mercies" (for example, in Psalm 103:4).

From such feelings, it is but a short step to *love*; indeed, love is implicit in *racham*. There is, however, a specific Hebrew word for love, *ahabah* (and the verb *aheb*). It can apply to love of food (Genesis 27:4), the love of God's law (Psalm 119:97), the love of a servant for his master (Exodus 21:5), or that between man and woman (Song of Solomon 3:1), and also the love of God for His people: "Because he loved thy fathers, therefore he chose their seed after them, and brought thee out ..." (Deuteronomy 4:37; 7:7,8). And that love was to be reflected by God's people: "Thou shalt love the LORD thy God with all thine heart" (6:5).

It might seem from this brief survey of words connected with God's compassion, mercy and love, that there was hardly a need for additional terms. It is at this stage, however, that scripture lifts us, as it were, onto a higher plane, and teaches us another word which, in a sense, spans all that we have been saying – and yet says something more: it is a word which has been mentioned already, *chesed*. There can hardly be a word in the world of sublimer meaning than this, variously translated in the KJV by the English words "goodness", "kindness", "mercy", "merciful kindness", or "loving kindness"; in the RSV, often by "steadfast love"; in the NIV, by "unfailing love". We should not complain that the translators are inconsistent in not keeping to just one rendering, for there is nothing in our language like *chesed*: it embraces certainly all of the meanings just given, yet all of those meanings, singly or together, are insufficient to convey the full sense of the original. To say that it is a complex Hebrew word with no clear equivalent in English may be true, but misses the point that Hebrew is uniquely God's language, with a vocabulary attuned to divine things. And even that statement must immediately be qualified, for Hebrew words are rarely just 'theological' and *chesed* finds a place in ordinary human relations too.

Perhaps it is here, then, that we should begin – noting how *chesed* is applied, for example, to the deeds of men like Hezekiah and Josiah:

> "Now the rest of the acts of Hezekiah, and his *goodness*, behold, they are written in the vision of Isaiah ..."
> (2 Chronicles 32:32)

> "Now the rest of the acts of Josiah, and his *goodness*, according to that which was written in the law of the LORD ... they are written in the book of the kings." (35:26,27)

In both places, "goodness" is rendered "good deeds" in the RV, and "kindnesses" in the KJV margin. Other alternatives are "deeds of faithful love" (New Jerusalem Bible); "acts / deeds of devotion" (NIV / NASB); "works of piety" (NEB and REB). Again, the inner meaning of the original is more than any or all of these, for there is something intensely and specifically Jewish that is lost in the translation; what is missing is the idea that the deeds of these good kings reflect and reciprocate a divine quality.

Covenant love

What, then, is the divine quality that lies behind this word? Without question, "piety" falls far short; "goodness" and "kindness" are but part of the whole; "[deeds of] faithful love" comes closer. But the meanings so far suggested are still deficient in one essential respect: *chesed* has to do with God's *covenant* relation with His people. Expanding the meaning to "covenant love", "covenant mercy", or "covenant faithfulness" brings us very much closer to the understanding we are seeking.

As in any study of Bible words, of course, meanings are ultimately to be found only by looking at the scripture context itself, so let the scriptures speak; let us follow the development of *chesed*, as we have followed other words, from its earliest use to its employment in the hands of psalmist and prophet, and then in their outworking in God's manifestation of Himself in Christ and the saints.

When the angels directed Lot away from the judgements to be brought upon the cities of the plain, he stayed to argue as to whether he could not flee to Zoar:

> "Behold now, thy servant hath found grace in thy sight, and thou hast magnified thy *mercy*, which thou hast shewed unto me in saving my life ... behold now, this city is near to flee unto ..." (Genesis 19:19)

Previously we saw how Noah, Abraham and Moses "found grace" in God's sight and understood the divine favour that had been granted to them; so now does Lot. And confident in God's grace, Lot can plead also for His mercy (*chesed*). The covenant was first with Abraham, yet Lot, for all his unwise choices, knew Abraham's God and evidently the terms of the covenant also; he acknowledged with gratitude that he owed his salvation to God's mercy. Here, then, early in the revelation of God's purpose, we see "grace", mercy, and "salvation" brought together: "mercy" is the linking word in this sequence.

Chesed appears next in the context of Abraham's dealings with Abimelech (20:13; 21:23), and then in the language used by Abraham's servant on his mission to seek a wife for Isaac (24:12,14,27,49). Genesis 24 is especially interesting, for Abraham's servant is clearly at home using *chesed* both for the human kindnesses shown to him by Rebekah's family, and the loving kindness of God Himself:

> "Blessed be the LORD God of my master Abraham, who hath not left destitute my master of his *mercy* and his truth." (verse 27)

> "And now if ye [Bethuel and Laban] will deal *kindly* and truly with my master, tell me: and if not ..." (verse 49)

Jacob, fearful of his reunion with Esau, prays to God: "I am not worthy of the least of all thy *mercies*, and of all the truth, which thou hast shewed unto thy servant ... Deliver me, I pray thee ..." (32:10,11). And Jacob again, when he was about to die, "called his son Joseph, and said unto him, If now I have found grace in thy sight, put, I pray thee, thy hand under my thigh, and deal *kindly* and truly with me ..." (47:29). Note, in the first of these quotations how *chesed* once more appears in conjunction with the idea of deliverance; and, in the second passage, alongside "grace" and "truth".

Exodus 34 has become a regular staging post in our exploration of the attributes of God, and we shall find *chesed* among the many names and characteristics revealed to Moses. The fact that (in the KJV) different English renderings are used slightly spoils the impact of the original Hebrew word in verses 6 and 7: "The LORD, the LORD God, merciful [*rachum*] and gracious, longsuffering, and abundant in goodness [*chesed*] and truth, keeping mercy [*chesed*] for thousands, forgiving iniquity and transgression and sin ..." (see also Numbers 14:18; Deuteronomy 7:9).

Yet again we see how the same characteristics of God appear together – *chesed* in close relationship with truth and salvation – here, particularly, salvation from sin.

Naomi understood God's merciful lovingkindness, and instructed her daughters-in-law also in its meaning:

"Go, return each of you to her mother's house: the LORD deal *kindly* with you, as ye have dealt with the dead, and with me ... Blessed be he of the LORD, who hath not left off his *kindness* to the living and to the dead." (Ruth 1:8; 2:20)

So well, in fact, had Ruth learned the loving kindness of the Lord, that Boaz could praise her for exhibiting that quality in her own actions:

"And he said, Blessed be thou of the LORD, my daughter: for thou hast shewed more *kindness* in the latter end than at the beginning ..." (3:10)

When God promised to establish the throne of David's kingdom, He said (through Nathan), "My *mercy* shall not depart from him, as I took it from Saul" (2 Samuel 7:15). Solomon, having brought up the ark of the covenant into the newly constructed temple –

"stood before the altar of the LORD in the presence of all the congregation of Israel, and spread forth his hands toward heaven: and he said, LORD God of Israel, there is no God like thee, in heaven above, or on earth beneath, who keepest covenant and *mercy* with thy servants that walk before thee with all their heart." (1 Kings 8:23)

Here we see *chesed* specifically in the context of the covenant and the kingdom.

"Goodness and mercy"

As always, what we discover from the books of the law is reinforced in the Psalms and the Prophets, but now with a future prospect, as the inspired writers assure themselves of the continuance of God's mercies in the coming of Messiah and, finally, of the kingdom:

"Surely goodness [*tob*] and mercy [*chesed*] shall follow me all the days of my life: and I will dwell in the house of the LORD for ever." (Psalm 23:6)

"I will sing aloud of thy mercy [*chesed*] in the morning ... For God is my defence, and the God of my mercy." (59:16,17)

> "LORD, thou hast been favourable unto thy land ... Turn us, O God of our salvation ... Shew us thy mercy [*chesed*], O LORD, and grant us thy salvation. I will hear what God the LORD will speak: for he will speak peace unto his people, and to his saints [*chasid*] ... Mercy [*chesed*] and truth are met together; righteousness and peace have kissed each other. Truth shall spring out of the earth; and righteousness shall look down from heaven." (85:1,4,7-11)

There is much to learn from Psalm 85 particularly: see how "mercy", as so often, comes together with "favour" (grace), "righteousness", "salvation", "peace" and "truth". Note, moreover, the Hebrew *chasid* for "saints" – a word from the same root as *chesed* and therefore clearly associated in meaning. The other word for "saints" is *qadosh* which signifies those 'set apart, separate, holy' (for an example, see Psalm 89:5-7). *Chasid* has a meaning which some have interpreted as 'kind, or pious, ones' – that is the significance attached to the religious 'Hasidim' in Israel today. But there is more to the word than the idea of piety: does not the connection with *chesed* suggest 'those in God's covenant love'? That would fit the usage of the word in Psalm 85 (see also Psalm 145:10), and of course the meaning attached to "saints" in its New Testament context.

In the next chapter we shall explore the use of *chesed* in the prophets; and then attempt a summary of its Old Testament meanings – and look at equivalents in the New Testament.

7 |

"The multitude of His mercies"

BEFORE we look at occurrences of *chesed* in the prophets, we should take a last brief look at its use in the Psalms. Our example is Psalm 89, which from start to finish echoes with the names and attributes of God, and always in the context of His covenant:

> "I will sing of the mercies [*chesed*] of the LORD for ever: with my mouth will I make known thy faithfulness to all generations ... I have made a *covenant* with my chosen, I have sworn unto David my servant ... O LORD God of hosts, who is a mighty one, like unto thee, O JAH? Righteousness and judgement are the foundation of thy throne: mercy [*chesed*] and truth go before thy face ... Thou spakest in vision to thy holy one [*chasid*] ... I have found David my servant; with my holy oil have I anointed him ... My faithfulness and my mercy [*chesed*] shall be with him ... My mercy [*chesed*] will I keep for him for evermore, and my *covenant* shall stand fast with him ... My lovingkindness [*chesed*] will I not utterly take from him, nor suffer my faithfulness to fail. My *covenant* will I not break, nor alter the thing that is gone out of my lips."
>
> (verses 1,3,8(RV),14(RV),19,20,24,28,33,34)

Chesed is God's firm and lasting love to those within His covenant, His constant and forgiving grace. And while it describes God's feelings for His people, it also defines the response that is due from them – in worship and devotion to Him; and in acts of kindness to their fellows.

No passage of scripture could convey more eloquently than this the meaning of the word *chesed*. Here it has its setting in God's choice of David, and in the covenant promise – "my *mercy* shall not depart from him" – which came to him through Nathan (2 Samuel 7:15). But above and beyond this immediate context towers David's greater Son, "my firstborn, higher than the kings of the earth" (Psalm 89:27), with whom God's covenant would continue for ever. And the point of the Psalm is surely that all the names and qualities, and promises, of God find their fulfilment and embodiment in him. He, the Lord Jesus Christ, is the covenant Son; in him were revealed, without measure, those characteristics of mercy, faithfulness, righteousness, salvation, judgement and truth, so strongly emphasised in this psalm.

Singing of the mercies of the Lord, the psalmist is confident that all that was promised will surely be fulfilled – in spite of that ancient Jewish cry in verse 46, "How long, O LORD ...?" Indeed the last few verses of the Psalm are surely not so much a cry of doubt as an expression of longing, the yearning of a child of God for that day when the covenant promises will finally come true: "Lord, where are thy former lovingkindnesses, which thou swarest unto David in thy truth?" (verse 49). Any doubts give way, at the end of the psalm, to supreme confidence in "thine anointed" and in the reproach by which the hopes of all men would be fulfilled.

We may have seemed to stray off course so far as our study of *chesed* is concerned, but we have already learned that no attribute of God can be considered in isolation. *Chesed* yields its secret only after a close examination of its context, and Psalm 89 has served particularly to show this very special attribute inextricably bound up with the eternal promises and faithful covenant of God.

"A throne shall be established in mercy"

Now let us continue our exploration of *chesed* in the prophets. The first occurrence in Isaiah is in a verse which follows on well from Psalm 89: "And a throne shall be established in mercy [*chesed*], and one shall sit thereon in truth, in the tent of David; judging, and seeking judgment, and swift to do righteousness" (Isaiah 16:5, RV). Here, too, the words speak of the son of David, the Son of God, the living expression of the Father's covenant-love.

The connection between *chesed* and covenant is evident from verses of profound depth and beauty in Isaiah 54:

> "For a small moment have I forsaken thee; but with great mercies [*rachamim*] will I gather thee. In a little wrath I hid my face from thee for a moment; but with everlasting kindness [*chesed*] will I have mercy on thee, saith the LORD thy Redeemer. For this is as the waters of Noah unto me: for as I have sworn that the waters of Noah should no more go over the earth; so have I sworn that I would not be wroth with thee, nor rebuke thee. For the mountains shall depart, and the hills be removed; but my kindness [*chesed*] shall not depart from thee, neither shall the covenant of my peace be removed, saith the LORD that hath mercy on thee." (54:7-10)

Here the context is God's covenant with Noah, and the kindness promised is that infinite kindness shown to Noah and his family when the earth and the rest of its inhabitants were destroyed.

The passages we have examined so far should prepare us for a curious phrase, "the sure mercies [*chesed*] of David", which we meet in Isaiah 55. With the background of Psalm 89 and Isaiah 16, we should have no difficulty: it is of course *God's* sure mercies that are actually being referred to, but David himself, as a party to the covenant, reflected that covenant-love which God had revealed to him. And if David could show forth the quality of *chesed*, how much more would his promised Son? –

> "I will make an everlasting covenant with you, even the sure mercies of David. Behold, I have given him for a witness to the people, a leader and commander ..." (Isaiah 55:3,4)

"The covenant of my peace"

Each occurrence of *chesed* in the Old Testament helps to widen and deepen its meaning: we have seen how it is used to denote faithfulness, kindness, mercy and love – but in particular the mercy and love manifested in God's covenant with His children. There was another interesting association in the passage we quoted from Isaiah 54 which we passed over but should now return to: it lies in the expression "the covenant of my *peace*". Those in covenant relationship with God, recipients of His mercy, find peace with God, a truth reinforced in a parallelism to be found in Jeremiah 16: "I have taken away my peace from this people, saith the LORD, even lovingkindness [*chesed*] and tender mercies" (verse 5). When God's covenant-love in removed, there is no peace; when there is *chesed*, there is peace. Or, as Paul expounds to those who have entered into covenant relationship with Christ:

> "Being justified by faith, we have peace with God through our Lord Jesus Christ." (Romans 5:1)

We cannot, moreover, study *chesed* without discovering, as we do in connection with all the attributes of God, that though each divine quality is wholly positive, there is a negative side to be faced by those who turn away. Remember Exodus 20, and God's promise that He will shew "mercy [*chesed*] unto thousands of them that love me"; but where it is also revealed that He is "a jealous God, visiting the iniquities of the fathers upon the children" (verses 5,6). Or consider Lamentations 3:

> "It is of the LORD's mercies [*chesed*] that we are not consumed, because his compassions [*rachamim*] fail not. They are new every morning: great is thy faithfulness [*emunah*] ... For the Lord will not cast off for ever: but though he cause grief, yet will he have compassion [*racham*] according to the multitude

> of his mercies [*chesed*]. For he doth not afflict willingly ..." (verses 22,23,32; cf. Joel 2:13)

God's mercy is the greater if we can understand His jealousy; His compassion far outweighs any grief and affliction which may be brought upon man for discipline; we have seen already that His wrath is "for a moment", but His kindness is "everlasting".

"Your goodness is as a morning cloud"

Hosea expounds God's love in the context of marriage – itself, of course, a covenant relationship:

> "I will betroth thee unto me for ever ... in righteousness, and in judgment, and in lovingkindness [*chesed*]." (2:19)

For their part, alas, God's people had become unfaithful to that covenant:

> "O Ephraim, what shall I do unto thee? O Judah, what shall I do unto thee? for your goodness [*chesed*] is as a morning cloud ... For I desired mercy [*chesed*] and not sacrifice; and the knowledge of God more than burnt offerings." (6:4,6; cf. Micah 6:8)

In his penetrating series of articles on "The Knowledge of God" (*The Christadelphian*, 1967) Brother Fred Pearce wrote the following in connection with *chesed* and the marriage covenant:

> "In Old Testament times it was marriage which best illustrated in human experience the divine *chesed*. In the Middle East, as indeed elsewhere, the future bride had little choice as to the man who was to become her husband; for it was he who took the initiative, choosing her first as one who would make a desirable wife, and approaching her father to get his consent. From the beginning of their relationship, therefore, it was the wife who had received grace and favour and was being offered the loyal love [*chesed*] of her husband; in return the Eastern wife owed humble love, and loyalty, which was her *chesed*. It was this clear conception of the relationship in marriage

which made it possible for God to use the figure so boldly to illustrate His own tie with Israel." (page 254)

Covenant-love in the New Testament

What happens to the idea of God's covenant-love when we turn to the New Testament? The *idea*, of course, continues: can we not hear the sentiments of the psalmist and the prophets in words from the apostles? In each of the following quotations, though Greek words are being used, the characteristics of God that are mentioned are those revealed through the Hebrew scriptures – and in the first quotation, there is even a link with the "covenants of promise", as was so often the case in the Old Testament:

> "God, who is rich in mercy, for his great love wherewith he loved us ... By grace are ye saved through faith ... Ye were without Christ, being aliens from the commonwealth of Israel, and strangers from the *covenants of promise* ... But now in Christ Jesus ye who were sometimes were far off are made nigh by the blood of Christ. For he is our peace ..."
> (Ephesians 2:4-13)

> "Be ye kind [*chrestos*] one to another, tenderhearted, forgiving one another, even as God for Christ's sake hath forgiven you."
> (Ephesians 4:32)

> "As newborn babes, desire the sincere milk of the word, that ye may grow thereby; if so be that ye have tasted that the Lord is gracious [*chrestos*]." (1 Peter 2:2,3)

When the Lord Jesus Christ himself quotes from Hosea 6, he may originally have used an Aramaic equivalent of *chesed*, but Matthew records the Greek word *eleos* (9:13; 12:7). The writers of the Gospels and epistles are limited by what the Greek language can convey. (Translations of the New Testament into Hebrew are now available, and it is reassuring that *chesed* is faithfully employed in passages such as Luke 1, where first Mary, and then Zacharias, reflect on God's covenant faithfulness fulfilled in the coming of Messiah – verses 50,54,58,72,78.)

Though Greek has at least three words for "love", and other words for "mercy" and "kindness", there was no word in Greek (nor is there in English [or most other Western languages]) to express the unique and distinctive quality of *chesed*. *Chrestos* (used in two of the quotations above) may well come closest to *chesed*. The Septuagint translators used *eleos* ('mercy') to render *chesed*, for example in Psalm 89, Isaiah 54 or Lamentations 3; but they also used *eleos* to translate *chanan* in Psalm 51:1 – "Have mercy upon me, O God ..." The special quality of covenant-mercy, as distinct from mercy in a general sense, is therefore lost.

Summary

So how can we sum up the meaning of the word *chesed*? It would be wrong to conclude that it belongs only to rarified discussions of theology: it is after all, as we saw in the previous chapter, a word used by the dying Jacob speaking as a father to his son Joseph; by Boaz when commending the lovely character of Ruth. Yet it is very special and distinctive. It is said that the root meaning has to do with strength, persistence and firmness – hence the translation "*steadfast* love". But steadfastness extends to faithfulness, loyalty and confidence – the basis of God's covenant with His people. Faithfulness, moreover, overflows into covenant-love, grace, and mercy.

Chesed is God's firm and lasting love to those within His covenant, His constant and forgiving grace. And while it describes God's feelings for His people, it also defines the response that is due from them – in worship and devotion to Him; and in acts of kindness to their fellows.

8 |

"I have loved thee with an everlasting love"

CHAPTER 31 of Jeremiah speaks eloquently of God's love for His people. The short phrase quoted in the above heading is but one of a succession of statements which confirm God's constant affection for Israel and Judah. There are other passages in Jeremiah and elsewhere in the writings of the prophets, but this chapter is superlative in its depiction of a God who loves "with an everlasting love" (31:3); who was a "father to Israel" (31:9,20), "a shepherd" (31:10), "a husband unto them" (31:32), the Lord who "redeemed Jacob, and ransomed him from the hand of him that was stronger than he" (31:11). He was a God whose "bowels are troubled" for Ephraim (31:20); and at the same time a God who disciplined those upon whom He had compassion, who "chastised" and "instructed" (31:18,19).

Divine emotions

In order to begin to do justice to the exalted subject of God's love, we must recognise that the feelings and emotions of man's experience are those of God as well: man, after all, is made in the image of God and has been endowed with responses corresponding to those of his Creator. Man sometimes hesitates to associate tender feelings and passions with the Almighty God, but such hesitation is a reflection not of Bible truth but of the distorted values and definitions of our age, where love and kindred emotions are thought to be weak and sentimental.

The emotion that bound together Jacob and Benjamin was expressed thus by Judah: "His life is bound up in the lad's life" (Genesis 44:30). The brotherly affection between David and Jonathan is referred to in these terms: "The soul of Jonathan was knit with the soul of David" (1 Samuel 18:1). Such – and of course more so – is the affection of God for His children:

> "In all their affliction he was afflicted, and the angel of his presence saved them: in his love and in his pity he redeemed them; and he bare them, and carried them all the days of old."
> (Isaiah 63:9)

> "When Israel was a child, then I loved him, and called my son out of Egypt ... I took them on my arms ... I drew them with cords of a man, with bands of love." (Hosea 11:1,4, RV)

Israel, sadly, did not always reciprocate God's love:

> "I have loved you, saith the LORD. Yet ye say, Wherein hast thou loved us?" (Malachi 1:2)

A jealous love

What is this "love" of God? One writer has expressed it thus:

> "The love which is commended in the Old Testament is the jealous love which chooses one object among thousands and holds it fast with all the strength of its passion and its will, brooking no relaxation of the bond of loyalty. It is just this jealousy which reveals the divine strength of such love." (Quell & Stauffer, *Bible Key Words – Love*)

In the Old Testament, the noun "love" is usually *ahabah*; the verb "to love" is *aheb*. Both words are widely used and (as we have seen in a previous chapter) they portray love in the most general sense. *Aheb* is used of Abraham's love for Isaac (Genesis 22:2), of Isaac's love for Esau and Rebekah's love for Jacob (25:28), of Jonathan's love for David (1 Samuel 18:1) and the love between the Shulamite and the shepherd in the Song of Solomon. Equally appropriately, *aheb* depicts God's love for His people, and their love for Him:

> "Because he *loved* thy fathers, therefore he chose their seed after them ... And thou shalt *love* the LORD thy God with all thine heart, and with all thy soul, and with all thy might."
> (Deuteronomy 4:37; 6:5; 10:12-15)

One of the first questions we are bound to ask is how the quality described above stands in relation to the covenant-love (*chesed*) which we considered previously. It is interesting that both "love" and "lovingkindness" occur in verse 3 of Jeremiah 31 from which we have already quoted: "I have loved [*aheb*] thee with an everlasting love [*ahabah*]: therefore with lovingkindness [*chesed*] have I drawn thee" (31:2,3 – "drawn" is the same word as "drew" in Hosea 11:4, quoted above).

In a moving narrative in Ezekiel, the Lord reflects upon His love for Israel, as one who has compassion on an abandoned newborn babe:

> "None eye pitied thee ... to have compassion on thee ... Now when I passed by thee, and looked upon thee, behold, thy time was the time of love; and I spread my skirt over thee, and covered thy nakedness: yea, I sware unto thee, and entered into a covenant with thee, saith the Lord GOD, and thou becamest mine." (16:5,8)

The imagery here is a vivid portrayal of God's love for Israel, sealed by the covenant that He made with them. Interpreting the allegory, one could say that it was God's eternal and unconditional love (*ahabah*) which initially moved Him to have compassion on His people, and God's lovingkindness (*chesed*) which in due time was expressed in the covenant relationship. Or, as Brother Fred Pearce put it, "The love [*ahabah*] of God was the cause of the covenant, but His faithfulness [*chesed*] was the means of its continuance" ("The Knowledge of God", Part 5, *The Christadelphian*, 1967, page 255).

The wonder of God's love is that it is unconditional. God does not love the righteous because of his righteousness; nor does he diminish His love for the sinner in proportion to his sin. The people whom Balaam was called to curse were spared that curse not for their virtue, but as Moses later recalled:

> "The LORD thy God would not hearken unto Balaam; but the LORD thy God turned the curse into a blessing unto thee, *because the LORD thy God loved thee.*" (Deuteronomy 23:5)

Nor indeed is it a matter of God only loving Israel: rather, He loves all mankind, but loves Israel more.

Ahabah, one might say, is the quality which God has exercised throughout history and to all whom He has favoured (including Israel); *chesed* is an attribute shown specifically to those in covenant relationship with Himself (especially Israel).

God's love in the New Testament

What Greek word can do justice to the Old Testament quality of divine love? *Eros* had the connotation of sensual and mystical ecstasy – it is never used in the New Testament. *Phileō* (and related words) conveys the sense of liking or caring – and this is quite often used:

> "He that loveth father or mother more than me is not worthy of me." (Matthew 10:37)

> "Then said the Jews, Behold how he loved him!" (John 11:36)

Then there is the noun *agapē* and the verb *agapaō* which, for the Greeks, are said to have been "colourless and indefinite" in meaning, lacking the sensuality of *eros* and the warmth of *phileō*; at most suggesting "sympathy, the mutual respect and friendship of equals". This lack of depth, however, proved an advantage. The Septuagint translators, when they set about rendering the Old Testament into Greek, chose almost always to use *agapaō* for *aheb*, and *agapē* frequently for *ahabah*. What appears to have happened is that Jewish scholars, and certainly the Lord Jesus and his apostles, adopted a root-word which was untainted by overtones of pagan excess; and through usage it came to convey the quality of divine love, and of human love on a spiritual plane.

The following examples, a small selection from the many to be found in the New Testament, illustrate how rich in meaning *agapaō* and *agapē* became in the hands of New Testament writers

– capable of expressing all aspects of God's love to man, man's returning love to God, and the love which was to be cultivated in the newly emerging ecclesias of the risen Lord:

> "Thou shalt love thy neighbour as thyself."
> (Matthew 19:19; 22:39)

> "God so loved the world, that he gave his only begotten Son."
> (John 3:16)

> "If ye love me, keep my commandments." (14:15)

> "Thou lovedst me before the foundation of the world ... And I have declared unto them thy name, and will declare it: that the love wherewith thou hast loved me may be in them, and I in them." (17:24,26)

The combined testimony of these and countless other examples confirms, then, that the Old Testament quality of divine love, far from being lost as we turn over the pages to the New Testament, is preserved – indeed enhanced – in the New. And the converse of this argument is also true: the love which Christ taught was not unknown in former times; it was discerned by the faithful, who anticipated the fuller revelation of God's love that the coming of Messiah would bring.

At his coming, the Lord Jesus Christ did indeed teach the love of God; but it was in his voluntary death that his love, and God's love through him, were shown to the full – and shown to the world, not just to Jewry. Strangely, the word "love" does not once occur in Acts, yet it was because of God's love in Christ that the apostles were impelled to go forth to preach the Gospel, speaking of God's love – albeit using other terms:

> "Ye are the children of the prophets, and of the covenant ... Unto you first God, having raised up his Son Jesus, sent him to bless you, in turning away every one of you from his iniquities." (3:25,26)

> "God ... giveth to all life, and breath, and all things ... that they should seek the Lord, if haply they might feel after him,

> and find him, though he be not far from every one of us."
> (17:24-27)

Both Peter in Jerusalem, and Paul in Athens, even if for some reason they do not use the word, speak clearly enough of God's love, and man's natural desire and duty to return it.

In the epistles, there is no hesitation to extol the love of God and to exhort the infant communities to show forth that love in their ecclesial life:

> "God commendeth his love [*agape*] toward us, in that, while we were yet sinners, Christ died for us." (Romans 5:8)

> "God, who is rich in mercy, for his great love wherewith he loved us, even when we were dead in sins, hath quickened us together with Christ ... that in the ages to come he might show the exceeding riches of his grace in his kindness toward us." (Ephesians 2:4-7)

The words are the words of the Lord's apostles; they are written in the new dispensation, when the Saviour, by his death and resurrection, has revealed God's love anew – and yet the language in which it is now presented, especially in this quotation from Ephesians, still echoes with Old Testament terms – "mercy", "love", "grace" and "kindness".

"God is love"

And in the same way as the Old Testament taught first the love of God, and then – as a command arising from it – the love of one's neighbour (Leviticus 19:18), so in many New Testament passages it is presumed that the love of God "shed abroad in our hearts" (Romans 5:5) will lead the disciple to love his fellows:

> "As touching brotherly love ye need not that I write unto you: for ye yourselves are taught of God to love one another."
> (1 Thessalonians 4:9)

> "Beloved, let us love one another: for love is of God; and every one that loveth is born of God, and knoweth God. He that loveth not knoweth not God; for God is love ... Herein is love,

> not that we loved God, but that he loved us, and sent his Son to be the propitiation for our sins. Beloved, if God so loved us, we ought also to love one another ... For this is the love of God, that we keep his commandments." (1 John 4:7-11; 5:3)

"Beloved of his God"

In considering the love of God we have largely concentrated on its revelation to the people of God as a whole – to Israel, and latterly through Christ to all who will believe. Of Israel Paul said that they were "*beloved* for the fathers' sakes" (Romans 11:28). We in turn are privileged to be called "the elect of God, holy and *beloved*" (Colossians 3:12). It is good, however, to recall that there were from time to time particular individuals to whom and in whom was specially manifested the love of God – a few singled out to be called "beloved". Of Solomon, Nehemiah said: "Among many nations was there no king like him, who was beloved of his God [Jedidiah, see 2 Samuel 12:25]" (Nehemiah 13:26). Daniel was "a man greatly beloved" (9:23; 10:11,19).

In the New Testament, we find the enigmatic figure to whom Luke addressed both his Gospel record and the Acts – Theophilus, whose name means 'loved of God'. But all are eclipsed by "my servant, whom I uphold; mine elect, in whom my soul delighteth" (Isaiah 42:1); "my beloved Son, in whom I am well pleased" (Mark 1:11; 2 Peter 1:17).

It is, then, with the Lord Jesus Christ, God's "well-beloved" (Mark 12:6), that our thoughts conclude: it is in him that we see the attribute of God's love revealed to its highest extent – love totally committed to the Father's will, love deep and abiding, selfless, and self-giving; a love which shows to us how God loves us, and how He would have us love.

> "Ye, beloved, building up yourselves on your most holy faith, praying in the Holy Spirit, keep yourselves in the love of God, looking for the mercy of our Lord Jesus Christ unto eternal life." (Jude 20,21)

9 |

"He is become my salvation"

FOR the Apostle Paul, the title "God our Saviour" seems to have had special appeal. Salvation is, of course, one of the themes of his letter to the Romans, but it is in the Pastoral Epistles that "Saviour" most frequently occurs – sometimes in relation to the Lord Jesus Christ, but also as an attribute of the Father.

The First Epistle to Timothy opens with the words: "Paul, an apostle of Christ Jesus according to the commandment of God our Saviour, and Christ Jesus our hope ..." (1:1, RV; see also Titus 1:3). Then in 1 Timothy 2 the apostle goes on to refer to God our Saviour, "who will have all men to be saved, and to come unto the knowledge of the truth". Could the purpose of God and the message of the Gospel be expressed more succinctly? From creation, God's sole desire for man is that he should be saved – and that desire has been fulfilled in the coming of His Son. There is of course no difficulty in appreciating that God Himself is Saviour – for He, after all, sent His Son for the salvation of mankind – and that Jesus too is Saviour, the chosen instrument of that saving and redeeming work:

> "*God hath saved us*, and called us with an holy calling, not according to our works, but according to his own purpose and grace, which was given us in Christ Jesus before the world began, but is now made manifest by the appearing of *our Saviour Jesus Christ*, who hath abolished death, and hath

> brought life and immortality to light through the gospel."
> (2 Timothy 1:9,10)

"The kindness and love of God our Saviour"

And if this passage is not already rich enough in its vocabulary, then there is another in Paul's letter to Titus, where the wonder of salvation is expounded in even more exultant language:

> "But after that the kindness and love of God our Saviour toward man appeared, not by works of righteousness which we have done, but according to his mercy he saved us ... that being justified by his grace, we should be made heirs according to the hope of eternal life." (3:4-7)

But it would be wrong to suggest that Paul is merely being carried away by emotion as he considers God as Saviour: what we have in these passages is a clear chain of thought which connects salvation with "kindness", "love", "mercy" and "grace"; and which shows that these have been displayed in spite of the lack of "works of righteousness which we have done". Salvation, in other words, is directly related to the redemptive attributes of God which we have been examining in this series.

From the beginning of the world God has been a Saviour: in the days of Noah, "the world that then was, being overflowed with water, perished" (2 Peter 3:6); but "Noah, being warned of God of things not seen as yet, moved with fear, prepared an ark to the saving of his house" (Hebrews 11:7). Through the might of God, the Hebrews crossed the Red Sea unharmed, and "the LORD saved Israel that day out of the hand of the Egyptians" (Exodus 14:30). Moses and the children of Israel could thus rejoice in their deliverance:

> "I will sing unto the LORD, for he hath triumphed gloriously: the horse and his rider hath he thrown into the sea. The LORD is my strength and song, *and he is become my salvation*." (1:1,2)

When the ark of God was brought up into the city of David, Asaph and his brethren gave voice to their song in words which included:

> "O give thanks unto the LORD; for he is good: for his mercy endureth for ever. And say ye, Save us, O God of our salvation, and gather us together, and deliver us from the heathen, that we may give thanks to thy holy name, and glory in thy praise."
> (1 Chronicles 16:34,35; Psalm 106:1,47)

"God is my salvation"

The Psalmist speaks often of the salvation of the Lord:

> "Truly my soul waiteth upon God: from him cometh my salvation [*yeshuah*]. He only is my rock and my salvation [*yeshuah*] ... In God is my salvation [*yesha*] and my glory: the rock of my strength, and my refuge, is in God." (62:1,2,7)

Psalm 118 quotes the verse from Exodus on which our title is based: "The LORD is my strength and song, and is become my salvation" (verse 14); while in verse 25, in the expression "Save now [*Hosanna*]", we have the cry of those who welcomed into Jerusalem the king riding upon an ass's colt:

> "Hosanna; Blessed is he that cometh in the name of the Lord ... Hosanna in the highest." (Mark 11:9,10)

But no part of the Old Testament is so full of the idea of salvation and the concept of God as Saviour as is Isaiah – not surprisingly, in fact, when we reflect that the prophet's name means 'Yahweh saves'. In Isaiah 12, there is yet another echo of that Song of Moses after the crossing of the Red Sea:

> "Behold, God is my salvation; I will trust and not be afraid: for the LORD JEHOVAH is my strength and my song; he also is become my salvation. Therefore with joy shall ye draw water out of the wells of salvation." (12:2,3)

> "And it shall be said in that day, Lo, this is our God; we have waited for him, we will be glad and rejoice in his salvation."
> (25:9)

"I, even I, am the LORD; and beside me there is no saviour" (43:11; 45:21). And coupled with the title of Saviour is the divine title of Redeemer – again one that is prominent in Isaiah:

> "And all flesh shall know that I the LORD am thy saviour and thy redeemer, the mighty one of Jacob."
> (49:26; see also 41:14; 44:6,24; 48:17; 54:5)

"Our father, our redeemer"

In Isaiah 63 we have one of the most exquisite passages of all scripture, in which God's saving love, His redeeming pity, are set in the context of those many other attributes we have learned to associate with God's dealings with His people. These are verses we have referred to already, but they bear repetition for their beauty and deep meaning – a meaning we can take to ourselves as well:

> "I will mention the lovingkindnesses [*chesed*] of the LORD, and the praises [*tehillah*] of the LORD ... the great goodness [*tub*] toward the house of Israel, which he hath bestowed on them according to his mercies [*rachamim*] ... So he was their Saviour [*yasha*] ... In all their affliction he was afflicted, and the angel of his presence saved them: in his love [*ahabah*] and in his pity [*chemlah*] he redeemed them; and he bare them, and carried them all the days of old ... Look down from heaven, and behold from the habitation of thy holiness and of thy glory: where is thy zeal and thy strength, the sounding of thy bowels and of thy mercies toward me? ... Thou, O LORD, art our father [*ab*], our redeemer [*gaal*]; thy name is from everlasting." (verses 7-9,15,16; cf. Jeremiah 15:20; 30:11)

But how does the Lord God redeem? how does He save? In the pilgrimage of the patriarchs, the wanderings of Israel, and their sojourn in the Land, God was ever at their side; "he bare them, and carried them all the days of old". That, however, does not refer particularly to salvation from sin and death: was there a hint of how this would ultimately be accomplished? In verse 5 of this same chapter 63 of Isaiah, and more especially in chapter 59, we have the promise not just of God's physical protection, but of His forgiveness – salvation from sin:

> "Behold the LORD's hand is not shortened, that it cannot save; neither his ear heavy, that it cannot hear: but your iniquities

> have separated between you and your God, and your sins have hid his face from you, that he will not hear ... And the LORD saw it, and it displeased him that there was no judgment [*mishpat*]. And he saw that there was no man, and wondered that there was no intercessor: therefore his own arm brought salvation [*yasha*] unto him; and his righteousness [*tsedaqah*], it sustained him ... And the redeemer shall come from Zion, and unto them that turn from transgression in Jacob." (59:1,2,15,16,20)

"He shall save his people from their sins"

And so, in the fulness of time, God sent forth His Son. Mary his mother, having received and believed the angel's promise, went into the hill country to share her glad news with Elisabeth.

> "And Mary said, My soul doth magnify the Lord, and my spirit hath rejoiced in God my Saviour ... For he that is mighty hath done to me great things; and holy is his name. And his mercy is on them that fear him." (Luke 1:46-50)

Zacharias, the father of John the Baptist, was filled with the Holy Spirit, and prophesied, saying:

> "Blessed be the Lord God of Israel; for he hath visited and redeemed his people, and hath raised up a horn of salvation for us ... that we should be saved from our enemies ... [and] serve him without fear, in holiness and righteousness before him, all the days of our life ..." (1:68-75)

Simeon too, acknowledged with gratitude that God had visited His people – embracing the Gentiles also in His saving grace: "For mine eyes have seen thy salvation, which thou hast prepared before the face of all people; a light to lighten the Gentiles, and the glory of thy people Israel" (2:30-32). And Anna, the aged prophetess, spake of the child Jesus "to all them that looked for redemption in Jerusalem" (2:38).

The Redeemer had come to Zion! And to Joseph it was commanded: "Thou shalt call his name Jesus: for *he shall save his people from their sins*" (Matthew 1:21). The one born to be Saviour was given a name which, in its Hebrew form *Yehoshuah*, means 'Yahweh is salvation' or 'Yahweh saves'.

Through his ministry, his death and resurrection, and his ascension to the right hand of the Father, the Lord Jesus Christ accomplished the work which God had given him to do. The apostles then went forth with fire and vigour to preach the Gospel of salvation from sin and death. In Jerusalem, for example, Peter proclaimed: "Him hath God exalted with his right hand to be a Prince and a Saviour, for to give repentance to Israel, and forgiveness of sins" (Acts 5:31). Paul's preaching in the Gentile world was similar: "Of this man's (David's) seed hath God according to his promise raised unto Israel a Saviour, Jesus" (13:23).

When we turn to the epistles, we find Paul reflecting on the work of salvation which had been accomplished through God's purpose in Christ:

> "For I am not ashamed of the gospel of Christ: for it is the power of God unto salvation to every one that believeth; to the Jew first, and also to the Greek." (Romans 1:16)

In the letter to the Romans especially, Paul expounds the doctrine of justification – salvation – by faith; and in the process he shows how man's redemption has been achieved notwithstanding the holiness and righteousness of God:

> "If thou shalt confess with thy mouth the Lord Jesus, and shalt believe in thine heart that God hath raised him from the dead, thou shalt be saved. For with the heart man believeth unto righteousness [*dikaiosunē*]; and with the mouth confession is made unto salvation [*sōtēria*]." (10:9,10)

Paul, of course, uses Greek words to express these truths, but in their New Testament usage *dikaiosunē* (righteousness) and *sōtēria* (salvation) are equivalent to the Hebrew *tsedaqah* (righteousness) and *yeshuah* (salvation).

God is a Saviour to those who believe and confess the Lord Jesus Christ: without in any way compromising His own righteousness and judgement, God forgives those who come to Him in faith through the appointed Mediator; He grants them salvation and by His grace they are restored to a right relationship with Him. This is the wonder of salvation: the renewal of fellowship between a man and his Maker, between a sinner and God his Saviour.

Righteousness and salvation

Having seen the outworking of God's purpose in Christ, we are now in a position to return to the Old Testament and find new meaning in a number of passages in the psalms and prophets. What is so striking as we look at the Old Testament, and especially the psalms and the prophets, is the way "salvation" and "righteousness" are coupled – often in typical Hebrew parallelisms. In Psalm 40, for example, a clearly Messianic Psalm, we have: "I have not hid thy *righteousness* within my heart; I have declared thy faithfulness and thy *salvation*: I have not concealed thy lovingkindness and thy truth" (verses 7-11). And in Psalm 98: "The LORD hath made known his *salvation*: his *righteousness* hath he openly showed in the sight of the heathen ... all the ends of the earth have seen the salvation of our God" (verses 2,3).

The same parallelism between God's righteousness and His salvation is seen again in Isaiah: "Thus saith the LORD, Keep ye judgement, and do justice: for my *salvation* is near to come, and my *righteousness* to be revealed" (56:1). "For Zion's sake will I not hold my peace, and for Jerusalem's sake I will not rest, until the *righteousness* thereof go forth as brightness, and the *salvation* thereof as a lamp that burneth" (62:1). And from Micah: "Therefore I will look unto the Lord; I will wait for the God of my *salvation* ... he will bring me forth to the light, and I shall behold his *righteousness*" (7:7).

"The only wise God our Saviour"

So close is this parallelism, in fact, that we can reasonably say that "salvation" is the expression of God's righteousness; He is a Saviour because He is Himself righteous, and desires man

– estranged through sin – to be restored to righteousness and fellowship with Him. That goal has been accomplished through the righteousness of Jesus, the one who bears God's Saving Name; and it will be made a living reality in the day when he appears "the second time without sin unto salvation" (Hebrews 9:28).

> "Now unto him that is able to keep you from falling, and to present you faultless before the presence of his glory with exceeding joy, to the only wise God our Saviour, be glory and majesty, dominion and power, both now and ever. Amen".
>
> (Jude 25)

10 |

"Behold the goodness and severity of God"

GOODNESS is one of the first qualities to be mentioned in scripture. When the work of creation was finished, God declared it "very good" (Genesis 1:31). All that the Lord God had made was good, reflecting His own goodness; the perfection, the excellence which belongs to the Creator Himself. And what about "severity"? The word occurs (in the KJV) only in the one verse, Romans 11:22, from which our title is taken. It does, however, sum up the concept of the judgements and wrath of God which is present from the very beginning of His dealings with mankind. As early as Genesis 2, there is the first hint of divine judgement, though as yet there was no transgression and no cause for punishment: "In the day thou eatest thereof thou shalt surely die" (2:17). We need only to turn to Genesis 3, however, to encounter both the first sin and the first act of judgement. Divine displeasure is implicit in God's question to Adam: "Where art thou?" – a challenge which was followed up by the more searching question: "Who told thee that thou wast naked?", and then with the sad pronouncement of the first punishments which God had to inflict upon His creation: the curse upon the ground, and banishment for the man and his wife.

"The fear of the Lord"

What a tragedy, then, was the Fall of man – yet each subsequent generation has repeated and magnified that first disobedience;

and as man has sinned, so the Almighty has been obliged to react. Sin entered the world when man chose to misuse the free will which God had granted him; sin arose when man failed to appreciate "the fear of the LORD". As Paul says in connection with man's depravity: "There is no fear of God before their eyes" (Romans 3:18, quoting Psalm 36:1).

Did Adam and Eve not know the fear of the Lord? Surely, when the man and his wife hid themselves, they were experiencing guilt: they were acknowledging that God required of them a standard of obedience to match His holiness; and that if they failed in living up to that standard then God would show His displeasure? They did indeed recognise the supremacy and holiness of God, and had begun to learn of the fear of the Lord – but they, like every man and woman since (with one exception), had evidently not learned the fear of God in a measure sufficient to withstand sin.

What precisely is this fear? Adam and Eve were frightened and hid themselves, but true Godly fear is not just being afraid. The people of God had awe-inspiring experiences, at which they trembled – Moses drew back from the burning bush; Israel stood quaking at the foot of Sinai, and so on – and although this is not "the fear of the Lord", such experiences did provide vital lessons for a generation who needed to learn the true "fear of God". Those who matured in their understanding of the character of God, learned to approach Him with a reverential awe which is a very different emotion from human fright or fear:

> "The people saw the thunderings, and the lightnings, and the voice of the trumpet, and the mountain smoking ... And they said unto Moses, Speak thou with us, and we will hear: but let not God speak with us, lest we die. And Moses said unto the people, Fear not [*yare*]: for God is come to prove you, and that his fear [*yirah*] may be before your faces, that ye sin not."
>
> (Exodus 20:18-20)

Time and again, and most particularly in the book of Deuteronomy, we hear Israel being exhorted to "fear the LORD thy God", but the fact that the exhortation is repeated throughout the Old Testament shows how slow the people were to learn: "Ye shall not fear other gods ... but the LORD your God ye shall fear ... Howbeit they did not hearken" (2 Kings 17:37-40). So basic was the principle of Godly fear, that through the inspired words of Jacob "Fear" becomes one of the divine titles: "Except the God of my father, the God of Abraham, and the Fear [*pachad*] of Isaac, had been with me ... And Jacob sware by the Fear of his father Isaac" (Genesis 31:42,53). Jacob, through bitter and humbling experiences, had begun to learn the truth that, "The fear of the LORD is the beginning of wisdom" (Psalm 111:10; Proverbs 1:7).

Though there are many more references one could quote, sufficient have been cited to show that the Old Testament idea of "the fear of God" is another of those profound and unique Hebrew idioms. Like *chesed* (covenant-love), which we considered in an earlier chapter, *yirah* and *pachad* also proved difficult to render into New Testament Greek – and are similarly almost untranslatable into modern languages. When Mary said, "His mercy is on them that *fear* him from generation to generation" (Luke 1:50), she will have used the Hebrew (or Aramaic) idiom, but in the Greek text through which her words have come down to us, the word for "fear" is *phobeō*, which meant 'to terrify' or 'to cause fear' (compare the English word 'phobia'). This word is really far from adequate to convey the true sense of "them that *fear* him". Similarly, in Paul's address to the men of Antioch, *phobeō* does not altogether do justice to the intensely Hebrew idea of 'Godfearers': "Men and brethren, children of the stock of Abraham, and whosoever among you *feareth* God ..." (Acts 13:26). And when John writes, "There is no fear in love; but perfect love casteth out fear" (1 John 4:18), he is trying to express the Old Testament idea of reverential awe rather than the Greek idea of 'terror' or 'fear' conveyed by the original word *phobos*.

There are other Greek words, though these are less frequently used. Cornelius was "a devout [*eusebēs*] man, and one that feared [*phobeō*] God" (Acts 10:2): here, *eusebēs* conveys quite well the Old Testament idea of 'reverential'. It is significant that the Septuagint translators, when faced with the same problem of finding a Greek word for "fear" in its Old Testament sense, sometimes preferred *eusebia* ('piety', 'reverence') – in Proverbs 1:7, for example; and also in the following passage:

> "The spirit of the LORD shall rest upon him, the spirit of wisdom and understanding ... the spirit of knowledge and of the *fear of the LORD*; and shall make him of quick understanding in the *fear of the LORD*." (Isaiah 11:2,3)

In this prophecy of Messiah it was important to convey the true idea of the fear of God.

God's judgements

But we must return to our main theme, and to Genesis. God's displeasure was evident, as we have seen, in the judgements uttered in the Garden of Eden, in the expulsion of Adam and Eve from that paradise, and in the placing of "cherubim, and a flaming sword ... to keep the way of the tree of life" (3:24). In each of these ways God's disapproval was shown – and yet there is no record in these early chapters of God being angry. The first time that we encounter the idea of wrath, it is Cain's wrath, not God's. Genesis 4 does, nonetheless, introduce words like "punishment" and "vengeance" (verses 13,15) and it is not long before other aspects of divine judgement are manifested. The Flood came because "God saw that the wickedness of man was great in the earth ... And it repented the LORD that he had made man on the earth, and it grieved him at his heart. And the LORD said, I will destroy man whom I have created" (6:5-7). Again, faced with the wickedness of the men of Babel, God was forced to confound their language and scatter them abroad (11:6-9). And so the sad history of mankind unfolds, marked at certain times by noble leadership and high resolve, but at other times by godlessness and evil.

Divine jealousy

It is unfashionable to speak of the wrath of God, but for those who read their scriptures – both the Old Testament and the New

– there is no escaping the concept of the righteous judgements of God. Though we may prefer to dwell on His love, grace, mercy and goodness, we must acknowledge His fury, indignation, anger, jealousy and zeal. And the way to understand these attributes, and not to be altogether downcast by reading of them, is to delve a little more deeply into their meaning. Thereby we discover that God is not an implacable deity who must be appeased, but a God who seeks, by acts of grace as well as judgement, to restore His children to Him.

A rewarding train of thought can be followed by considering divine jealousy. There is a Hebrew word, *qinah* (and other related words), translated "jealousy", "envy" or "zeal". Where "jealousy" occurs in the Old Testament, it is invariably in connection with divine judgements and especially with Israel's tendency to go after other gods: "For I the LORD thy God am a jealous [*qanna*] God, visiting the iniquity of the fathers upon the children ..." (Exodus 20:5; also Deuteronomy 5:9). "Jealous" even becomes one of the divine titles: "Thou shalt worship no other god: for the LORD, whose name is Jealous, is a jealous God" (Exodus 34:14; Deuteronomy 6:15). The opening verses of Nahum's prophecy reinforce the association of jealousy with judgement – it would be hard to find a scripture passage that is more evocative of divine wrath:

> "The LORD is a jealous God and avengeth; the LORD avengeth and is full of wrath ... Who can stand before his indignation? and who can abide in the fierceness of his anger? his fury is poured out like fire ... He will make an utter end." (1:2-9)

In Ezekiel 5, the word translated "jealousy" in Nahum is now translated "zeal":

> "Thus shall mine anger be accomplished, and I will satisfy my fury upon them, and I will be comforted: and they shall know that I the LORD have spoken in my zeal [*qinah*], when I have accomplished my fury upon them." (5:13; cf. 16:42)

Once again we see God's "zeal" (or "jealousy") associated with anger and fury – but what is the significance of the unexpected phrase, "*and I will be comforted*"? In what sense does God take comfort from the judgements which He executes, in this case upon Jerusalem? There is a parallel verse in Isaiah: "Therefore saith the Lord, the LORD of hosts, the mighty One of Israel, Ah, I will ease me [*nacham*] of mine adversaries, and avenge me of my enemies" (1:24). Moffatt has, "I will have the comfort of vengeance on my foes"; the RSV, "I will vent my wrath on my enemies".

"I will be comforted"

In some sense, it is true that God gains satisfaction when justice is done and vengeance is taken on those who oppose His will. But there is a deeper sense to be explored, and a closer examination of the phrase "I will be comforted" will help us to marvel once again at the character of the God of Israel. God's judgements are real, but always limited in duration and qualified by mercy:

> "Have I any pleasure in the death of the wicked, saith the Lord GOD: and not that he should return from his way, and live?"
> (Ezekiel 18:23,32; 33:11; cf. 2 Peter 3:9)

> "In overflowing wrath I hid my face from thee for a moment; but with everlasting kindness will I have mercy on thee, saith the LORD, thy redeemer." (Isaiah 54:8, RV)

What, then, is behind the word "comforted" in Ezekiel 5:13? The Hebrew word *nacham* appears in familiar passages such as, "Thy rod and thy staff they *comfort* me" (Psalm 23:4) and "*Comfort* ye, *comfort* ye, my people, saith your God" (Isaiah 40:1). There are, however, alternative meanings, very different from the idea of 'ease' or 'consolation' – in fact, almost the opposite. *Nacham* means literally 'to give vent to one's sighs', 'to draw breath'; and it can be used positively to express fulfilment and satisfaction, or negatively to describe a reaction to some present or impending evil. A related word is translated "sighing", "groaning" or "mourning". When Job says, "My stroke is heavier than my groaning [*anachah*]", he is certainly not speaking of "comfort" in the usual sense; nor is Isaiah when he prophesies, "Sorrow and sighing [*anachah*] shall flee away" (35:10; 51:11).

"He repenteth him of the evil"

But even this does not exhaust the range of meaning associated with *nacham*. Turning to a lexicon we discover that while *nacham* is translated sixty-seven times by "comfort", it is rendered over forty times by "repent":

> "It *repented* the LORD that he had made man on the earth."
> (Genesis 6:6)

> "Turn unto the LORD your God: for he is gracious and full of compassion, slow to anger, and plenteous in mercy, and *repenteth* him of the evil ..."
> (Joel 2:13,14; cf. Jonah 3:9,10; etc.)

Thus a single word can give expression to a whole range of emotions, from pleasurable "comfort", through "sighing", to "repenting". We began with one instance of "comforted" in Ezekiel 5:13, and explored its significance in the context of "anger" and "fury" Having examined other contexts we can now appreciate the many overtones of the word, and understand some of the many facets of God's emotions. He experiences satisfaction when His laws prevail and those who oppose Him are judged; as a Father He feels distress as He sighs over the condition of the human race; and at the same time, if man will but turn to heed His will, He will repent of the evil.

The anger and compassion of Jesus

We have ventured, with awe and (it is hoped) with reverence, into the sphere not just of God's attributes but also of His feelings. We have looked chiefly at the Old Testament, for it is there that the rich significance of God-given words is most apparent; but let us not forget that the God of the New Testament is the same God, and His characteristics are there even more fully revealed in His Son. Did not the Lord Jesus Christ, during his ministry, manifest the Father's goodness and severity? did he not show forth the same emotions? He could be angry with the scribes and Pharisees, and show tender compassion on the meek. Sometimes, he was able to rejoice at the faith of his followers; at other times, he "sighed deeply in his spirit" (Mark 8:12); "he groaned in the spirit, and was troubled" (John 11:33). In every action, in every word, he revealed to us the Father.

11 |

"My rock and my fortress ... my strength"

MAN cannot walk in his own strength: he has to learn to recognise his insufficiency and acknowledge the might of His Creator. That might, that strength, is emphasised throughout scripture, and appears in an amazing variety of expressions. The psalm from which our title comes, conveys the all-sufficiency of Israel's God in a succession of words and phrases:

> "I will love thee, O LORD, my strength. The LORD is my rock, and my fortress, and my deliverer; my God, my strength, in whom I will trust; my buckler, and the horn of my salvation, my high tower ... For who is God, save the LORD? and who is a rock, beside our God? It is God that girdeth me with strength ... Thou hast also given me the shield of thy salvation: and thy right hand hath holden me up, and thy gentleness hath made me great." (Psalm 18:1,2,31-35)

Such passages tell of the strength of God, a strength that can manifest itself in mighty deeds and acts of creation – and destruction; but also in that gentle strength, in which David trusted, and upon which every believer can depend.

The Almighty

Strength is part of the larger topic of God's power – His omnipotence. To Abraham God revealed Himself as El Shaddai, one of the divine names translated in most Bibles as "God Almighty": "I am God Almighty; walk before me, and be thou perfect" (Genesis 17:1, RV). It is a title used forty-eight times in the Old Testament. While the significance of the names of God is outside the remit of these articles, it can be noted that El Shaddai almost certainly had a meaning which, though including the idea of 'Almighty', extended far beyond it: Brother Alfred Nicholls, in *The Name that is above every Name* (pages 6,7), shows how it is particularly used in the context of fruitfulness and blessing, and yet also appears in the context of judgement and destruction. That, of course, is entirely in keeping with what we have seen already in connection with other attributes of God: often there are opposite and seemingly contradictory aspects to the same feature of the divine character. As we saw previously, He is a God of both goodness and severity.

Only once does the word "omnipotent" appear in the King James Version, in the New Testament: "Alleluia: for the Lord God omnipotent reigneth" (Revelation 19:6). Here the original word is the Greek *pantokratōr*, which literally means 'all-powerful'. This same word is translated "Almighty" in nine other places in the New Testament, most of them in Revelation. It is especially interesting to note that *pantokratōr* was the word chosen by the Septuagint translators to render *Shaddai* in the Old Testament – confirmation that "Almighty" is at least a part of its ancient meaning.

"The Mighty One of Jacob"

God, besides being referred to in our scriptures as the Almighty, is very frequently termed "mighty", or "the mighty one". The basic Hebrew word for "God", *el*, itself means 'mighty one'; but there are in addition several more words translated in our scriptures by "mighty". Among the blessings of Jacob is the following concerning Joseph: "His bow remained steady, his strong arms stayed supple, because of the hand of the Mighty One [*abir*] of Jacob, because of the Shepherd, the Rock of Israel" (Genesis 49:24, NIV). (The other five occurrences of the word *abir*, in the Psalms and Isaiah, are also in the phrase "the Mighty One of Jacob".)

Gibbor is the next word we come across, translated "mighty" in passages such as, "The LORD your God is God of gods, and Lord of lords, a great God, a mighty [*gibbor*], and a terrible, which regardeth not persons, nor taketh reward" (Deuteronomy 10:17; cf. Nehemiah 9:32). Another familiar quotation is from Isaiah 9:6: "Unto us a child is born ... his name shall be called Wonderful, Counsellor, The mighty God [*gibbor*], The everlasting Father, The Prince of Peace" – ascriptions which, of course, in the first place belonged to God Himself, but are here applied prophetically to His Son.

Then there is *geburah* – "Thou hast a *mighty* arm" (Psalm 89:13); *gadol* – "The LORD thy God is among you, a *mighty* God" (Deuteronomy 4:37); *chazaq* – "Thou hast brought thy people forth out of the land of Egypt with a *mighty* hand" (Daniel 9:15); and *kabbir* – "Behold, God is *mighty* ... *mighty* in strength and wisdom" (Job 36:5). All these (and there are yet other Hebrew words besides) are used to express the might of the God of Israel.

By comparison, there are fewer Greek words, so that in the New Testament, God's might is conveyed by *ischus* in, for example, Ephesians 6:10 – "Be strong in the Lord, and in the power of his *might*"; *dunatos*, for example in Luke 1:49 – "He that is *mighty* hath done to me great things"; or *krataios*, for example in 1 Peter 5:6 – "Humble yourselves therefore under the *mighty* hand of God".

> "It is God that girdeth me with strength ... thy gentleness hath made me great." (Psalm 18:32,35)

"Great in power"

When we look in our concordances for the word "power" we find a further spectrum of words, some of which we have already encountered in our examination of "might". Just a few examples should suffice: "They shall speak of the glory of thy kingdom, and talk of thy power [*geburah*]" (Psalm 145:11). "Thy people shall be willing in the day of thy power [*chayil*, elsewhere translated force, valour, host, army etc.]" (110:3). "The LORD is slow to anger, and great in power [*koach*] ... a strong hold in the day of trouble; and he knoweth them that trust in him" (Nahum 1:3,7). "Praise God in his sanctuary: praise him in the firmament of his power [*oz*]" (Psalm 150:1). And in the New Testament: "Upholding all things by the word of his power [*dunamis*]" (Hebrews 1:3); "It is not for you to know the times or the seasons, which the Father hath put in his own power [*exousia*, often translated 'authority']"; "The blessed and only Potentate [*dunastēs*, 'one that is powerful'], the King of kings, and Lord of lords ... to whom be honour and power [*kratos*] everlasting" (1 Timothy 6:15,16).

The Spirit of God

Having introduced the word "power", we are of course bound to touch on the subject of the Holy Spirit: indeed, "power" (usually *dunamis*) appears several times in the New Testament in conjunction with the (Holy) Spirit (for example, in Acts 1:8; 10:38; Romans 15:19). In this article, we cannot begin to do justice to the Spirit of God, which is in any case better seen as an aspect of His being rather than an attribute of His character, like holiness or mercy. In defining the Holy Spirit, and in countering the Trinitarian belief in the personification of the Spirit, we very properly refer to the Holy Spirit as the power of God: it is the means whereby God can reveal His might and show forth His strength. Having said that, however, God's strength and might and power are talked about in the Scriptures very commonly without any reference to the Holy Spirit – a term reserved for particular manifestations of divine power.

"By strength of hand"

Let us now explore further the concept of God as man's source of *strength*, his stay, his rock and fortress: this, we shall now find, is a rich seam for further study. Yet again, the range of Hebrew and Greek words (particularly the former) is impressive, though each one, in its original usage, will have conveyed a particular nuance of meaning. Our opening quotation from Psalm 18 began with David's phrase, "I will love thee, O LORD, my strength [*chezeq*]". Centuries before, Moses had reminded the people of "the strength of hand" by which the Lord had redeemed Israel in the Exodus: "Remember this day, in which ye came out from Egypt, out of the house of bondage; for by strength [*chozeq*] of hand the Lord brought you out ..." (Exodus 13:2,14,16).

After the exile, when Ezra received a generous letter from King Artaxerxes, he thanked God for the turn of events:

> "Blessed be the LORD God of our fathers, which hath put such a thing as this into the king's heart ... and I was strengthened [*chazaq*] as the hand of the LORD my God was upon me."
> (Ezra 7:27,28)

A little later, when Sanballat and his company tried to weaken the hands of those who were rebuilding Jerusalem, Nehemiah sought strength from His God: "They all would have made us afraid ... But now, O God, strengthen [*chazaq*] thou my hands" (Nehemiah 6:9).

"My strength and song"

From the same passage in Psalm 18 comes one of the words we saw in connection with "power": "It is God that girdeth me with strength [*chayil*] ... thou hast girded me with strength unto the battle" (verses 32,39). Another word translated "power" was *oz*, which is also frequently rendered "strength":

> "The Lord is my strength [*oz*] and song, and he is become my salvation ... Thou hast guided thy people in thy strength [*oz*] unto thy holy habitation." (Exodus 15:2,13)

> "The king shall joy in thy strength [*oz*], O LORD; and in thy salvation how greatly shall he rejoice!" (Psalm 21:1)

The coupling of the ideas of joy and strength occurs also where *maoz* is the word for "strength":

> "The day is holy unto our Lord: neither be ye sorry; for the joy of the LORD is your strength [*maoz*]." (Nehemiah 8:10)

Strength and joy; strength and song; strength and salvation: these associations are made not just for poetic effect, but because of the fundamental truth that in our weakness we can call upon God's strength, finding salvation and joy in Him: "Only in the LORD ... is righteousness and strength [*oz*]" (Isaiah 45:24). And this is the more so through our Lord Jesus Christ. If the Psalmist could say, "Unto thee, O my strength [*oz*], will I sing: for God is my defence, and the God of my mercy" (59:17), how much more may we who have obtained mercy through the sacrifice of the Saviour: "For when we were without strength [*asthenēs*], in due time Christ died for the ungodly" (Romans 5:6).

"Underneath are the everlasting arms"

We have by no means exhausted the rich vocabulary, particularly in the Old Testament, used to express the might and power and strength of God. There are, moreover, many other metaphors which convey the same truths. There are countless references to "the *hand* of the LORD"; there are many others to "the *arm* of the LORD". God took for Himself a nation "by wonders, and by war, and by a mighty hand, and by a stretched out arm" (Deuteronomy 4:24). "The eternal God is thy refuge, and underneath are the everlasting arms" (33:27). And even if hand or arm is not actually mentioned, the image of a Father carrying His children in His arms is often present:

> "In his love and in his pity he redeemed them; and he *bare* them, and *carried* them all the days of old." (Isaiah 63:5)

> "The everlasting God ... fainteth not, neither is weary ... To them that have no might he increaseth strength ... They that wait upon the LORD shall renew their strength; they shall mount up with wings as eagles; they shall run, and not be weary; and they shall walk, and not faint." (40:28-31)

Our God is strong to help, mighty to save; His strength, as Paul learnt, is "made perfect in weakness" (2 Corinthians 12:9). And often, like Paul and so many other Godly men and women, we shall experience that strength only in the measure that we admit our weakness and accept help through His word:

> "The God of all grace, who called you unto his eternal glory in Christ, after that ye have suffered a little while, shall himself

> perfect, stablish, strengthen, settle you. To him be glory and dominion for ever and ever." (1 Peter 5:10,11)

The words of Hymn 49, by Brother David Brown, capture very well that recognition of divine strength which should be ours:

> "Strength, honour, majesty, / Ever beseemeth Thee, / Uncreate unity, / Fountain of life: / Mighty of mighties, Thou, / From Thee all blessings flow / To all – above – below, / Healer of strife."

"The Strength of Israel"

If God is strong, then no wonder that in a couple of places "Strength" actually becomes one of the divine titles. There is a significant passage in 1 Samuel: "The Strength [*netsach*] of Israel will not lie nor repent: for he is not a man, that he should repent" (15:29). *Netsach* is yet another of the many Hebrew words translated "strength", though its primary meanings are more to do with 'preeminence', 'eternity' or 'victory'. In a further passage, *netsach* is in fact rendered "victory" –

> "Thine, O LORD, is the greatness, and the power [*geburah*], and the glory, and the victory [*netsach*], and the majesty ... in thine hand is power [*koach*] and might [*geburah*]; and in thine hand it is to make great, and to give strength [*chazaq*] unto all." (1 Chronicles 29:11,12)

In the kingdom age, God will "swallow up death in victory [*netsach*]" (Isaiah 25:8). Our prayer, "Thine is the kingdom, and the power, and the glory" (Matthew 6:13) will then be fulfilled; for while strength and power and might have been God's from the beginning, they are complete and all-pervading only when sin and opposition to divine rule are put down, when thousands upon thousands sing, "Worthy is the Lamb that was slain to receive power, and riches, and wisdom, and strength, and honour, and glory, and blessing" (Revelation 5:12).

12 |

"From everlasting to everlasting, Thou art God"

GOD is not limited by time: He is the Ancient of days (Daniel 7:9,13,22); He is "the first and the last" (Isaiah 41:4; 44:6; 48:12). "Before me there was no God formed, neither shall there be after me" (43:10). From age to age, "from everlasting to everlasting" (Psalm 41:13; 93:2; 103:17; 106:48; etc.), He is God:

> "Lord, thou hast been our dwelling place in all generations. Before the mountains were brought forth, or ever thou hadst formed the earth and the world, even from everlasting to everlasting, thou art God ... For a thousand years in thy sight are but as yesterday when it is past, and as a watch in the night ..." (Psalm 90:1-4)

By contrast man is of few days, a mortal creature:

> "We spend our years as a tale that is told ... So teach us to number our days, that we may apply our hearts unto wisdom." (verses 9-12)

"Which is and was and is to come"

It is no surprise that Moses understood the eternity of God: it was after all to him that God revealed Himself as "I am that I am" – that covenant name which, among other things, spelled out eternity. Though at first sight it may appear to refer only to the present, as the name is expounded in scripture we see that it comprehends God's past and future existence. "I am the Alpha and the Omega, saith the Lord God, which is and which was and which is to come, the Almighty" (Revelation 1:8, RV; 11:17; 16:5). Yahweh, the covenant name, speaks of God's eternity: there are, indeed, versions of the Bible, Moffatt's for example, which render "the LORD" of the KJV as "the Eternal". (French versions, similarly, use "L'Éternel".)

But the idea of God as the eternal, the everlasting, God goes back further – at least to the time of Abraham. In Genesis 17, God sought to reveal to Abraham the everlasting covenant which He would make with him and his descendants. To Abraham, at a time when he and Sarah were still childless, an everlasting covenant was hard to comprehend. It is the more significant, then, that very shortly after the birth of Isaac, the patriarch "called on the name of the LORD, *the everlasting God*" (21:33).

As we have discovered with other divine attributes, a variety of Hebrew and Greek words are used to convey the idea of eternity. One of these, in fact, is the word we were considering towards the end of the previous chapter: *netsach*. In the passages we looked at then, this word was translated "strength" and "victory", but we noted that its basic meaning had more to do with 'pre-eminence' or 'eternity'. An example of its use in connection with the everlasting purposes of God is in Psalm 68:16 – "This is the hill which God desireth to dwell in; yea, the LORD will dwell in it *for ever*."

"... that inhabiteth eternity"

Then there is the word *ad*, quite often translated "ever" but once rendered "eternity" (the only occurrence of "eternity" in the KJV): "Thus saith the high and lofty One that inhabiteth eternity, whose name is Holy ..." (Isaiah 57:15).

In the English language, words like "eternal" and "everlasting", used to describe the Almighty, can be used both of His past and His future eternity: Hebrew has a word which, unlike any word in English, refers specifically to the past: *qedem*. Young gives its meaning as 'what is before in time or place'. In Habakkuk, for example, we have: "Art thou not from everlasting [*qedem*], O LORD my God, mine Holy One?" (1:12). The word is also found in Deuteronomy 33, in the final blessings of Moses: "The eternal [*qedem*, same word as 'ancient' in verse 15] God is thy refuge, and underneath are the everlasting arms" (verse 27).

This verse, in turn, introduces us to another Hebrew original; for while "eternal" in Deuteronomy 33:27 is *qedem*, "everlasting" is a different word, *olam*. This is the word most commonly rendered "ever", "everlasting", or "evermore" in the Old Testament – it is a word of deep significance. When God promised the land to Abraham in perpetuity, He used this word: "To thee will I give it, and to thy seed *for ever*" (Genesis 13:15). Again, when God speaks to David through the prophet Nathan of the seed to come, a son greater than Solomon, he says: "He shall build a house for my name, and I will establish the throne of his kingdom *for ever*" (2 Samuel 7:13,16).

And so we could go on, through the Psalms and prophets especially, noting the use of this rather special word in respect of God and His eternal purpose – those things which are for ever. *Olam* is translated "everlasting" in Psalm 90:2, from which this chapter's title is taken. As a refrain throughout Psalm 136, we have "... for his mercy endureth for ever [*olam*]". In Isaiah, "Trust ye in the Lord for ever [*ad*]: for in the LORD JEHOVAH is everlasting [*olam*] strength" (26:4). "Hast thou not known? hast thou not heard? the everlasting [*olam*] God, the LORD, the Creator of the ends of the earth, fainteth not, neither is weary; there is no searching of his understanding" (40:28). And in Jeremiah, "The LORD is the true God, he is the living God, and an everlasting [*olam*] king" (10:10).

"All powerful, self-existent God,
Who all creation dost sustain!
Thou wast, and art, and art to come,
And everlasting is Thy reign."

"Remember the days of old"

Olam is, however, translated in a number of other ways. Its first occurrence is in Genesis 3:22, "... and live *for ever*". The second occurrence is when God says, "My spirit shall not always [*olam*] strive with man, for that he also is flesh" (6:3). Then we find it in connection with the covenant with Noah: "This (the rainbow) is the token of the covenant which I make with you and every living creature ... for perpetual [*olam*] generations" (9:12). It is rendered "ancient" in phrases like "the ancient landmark" (Proverbs 22:28; 23:10), "the ancient paths" (Jeremiah 18:15) and "the ancient high places" (Ezekiel 36:2). In a similar way, it is translated "old" in phrases such as "the old way" (Job 22:15), "the old waste places" (Isaiah 58:12; 61:4) and "the days of old" (Deuteronomy 32:7; Isaiah 63:9,11). When the Preacher refers to man going to his "long home" (Ecclesiastes 12:5), "long" is *olam*, in the sense of 'eternal' or 'age-lasting'.

We begin to see the range and richness of meaning in this Hebrew word: remember, this is a word – and there are of course many others – which has been used in connection with the Almighty and His purposes throughout His revelation to man. The root meaning has to do with something 'hidden' or 'concealed'; hence the idea of an unknown or undefined or limitless time, and thus 'eternity', 'world' or 'age'.

> "God ... hath set the world [*olam*; margin 'eternity'] in their heart, yet so that man cannot find out the work that God hath done from the beginning even to the end."
>
> (Ecclesiastes 3:11, RV)

"For ever and ever"

When we turn to the New Testament, the idea of 'world' or 'age' continues in the Greek word *aiōn*, and its derivatives. In looking at some of the attributes of God, such as "mercy" or "fear" we have noted how inadequate the Greek language can be in providing equivalents for Hebrew words and ideas: *aiōn*, though it may not have all the same features, is in fact a very close counterpart to *olam*.

We can put this to the test by observing how a quotation from the Old Testament is rendered in the New. There are several examples to be found in the epistle to the Hebrews: The well known verse from Psalm 110, "Thou art a priest for ever [*olam*] after the order of Melchizedek", becomes in Hebrews, "Thou art a priest for ever [*aiōna*] after the order of Melchizedek" (5:6; 6:20; 7:17,21). A similar transition is made when Psalm 45:6 is quoted in Hebrews 1:8 – "Thy throne, O God, is for ever and ever".

What these and other New Testament passages reveal, is that, like the Father from whom he inherits so many characteristics, the Lord Jesus Christ is heir to the everlasting divine nature; though made in the likeness of his fellow men, and inheriting their mortality, he was raised to life eternal – to live and reign *for ever*. The quality of eternity which is shared by the Father and His Son is expressed very clearly in the closing verses of the epistle to the Romans:

> "Now to him who is able to establish you by my gospel and the proclamation of Jesus Christ, according to the revelation of the mystery hidden for long ages [*aiōnios*] past, but now revealed and made known through the prophetic writings by the command of the eternal [*aiōnios*] God ... to the only wise God be glory for ever [*aiōna*] through Jesus Christ."
>
> (Romans 16:25-27, NIV)

Another example is in the opening verses of the letter to Titus, where Paul writes to his "son after the common faith", "... in hope of eternal [*aiōnios*] life, which God, who cannot lie, promised before times eternal [*aiōnios*]; but in his own seasons manifested his word in the message wherewith I was intrusted" (Titus 1:2,3, RV). Steeped in the language and ideas of the Old Testament, Paul is able to use Greek words to convey what are essentially Hebrew thoughts regarding the eternity of God, and the ages through which His purpose has moved towards its culmination in Christ.

"An everlasting dominion"

God is eternal; and the Son at His right hand has been granted that same eternal nature, and given the everlasting dominion that the Father determined should be his by virtue of his obedience:

> "I saw in the night visions, and, behold, one like the Son of man came with the clouds of heaven, and came to the Ancient of days, and they brought him near before him. And there was given him dominion, and glory, and a kingdom ... his dominion is an everlasting dominion, which shall not pass away." (Daniel 7:13,14)

The Son having been made immortal, the first-fruits of them that slept, it is the Father's will that those who seek salvation from death through him should in the fulness of time themselves inherit eternal life:

> "As Moses lifted up the serpent in the wilderness, even so must the Son of man be lifted up: that whosoever believeth in him should not perish, but have eternal life." (John 3:15)

> "The God of all grace, who hath called us unto his eternal glory in Christ Jesus ... stablish, strengthen, settle you. To him be glory and dominion for ever and ever." (1 Peter 5:10,11)

> "And this is the record, that God hath given to us eternal life, and this life is in his Son." (1 John 5:11).

In the age to come, when the elect stand at last before the Lamb, then praises will sound to God in and throughout eternity:

> "Blessing, and glory, and wisdom, and thanksgiving, and honour, and power, and might, be unto our God for ever and ever [margin, 'unto the ages of the ages']. Amen." (Revelation 7:12)

13 |

"Dwelling in light unapproachable"

ONE of the attributes of God which we might almost forget to mention is His invisibleness. It is one of those paradoxes of our faith that the great Creator – infinite, omniscient, and filling time and space – is not perceived by any of the physical senses with which He has endowed His creatures.

> "He only hath immortality, dwelling in light unapproachable; whom no man hath seen, nor can see: to whom be honour and power eternal." (1 Timothy 6:16)

> "Father and Friend, Thy light, Thy love
> Beaming through all Thy works we see:
> Thy glory gilds the heavens above,
> And all the earth is full of Thee."

The double paradox, however, is that though God remains hidden from our view, it is His chief desire to be manifested. The mighty works of creation – sun, moon and stars, this planet earth, the forms innumerable that teem upon it – these are the outward and visible evidences of God's majesty; but He is also revealed in ways perceived only by the spiritual senses:

> "That which may be known of God is manifest in them; for God hath showed it unto them. For the invisible things of him from the creation of the world are clearly seen, being understood by the things that are made, even his eternal power and Godhead; so that they are without excuse." (Romans 1:19,20)

Is not Paul saying that, though God is indeed proclaimed by the *visible* creation, the true revelation of Himself which He wants mankind to "see" is only fully understood through that which is *invisible*?

Life and light

The common factor in these two aspects of God's revelation of Himself is "light" – the physical light by which the things of creation are made visible; and the spiritual light "which lighteth every man that cometh into the world" (John 1:9).

God is the source of all light. "Let there be light [Hebrew, *or*]" (Genesis 1:3) was the Creator's first instruction. And when, in the fulness of time, He brought His only begotten Son into the world, it is as if that first command was repeated, for "in him was life; and the life was the light [Greek, *phos*] of men" (John 1:4). The apostle Paul makes this connection:

> "For God, who commanded the light to shine out of darkness, hath shined in our hearts, to give the light of the knowledge of the glory of God in the face of Jesus Christ."
>
> (2 Corinthians 4:6)

The point we are making is simply this: that though God does reveal Himself in visible ways, that is but the beginning of His self-manifestation. As Job says, "Lo, these are but the outskirts of his ways" (Job 26:14, RV). The fuller, deeper, revelation of the Almighty is not so much in tangible, visible things as in the illumination of the mind; the work of His Word to enlighten and transform those who bear His name and show forth, to whatever limited degree, His glory.

Let us, then, stay with the concept of "light". Light is energy; light is that which enlightens; light transforms – transfigures. No wonder that, in the simplest of phrases, John can say, "*God is light*, and in him is no darkness at all" (1 John 1:5). He is "the Father of lights, with whom can be no variation, neither shadow that is cast by turning" (James 1:17, RV). Each new dawn reassures us of God's care for His creation; the splendour of the rainbow reminds us of the covenant "between me and all flesh that is upon the earth" (Genesis 9:17). Light and glory are often equated: God's glory was evident in the burning bush, in the pillars of cloud and fire, in the glimpse which Moses was granted in the cleft of the rock – and reflected in the shining face of Moses after receiving the tables of testimony in the mount.

The association of "light" and "countenance" is an interesting theme which can be followed throughout scripture – and, as always, the psalms are a particularly rich source. Consider the sequence:

> "LORD, lift thou up the light of thy countenance upon us." (4:6)
>
> "God be merciful unto us, and bless us; and cause his face to shine upon us." (67:1,2)
>
> "Turn us again, O God, and cause thy face to shine; and we shall be saved." (80:3,19)
>
> "Righteousness and judgement are the foundation of thy throne: mercy and truth go before thy face. Blessed is the people that know the joyful sound: they walk, O LORD, in the light of thy countenance." (89:14,15, RV)

"His face did shine as the sun"

Perhaps we have not thought of such passages in the context of God manifestation, yet clearly this is what is behind the psalmist's thought: the light of God's countenance, His character, His glory, is not merely to be admired; it must also be absorbed by those who would be His servants. They are called "out of darkness into his marvellous light" (1 Peter 2:9). They are to "walk as children of light" (Ephesians 5:8). And in this they have the Lord Jesus Christ as their example: When he was transfigured, "his face did shine as the sun, and his raiment was white as the light" (Matthew 17:2). But even those who were not "eyewitnesses of his majesty" (2 Peter 1:16) still have before them the enduring example of Christ as the light of the world: "He that followeth me shall not walk in darkness, but shall have the light of life" (John 8:12).

The final manifestation of the God of Light awaits the Day when He is all in all, when "the earth shall be lightened with his glory" (Revelation 18:1).

> "And the city had no need of the sun, neither of the moon, to shine in it: for the glory of God did lighten it, and the Lamb is the light thereof. And the nations of them which are saved shall walk in the light of it ... for there shall be no night there."
> (21:23-25; 22:5)

Good marginal references will take us back from Revelation to Isaiah 60; and chapter 60 will almost certainly refer back to chapter 59; for here, especially, the prophet expounds the message of the Gospel in terms of "light".

> "We look for light, but behold darkness; for brightness, but we walk in obscurity. We grope for the wall like the blind, yea, we grope as they that have no eyes." (59:10)

But the same chapter speaks of the Lord bringing salvation (verse 16), and the Redeemer coming to Zion (verse 20), so that when we come to chapter 60 the gloom is dispelled:

> "Arise, shine; for thy light is come, and the glory of the LORD is risen upon thee. For, behold, darkness shall cover the earth, and gross darkness the peoples: but the LORD shall arise upon thee, and his glory shall be seen upon thee. And nations shall come to thy light, and kings to the brightness of thy rising."
> (60:3)

Then, towards the end of chapter 60, is the passage which parallels Revelation 21 and 22: "The sun shall be no more thy light by day ... but the LORD shall be unto thee an everlasting light, and thy God thy glory" (Isaiah 60:19,20).

In a wonderful exposition, Isaiah portrays the hopeless lot of mankind; the love of God; the promise of a Redeemer; righteousness, salvation, and the prospect of an earth filled with eternal light and glory – a theme which continues, of course, right to the end of the book, to the promise of new heavens and a new earth.

But let just one word detain us: it is the word "glory" in 60:19, which is not the usual Hebrew *kabod*, but *tipharah*, a word whose meaning is closer to 'beauty'. The same word occurs in a psalm we have already quoted: "Thou [LORD] art the glory (beauty) of their strength" (89:17; cf. 78:61). And thus we are introduced to yet another attribute of God. "Beauty" is a word which, like so many, has become debased; yet in connection with divine things, it has an exalted meaning. "Look down from heaven, and behold from the habitation of thy holiness and of thy glory [*tipharah*, beauty] ..." (Isaiah 63:15). The KJV sometimes actually translates *tipharah* by "beauty" (and also "honour"): "The LORD made the heavens. Honour [*hod*] and majesty [*hadar*] are before him: strength [*oz*] and beauty [*tipharah*] are in his sanctuary" (Psalm 96:5,6). "In that day shall the LORD of hosts be for a crown of glory [*tsebi*, 'beauty' or 'desire'], and for a diadem of beauty [*tipharah*], unto the residue of his people" (Isaiah 28:5).

Beauty and Excellency

One word leads to another: from "beauty" as a translation of *tipharah*, our concordance will take us to "beauty" as a translation of the word *noam* – "Let the beauty of the LORD our God be upon us" (Psalm 90:17); and again as a rendering of *yophi* – "Thine eyes shall see the king is his beauty" (Isaiah 33:17).

Finally, among the attributes to be considered this month, we look briefly at "excellency". Previously we have seen this associated with "glory", but it has other connotations too. When Moses sang in triumph at the drowning of the Egyptians, he said, "In the greatness of thy excellency [*gaon*, 'rising'] thou hast overthrown them that rose up against thee" (Exodus 15:7). But *gaon* also appears translated as "majesty", for instance in Isaiah 2: "Enter into the rock, and hide thee in the dust, for fear of the LORD, and for the glory of his majesty" (verses 10,19,21).

From light, through beauty, to excellency and majesty, we have reviewed just a few more of the limitless number of divine characteristics, and we are left marvelling with the psalmist:

> "O LORD our Lord, how excellent is thy name in all the earth! who hast set thy glory above the heavens ... When I consider thy heavens, the work of thy fingers, the moon and the stars, which thou hast ordained; what is man, that thou art mindful of him? and the son of man, that thou visitest him? ... O LORD our Lord, How excellent is thy name in all the earth!"
>
> (Psalm 8)

14 |

"Great is thy faithfulness"

OUR survey of the attributes of God is almost concluded. That is not, of course, to say that it is complete, or that there are no other characteristics of the Almighty that we could most profitably examine. There are indeed many more aspects of God's nature to explore but we must now begin to draw together the studies we have undertaken. This, however, cannot be done until we have looked, at least, at one very special word. That word is "truth".

The overall title we adopted for this series was "The God of Truth". This is a phrase which occurs several times in the scriptures: it is a phrase which concisely and conveniently summarises a number of facts about Almighty God – for example, that He is true, that He is the source and originator of truth, the revealer of Truth, the One who caused grace and truth to be manifested in His only begotten Son, and so on. Correct though all these statements are, however, they have not said the half of what needs to be said about The God of Truth.

As we have seen in connection with a number of other divine attributes, we need to look behind the English words. When we do this for the Hebrew (and for that matter also the Greek) words for "truth", we open up great vistas of meaning which, irrespective of the version we might use, do not come over completely in our western tongues.

Mercy and truth

But let us start by looking simply at occurrences of "truth" in the KJV (or RV); and commencing – as we have done so often, and with such benefit – with the earliest usages of the word. One such is when the servant of Abraham, sent to find a wife for Isaac, and meeting Rebekah by the well, said, "Blessed be the LORD God of my master Abraham, who hath not forsaken his mercy and his truth [*emeth*] toward my master" (Genesis 24:27, RV).

> "All the paths of the LORD are mercy and truth unto such as keep his covenant and his testimonies." (Psalm 25:10)

What a testimony to the instruction Abraham had given to members of his household, and to this servant in particular! A servant who had learned of "mercy" [*chesed*] and "truth" [*emeth*] was indeed well tutored: *chesed*, as we have seen, is one of the profoundest and loveliest of Hebrew words, conveying that covenant love which God has for those who are His; *emeth*, which we now consider for the first time, is no less profound – a very special Hebrew idea. Its meaning embraces 'faithfulness' and 'steadfastness'; it conveys something that is 'right', 'established', 'sure'. In the very same chapter of Genesis, when the servant is rehearsing before Laban and Bethuel the events that had just happened at the well, *emeth* is used twice more:

> "I worshipped the LORD, and blessed the LORD, the God of my master Abraham, which had led me in the *right* way to take my master's brother's daughter for his son. And now if ye will deal *truly* with my master, tell me ..." (Genesis 24:48,49)

Steadfastness, faithfulness, firmness

A few chapters further on we encounter Jacob, apprehensive at meeting his estranged brother Esau, but sensibly committing his fears to God:

> "And Jacob said, O God of my father Abraham, and God of my father Isaac ... I am not worthy of the least of all the mercies

[*chesed* again!], and of all the truth [*emeth*], which thou hast showed unto thy servant ..." (32:10)

How does God "show truth" to His servants? What quality is this that is so deeply engraven upon the mind of Abraham's servant, and that of Jacob; a quality that is coupled here, as it is in other places, with "mercy"? What God was showing to these men of faith in patriarchal times is His characteristic of steadfastness, faithfulness, and constancy, His firm adherence to the covenants of promise.

It should come as no surprise that our next staging-post is Exodus 34, for there (as we have noted several times in this series) we have the definitive proclamation of the Name and character of Yahweh: "The LORD, the LORD God, merciful and gracious, longsuffering, and abundant in goodness [*chesed*] and truth [*emeth*]" (verse 6). And then we could go on, through Kings and Chronicles, through the Psalms and Prophets, observing the use of "truth" in its peculiar Hebrew meaning, and realising with each occurrence the increasing richness of this word.

The mind of David was fully able to grasp the wonder of all God's attributes: in the psalms, he pours forth his appreciation of God's righteousness, His redemption, His salvation, His mercy and truth. Just one example is Psalm 31, where David extols his God and gives us an inspired glimpse of the character and work of Messiah:

> "In thee, O LORD, do I put my trust; let me never be ashamed: deliver me in thy righteousness ... For thou art my rock and fortress ... Into thine hand I commend my spirit: thou hast redeemed me, O LORD, thou God of truth." (verses 1-5, RV)

In Psalm 89, "lovingkindness" and "truth" are brought together, each one of them evocative of the covenant; but the association is driven home by the additional use of the actual word for covenant:

> "My lovingkindness [*chesed*] will I not utterly take from him, nor suffer my faithfulness [*emunah*, see also verses 1,2,5, 8,24] to fail. My covenant [*berith*] will I not break, nor alter the thing

> that is gone out of my lips. Once have I sworn by my holiness; I will not lie unto David; his seed shall endure for ever, and his throne as the sun before me. It shall be established for ever as the moon, and as a faithful [*aman* – related to *emeth*, and *amen*] witness in heaven." (verses 33-37)

"Thou wilt perform the truth"

Passing over several references in Isaiah and Jeremiah, we come to a classic instance of the use of *emeth* in Micah:

> "Thou wilt perform the *truth* [margin, thou wilt shew thy *faithfulness*] to Jacob, and the mercy [*chesed*] to Abraham, which thou hast sworn unto our fathers from the days of old." (7:20)

Here, surely, are echoes of the passage we have already quoted from Genesis 32 – and again we see how "truth" is bound up with God's covenant faithfulness.

Such, then, are the meanings and overtones of just one of the words in the Hebrew vocabulary of truth. There are, however, several other words in the same family. We have just indicated an occurrence in Psalm 89 of *emunah* (faithfulness), itself related to *emeth*, and related in turn to *omnam* (truly), *aman* (faithful) and *amen* ('so be it'). Another example of the first of these is as follows:

> "It is of the Lord's mercies [*chesed*] that we are not consumed, because his compassions [*rachamim*] fail not. They are new every morning: great is thy faithfulness [*emunah*]." (Lamentations 3:23)

"Faith" in the Old Testament

How many times does the word "faith" occur in the Old Testament? It may come as a surprise to discover that only twice is this word to be found in the English King James Version of the Hebrew scriptures: once in Deuteronomy 32:20 – "They are a very froward generation, children in whom is no faith"; and a second time in Habakkuk 2:4 – "But the just shall live by his faith". In the first of these the word for "faith" is *emun* (more often rendered "faithful"); in the second, *emunah* (usually translated "faithfulness" or "truth").

Is then the idea of "faith" unimportant under the old covenant? Decidedly not! The idea itself abounds in the Old Testament, especially in the form of the related verb "believe". The first occurrence of any of the "truth" family of words is in Genesis 15:6, where we read that Abraham "believed [*aman*] the LORD; and he counted it to him for righteousness". Doubtless we have all quoted this verse without stopping to consider that "believe" in reality is a verb closely associated with 'steadfast', 'faithful', 'true'. Belief in God, of course, is trust in His faithfulness. (It is a worthwhile exercise to examine all the other occurrences of "believe" in the Old Testament and listen for the overtones of "truth" each time *aman* is used.)

To ears which are more generally attuned to Greek ideas and to a New Testament which has been translated from the Greek, it seems odd that words which mean "faith" and "truth" should be, as it were, interchangeable: in Greek, after all, "truth" is *alētheia*, while "faith" is *pistis*, a different and distinct idea. Yet, far from Hebrew being the poorer for not having distinct words, in reality it is richer – simply because of the wide range of God-given meanings associated with the *emeth* / *emunah* family of words. In its awe-inspiring way, the Old Testament teaches us something that is totally lacking in Greek (or Latin, or English): namely, that "truth" and "faith" are twin concepts deriving from the same idea and the same root word. To the Greek, truth was merely the opposite of falsehood; to the Jew it had to do with the recognition and reciprocation of divine faithfulness.

"Truth", to the Hebrew mind, was no philosophical abstraction, but the practical assurance that he could rely on the faithfulness of God – and that he must seek to imitate it himself in faithful service. Psalm 31, from which we have already quoted the expression "thou God of truth", also contains the following verse: "O love the LORD, all ye his saints: for the LORD preserveth the *faithful*" (verse 23). By contrast, there was "a generation that set not their heart aright, and whose spirit was not *stedfast* with God ... Their heart was not right with him, neither were they *stedfast* in his covenant" (Psalm 78:8,37). Both "faithful" and "stedfast" are translations of *aman*. The *faithful* are those who respond to the God of *truth*, and who are in their own lives constant, steadfast ... *true*.

Nehemiah testifies to the character of "Hananiah the ruler of the palace", that "he was a faithful [*emeth*] man" (7:2, cf. 13:13): he was, in other words, 'a man of truth'. In the moving prayer of confession in Nehemiah 9, God is addressed: "Thou art the LORD the God, who didst choose Abram ... and foundest his heart faithful (*aman*) before thee, and madest a covenant with him" (9:6-8): here was a man whose own faithfulness sought to reflect the faithfulness of God.

"Truth is perished"

Jeremiah laments the decline in "truth" (*emunah*) in his day: "See ... if there be any that executeth judgment, that speaketh the truth ... O LORD, are not thine eyes upon the truth?" (5:1,3); "Truth is perished, and is cut off from their mouth" (7:28); "They are grown strong in the land, but not for truth" (9:3). In all these instances the "truth" that was lost sight of was not so much the first principles, which is what we tend to associate with the word, but the fidelity of service and worship that the God of truth requires.

Our survey would not be complete without considering what some may feel are 'curiosities' in the translation of the words under review. What, for example, do we make of "I will fasten him [Eliakim] as a nail in a sure [*aman*] place" (Isaiah 22:23,25)? Or "He that walketh righteously ... his waters shall be sure [*aman*]" (33:16)? What the prophet has to convey in each of these instances is the idea of something certain, something unmoveable (in the case of the nail) or unfailing (in the case of the water supply). Though here applied by metaphor to material things, the sense also holds for exalted themes – the unfailing constancy and unshakeable faithfulness of the God of Israel, *the God of truth*.

> "For all the promises of God in him are yea, and in him Amen, unto the glory of God by us." (1 Corinthians 1:20)

One final usage will conclude our review of Old Testament occurrences of 'truth'-related words. We have looked at *emeth*, at *emunah* and at *aman*; but there is also *amen* – another word for "truth", but with the overtone of 'assent' or 'affirmation'.

Amen

Amen, which has come down to us unchanged from the Hebrew, occurs in only a few places in the Old Testament – mostly at the conclusion of oaths, prayers and psalms (for example, Deuteronomy 27:15-26; Nehemiah 5:13; Psalm 106:48; etc.). In Jeremiah 11, the prophet responds to what God has said with "So be it (*amen*), O LORD" (verse 5). In Isaiah 65:16, there is a particularly powerful use of *amen*, though its significance is not immediately obvious in most versions: "He who blesseth himself in the earth shall bless himself in the God of *truth* [*amen*]; and he that sweareth in the earth shall swear by the God of *truth* [*amen*]." The meaning may appear to be the same as in other passages, but by using *amen* rather than *emeth* this verse carries a particularly emphatic declaration of the divine attribute: He is *the God of Amen* – the God whom man can trust, and to whom man can respond, as Jeremiah did, with confident affirmation.

Turning to the New Testament, we find passages where the idiom is clearly Greek; but there are many others, especially in John's Gospel and Epistles, which show that the Lord Jesus Christ and his apostles are still thinking in the Hebrew mould. Speaking of the Son of God, John says, "The Word was made flesh, and dwelt among us (and we beheld his glory, the glory as of the only begotten of the Father), full of grace and truth [*alētheia*]" (1:14,17). This is surely telling us that the God of truth is now revealed in His Son: he, like his Father, manifests the faithfulness and steadfastness upon which the believer can depend. "I am the way, the truth, and the life" (14:6), he later said, continuing the Old Testament usage of the idea of truth. "To this end was I born, and for this cause came I into the world, that I should bear witness unto the truth. Every one that is of the truth heareth my voice" (18:37). Again, the Lord is speaking, not of abstract Gentile notions of "truth", but of practical Jewish certainty. Pilate, not surprisingly, was out of his depth, and responded with the meaningless rhetorical question, "What is truth?" (verse 38).

"Verily, verily ..."

It can hardly be without significance that the Gospels record the Lord Jesus Christ one hundred times using *Amen* ("Verily" in the KJV) in the course of his teaching. That in itself reinforces the point that his message spelled out the truth of God, revealed in the words he spoke, and manifested in his life of personal faithfulness. When, at last, we reach the book of Revelation, "Amen" occurs for the last few times, and once more the usage is of wonderful and profound significance:

> "Unto the angel of the church of the Laodiceans write; These things saith the *Amen*, the *faithful* and *true* witness, the beginning of the creation of God ..." (3:14)

Does that not say it all? – here the Old Testament exposition of truth finds its ultimate meaning in Christ: all that was faithful and true in the Father is revealed now in the Son – and in the body of believers who by lives of faithfulness show forth the God of truth and await the coming of His Son.

> "Amen: come Lord Jesus!" (Revelation 22:20)

15 |

"Who hath known the mind of the Lord?"

IN a short series of chapters on the attributes of God, we have been able to do no more than begin to reflect on the greatness of God's character. But how rewarding such a study can be: how infinite is the Almighty; how immeasurable His qualities! Much, nonetheless, has had to be left out of our consideration: there has been no attempt to deal in detail with God's covenant Name, nor with the great themes of God Manifestation. There is, in fact, good reason for considering the divine attributes first, for how shall we fully understand the ways in which God manifests Himself without knowing the nature of those qualities He seeks to manifest?

The writer's hope is that enough has been said to encourage – if necessary, to rekindle – that desire in every one of us to know God better and to promote a more sensitive awareness of His goodness and severity. Is it possible that we have lost something of the reverence for the Lord God which our forbears had? Do brethren who lead us in prayer to the Father show sufficient consciousness of His majesty and holiness? In an age of cleverness, when mankind can boast of so many inventions, there is a danger that humility before our Maker, a simple faith in His infinite power and an awareness of our frailty, become forgotten – even despised.

There has been a pattern to the present studies. We tried to show that virtually every characteristic of God can, in the first place, be traced to Genesis: there we have the earliest indications of His holiness and glory; His mercy, truth and love. Then, in Exodus, comes the fuller exposition of those qualities in association with the divine Name; while from Exodus onwards, as God reveals Himself to judges, kings, poets and prophets, these attributes are amplified. By then they have become part of the life and language of Israel; they are the constant meditation of the psalmist, the delight and desire of all the prophets. And finally, and in their fulness, those same characteristics of Israel's God find expression in His Son:

> "For God, who commanded the light to shine out of darkness, hath shined in our hearts, to give the light of the knowledge of the glory of God in the face of Jesus Christ."
>
> (2 Corinthians 4:6)

"That they might know thee"

Thus it came about that the God "who at sundry times and in divers manners spake in time past unto the fathers by the prophets, hath in these last days spoken unto us by his Son ... the brightness of his glory, and the express image of his person" (Hebrews 1:1-3). But of what value was a fuller revelation of God to a dying race? The work of Jesus in manifesting the Father actually provided the means of reconciliation between God and man. Through the willing sacrifice of Christ, man at last had the prospect of life eternal, which in turn gave him a new appreciation of God. As Jesus said in prayer to his Father:

> "This is life eternal, *that they might know thee* the only true God, and Jesus Christ, whom thou hast sent ... I have declared unto them thy name, and will declare it: that the love wherewith thou hast loved me may be in them, and I in them."
>
> (John 17:3,26)

> "No man hath seen God at any time; the only begotten Son, which is in the bosom of the Father, he hath declared him."
>
> (1:18)

> "O the depth of the riches both of the wisdom and knowledge of God! How unsearchable are his judgments, and his ways past finding out! For who hath known the mind of the Lord? or who hath been his counsellor? or who hath first given to him, and it shall be recompensed unto him again? For of him, and through him, and to him, are all things: to whom be glory for ever. Amen." (Romans 11:33-36)

"Who hath known the mind of the Lord?" These studies may have taken us a little way towards an understanding of the mind of God. But one impression that must surely remain with us is that the God of Israel is a God who can be understood only by those who will take the trouble to grasp something of the idiom of the Old Testament. We have seen that concepts such as "lovingkindness", "mercy", "fear" are uniquely Hebrew in origin and sense; and we must remember that the Lord and his apostles, when they used Greek or Aramaic, the languages of their time, were still thinking, as it were, in Hebrew. The God of the Old Testament is the God of the New Testament too; the great proclamation at Sinai – "The LORD God, merciful and gracious, longsuffering, and abundant in goodness and truth, keeping mercy for thousands, forgiving iniquity and transgression and sin, and that will by no means clear the guilty ..." (Exodus 34:6,7) – is a proclamation which reverberates on through the Pentateuch, Psalms and Prophets, *and* into the Gospels and Epistles.

Moses spoke of "the faithful God, which keepeth covenant and mercy with them that love him" (Deuteronomy 7:9); David prayed, "Have mercy upon me, O God, according to thy lovingkindness: according unto the multitude of thy tender mercies blot out my transgressions ..." (Psalm 51:1); Solomon spread forth his hands toward heaven and said, "There is no God like thee, in heaven above, or on earth beneath, who keepest covenant and mercy ..." (1 Kings 8:22,23); Isaiah extolled "the loving-kindnesses of the LORD and the praises of the LORD ... our father, our redeemer" (63:7,16); Daniel, in his confession, referred to "the great and dreadful God" (9:4); Nehemiah to the "great, the mighty, and the terrible God, who keepest covenant and mercy" (9:32).

And the language of the New Testament is not suddenly different. The Master, who himself so wonderfully portrayed the virtues which belong to his Father, commended them to his followers: "Blessed are they which do hunger and thirst after righteousness ... the merciful ... the pure in heart" (Matthew 5:6-8). Paul wrote "that we should be holy and without blame before him in love" (Ephesians 1:6). What was commanded to Israel is reiterated for those who would be disciples of Christ: "Be ye therefore perfect, even as your Father which is in heaven is perfect" (Matthew 5:48; Genesis 17:1; Deuteronomy 18:13). And though we now have "peace with God through our Lord Jesus Christ ... access by faith into this grace wherein we stand" (Romans 5:1,2), yet the character of God is still that declared at Sinai; we must still be aware of "the goodness and severity of God" (11:22). The one who for Daniel was the "great and dreadful God" is still for the writer to the Hebrews "a consuming fire" (12:29).

Christadelphian writings

These are the truths about God which have been expounded by generations of Christadelphians and it would be wrong not to acknowledge the wealth of exposition which is already on record – most of it accessible to today's readers. We shall therefore conclude the series with representative extracts from the writings of others – making it clear that we are focusing especially on studies of the *attributes* of God:

> "God's goodness to His people, and severity upon His enemies, are the necessary result of His peculiar character. Hence His goodness and character are inseparable; so that to declare 'The Name' of the Lord is at once to make known His character and goodness, which stand related as effect and cause. Because of this it is written, 'I will make all *my goodness*

pass before thee, and I will proclaim *the name of the* LORD before thee; and I will be gracious to whom I will be gracious, and I will show mercy on whom I will show mercy' ... Such a God is Jehovah in His character, or relations of goodness to those whom He chooses for His people; but at the same time 'a consuming fire' to His enemies (Hebrews 12:29). He is a great and absolute sovereign in all His doings, having mercy upon whom He will, and hardening at His pleasure (Romans 9:18) ... All His promises emanate from the essential goodness of His nature, which is favour, forbearance, abounding in truth, faithfulness, pardoning, and corrective but not utterly destroying." (Brother John Thomas, "The Goodness of God", in *The Faith in the Last Days*)

"The God of Israel is a personal God. The Father of our Lord Jesus Christ is a personal Father, yet not a man, though we faintly borrow our image from Him. He is glorious and incorruptible in His substance; unchangeable in His nature, one with the universe, clothed with eternal light and power. He fills heaven and earth by His spirit, which is one with Him. By this He upholds all things, and knows and controls everything. 'Honour and majesty are before him: strength and beauty are in his sanctuary' (Psalm 96:6); 'Who in the heaven can be compared unto the LORD? who among the sons of the mighty can be likened unto the LORD?' (89:6); 'Great is the LORD, and greatly to be praised; and his greatness is unsearchable ... I will speak of the glorious honour of thy majesty ... to make known to the sons of men his mighty acts, and the glorious majesty of his kingdom' (145:3-12)." (Brother Robert Roberts, *The Ways of Providence*)

Hymns of praise

Other brethren of a century ago expressed the same truths in distinctively Christadelphian hymns:

> "Glory and blessing be
> Ever ascribed to thee,

Uncreate unity,
Father of all …
Thy grace and truth became
Flesh for a saving name,
Jehovah Elohim,
Never to cease …" (Brother David Brown,
Hymn 49: originally in *The Golden Harp*) [1]

"Lord, when we meet to worship thee,
Before us let Thy glory pass:
Proclaim Thy mercy rich and free;
In Jesus may we see Thy face …" (Brother J. Bland, Hymn
103: initially in the Suffolk Street Hymn Book of 1903) [2]

From a booklet *The Music of Faith*, published in the 1950s, we quote stanzas by Sister Jean Galbraith which capture the wondering awe of true worship:

"Thou wast the poet then, who made the world,
Within whose mind the first star's pulsing flame
Lived ere its travail started, or there came,
Through aeons long, to birth the embodied thought …
Thine was the Word, conceived so wondrous fair
It lay within Thy heart for ages long,
But far too wonderful, too pure and strong
To stay unbodied; fruitless till it lived.
Fruitless ere life, and yet, 'Except it die
Abiding by itself alone'. O Thou
Who didst conceive and clothe the Word, and now
Couldst let it die, 'that men might live in him' …"

Later writers continued the theme in magazine articles or books:

> "God is not an abstraction; a thought; an influence; simply power or energy; or a law of the world. The world is His; He causeth the sun to rise, and the grass to grow; and while He

1 In the current *Christadelphian Hymn Book*, 2002, Hymn 83.

2 Now Hymn 153.

is the Holy One inhabiting eternity, He looks on the poor and contrite in heart, who tremble at His word, to dwell with them. Through the Son we can know the Father, for he has revealed Him." (Brother John Carter, Editorial in *The Christadelphian*, April 1955)

"'I will be what I will be', God had named Himself. It was a promise as well as a declaration of His nature. The culmination was reached in the coming of the Son in whom the Father manifested Himself: Yahweh *became* the fullness of grace and truth in Christ Jesus. In His Son was the full revelation of compassion and steadfast love, for in him is the Lord's forgiveness and the Lord's salvation. When Christ Jesus had humbled himself and been obedient unto death – and that none other than the death of the cross – God 'highly exalted him' above all that is or can be except the Father Himself. He bestowed upon him 'the name that is above every name, that at the name of Jesus every knee should bow', even as it had been declared that they should bow to the Father. Grace and truth had always been in the Son; now the Yahweh Name itself became his not only by inheritance but by Divine fiat; of all creation he was made the head." (Brother L. G. Sargent, *The Christadelphian*, 1963: Conclusion of two studies on "The Name of the Lord")

Awe and wonder

We move to a more recent era, and the book *The Name that is above every Name* (1983), in which Brother Alfred Nicholls "expresses the hope that present-day readers will feel the same sense of wonder and awe that was experienced by an earlier generation of Christadelphians when they first began to know the Name and to put their trust in the Lord God of Hosts":

"Israel's God was the LORD – and there was only One like Him. He was Uncreate Unity, and yet He was their God – 'kind, yet requiring men to obey His law; loving and compassionate, yet will not tolerate the rebellious and the guilty; forgiving offences, yet jealous of the dignity, the glory, and supremacy of His Name ... eternal, unchangeable, infinite, glorious in power and majesty ...' (from *The Christadelphian Instructor*). All these attributes of their God the Israelites had seen in awesome manifestation in their life in the wilderness. And they had known that He was unchanging, and that when His compassion seemed to yield to His anger the change had been in their relationship to Him. ... When they entered the land filled with every blessing together with all forms of temptation, as their God was *one* LORD the nation's service and devotion had to be likewise complete and entire – with *all* their heart, and soul, and strength, and mind. Can *we*, who seek to know His Name, offer Him less?" (pages 53,54)

Conclusion

A last extract is from the pen of Brother Fred Pearce. We have quoted earlier from his fine studies on "The Knowledge of God" (*The Christadelphian*, 1967); the following is from his chapter "Concerning God" in *Studies in the Statement of Faith* (1991). What Brother Fred wrote regarding that chapter would very fittingly apply to what has been attempted in the present series:

> "Even our brief outline of the significance of God has been enough to reveal His sheer immensity. We have rather naturally become accustomed to thinking of 'the truth' as a series of doctrines to be understood, and so it is. But it is clear that the 'doctrine of God' is vastly greater than any one of them. The reason is not far to seek: the Lord God of heaven and earth stands behind all the teaching that has been revealed to us, from the creation of the world and of mankind, to the final phase of the Kingdom of God. For the faithful He has been the source of all light in their native darkness. The thought of Him has been their consolation, and faith in Him has been their strength in times of trial. The knowledge of Him, made clearer to them in the Person of His Beloved Son, has been a guide and an inspiration in their life of service."

How can we do justice to this immense subject in a few concluding words? Only by letting the inspired words of scripture do it for us – first, in the words of David, as he commits his son Solomon to the building of the house of God:

> "Blessed be thou, LORD God of Israel our father, for ever and ever. Thine, O LORD, is the greatness, and the power, and the glory, and the victory, and the majesty: for all that is in the heaven and in the earth is thine; thine is the kingdom, O LORD, and thou art exalted as head above all. Both riches and honour come of thee, and thou reignest over all ... We thank thee, and praise thy glorious name." (1 Chronicles 29:10-13)

And turning, finally, to Revelation we catch a glimpse of that future day when angels will stand round about the throne, worshipping God, and saying:

> "Salvation to our God which sitteth upon the throne, and unto the Lamb ... Amen: Blessing, and glory, and wisdom, and thanksgiving, and honour, and power, and might, be unto our God for ever and ever. Amen." (Revelation 7:10,12)

Section 3

Extracts from *Names and Titles of the Deity*

(W. H. Boulton)

Our third section is intended to be useful as an aid for further personal study. What follows are adapted extracts from the book *Names and Titles of the Deity* by Brother W. H. Boulton. In this book, based on the King James Version, Brother Boulton worked through the most familiar Hebrew and Greek titles of the Deity. Further beneficial study can be found by searching the scriptures for less frequently used titles not found below.

The titles of each section contain short, summary definitions based on Brother Boulton's comments. These definitions are those of the compiler of the present volume and not those of Brother Boulton. The compiler has slightly adapted some of the extracts with the aim of smooth reading, and it should be remembered during reading that what follows is not an exact replication of Brother Boulton's words. Finally, Brother Boulton noted in his Preface that he was not a trained linguist, but that his work aligned the comments of trained linguists with the doctrine of God Manifestation as expounded by Brother John Thomas.

---

1 | Hebrew, *El*

Strong's Number: H410.

Translation: Usually 'God' or 'god' (uncapitalized).

Essential meaning: 'Strength' or 'power' as well as 'a source from which power emanates'.

THE name *El*, constitutes what may be called the fundamental name of God, in that it expresses the main idea upon which any true conception of God must be based. It is derived from a root which is variously explained to mean to be first, to be strong, mighty. The primary idea of all the definitions is radically the same; the universal extension of power implies an original source from which that power flows, and its universality of extension implies absolute omnipotence in regard to the source.

[The source] must necessarily contain within it all the potential power of the universe, [as] is declared in the statement of Moses, the man of God, "Lord [*Adonai*], Thou hast been our dwelling-place in all generations. Before the mountains were brought forth, or ever Thou hadst formed the earth and the world, even from everlasting to everlasting Thou art *El*" (Psalm 90:1,2).

El is frequently qualified by an adjective; indeed, it is an almost, but not quite, invariable rule that when an adjective is found qualifying the name God, the word in the Hebrew is *El*. With the exception of "great," "living" and "high" these terms are very seldom applied to God when other names, such as *Eloah* and *Elohim* are used. There is something very fitting in this fact; it emphasises the essential idea that whatever may be the characteristic in view, the governing factor is the power and strength of *El*.

As might be anticipated, *El* is often used to designate God, when creation or formation is being referred to. Thus, we read of the *El* that formed thee (Deuteronomy 32:18), who created us (Malachi 2:10), and whose glory the heavens declare (Psalm 19:1).

It is also used when it is desired to express the difference that exists between God and man (e.g., Isaiah 31:3), whilst the essential divinity of God is declared in the statement "Before Me there was no *El* formed, neither shall there be after Me" (Isaiah 43:10). *Elohim* have been, and will be, formed after Him; but certainly no *El*, for there can be but one source of a universally extended and supreme power.

When the usage of this appellation of God is studied, it will be found that it is often used by those who were not of the race of Israel – e.g., Melchizedek (Genesis 14:18), Hagar (Genesis 16:13), Balaam (frequently in Numbers 23,24), Lucifer (Isaiah 14:13), and the Prince of Tyre (Ezekiel 28:2). In Job it is used over fifty times.

Occasionally *El* is used to designate a false God, but in these instances it is an accommodation to human thought and language (e.g., Deuteronomy 32:12). Really, there can be no false *El*, for there can be no second cause of infinite extension and power. God has, and can have, no rival.

For the name *El* used in combination with other names, see *El Shaddai* (page 211), and *El Elyon* (page 214). *El* is sometimes translated in other ways, such as "goodly" (Psalm 80:10), where we should read "Cedars of *El*" and "great" (Psalm 36:6), where reference is made to "Mountains of *El*".

---

2 | Hebrew, *Eloah / Elohim*

Strong's Number: H433 (*eloah*) and H430 (*elohim*).

Translation: Usually (*elohim*) or always (*eloah*) 'God' or 'god' (uncapitalized).

Essential meaning: 'Power' and so 'mighty one' (*eloah*) or 'mighty ones' (*elohim*).

AS the above are the singular and plural forms of the same word, it will be well to consider them together. The latter is the most commonly used term of all in relation to God, except His name *Yahweh*, occurring in all over 2,700 times. *Eloah* is used only in the instances cited in the Appendix below (page 230). Also in the Appendix are the passages where the Chaldee equivalent *Elah* is used. It will be noticed that with two exceptions the occurrences of *Eloah* are all in the poetic portions of the scriptures.

Eloah and *Elohim* are derived from *El*; and, therefore, signify mighty one and mighty ones respectively. The fact of this derivation is in accord with the actual relationship which the *Elohim* bear to *El*; they are possessed of a strength which is derived, not inherent. An important point in relation to the word *Elohim* is the fact that, although the word is plural, it is almost invariably used with a singular verb. The explanation for this will be seen by noting the use of the word in a large number of passages, some of which will be particularly referred to.

The translations of the two words into English are:

- *Eloah* – always God, or god.
- *Elohim* – God, god, gods, goddess, angels, exceeding, godly, great, judges, mighty.

It has been pointed out that the *Elohim* derive their strength from *El*. It might be said that He is in them, and that consequently their actions are really His. Jesus once said "I can of mine own self do nothing" ; all the *Elohim* may say the same. They are strong, glorious and immortal, but their strength, glory and immortality are derived from the *El* who created them and who works through them. He is the strength of these mighty ones, the First, the underived and Infinite One, who is from everlasting.

Among the translations given above is the word 'angels'. This rendering is only found in Psalm 8:5: "Thou hast made him a little lower than the angels [*Elohim*], and has crowned him with glory and honour." The Revised Version renders this 'but little lower than God' with a marginal reading 'or the angels; Heb. *Elohim*'. In this case we have the advantage of an inspired quotation and comment in the New Testament. In an argument designed to establish the superiority of Jesus above the angels (Hebrews 1,2) we read:

> "What is man, that thou art mindful of him? or the son of man, that thou visitest him? Thou madest him a little lower than, the angels; thou crownedst him with glory and honour, and didst set him over the works of thy hands ... But now we see not yet all things put under him, but we see Jesus, who was made a little lower than the angels for the suffering of death crowned with glory and honour." (Hebrews 2:6-9)

Thus, although there is only one instance in the Old Testament of *Elohim* being translated angels, there is no room to question the accuracy of the rendering. Moreover, this application of the word is strongly confirmed by other New Testament references to angels.

In another passage in the Epistle to the Hebrews there is a quotation from the Psalms in which this fact is apparent. In the Hebrews it is given as, "Let all the angels of God worship Him" (Hebrews 1:6). Looking back to the Old Testament this is found to be, "Worship Him all ye gods [*Elohim*]" (Psalm 97:7). Again, when God commissioned Moses from the burning bush we read:

> "And when the LORD saw that he turned aside to see, God [*Elohim*] called unto him out of the midst of the bush, and said ... I am the God [*Elohim*] of thy father, the God [*Elohim*] of Abraham, the God [*Elohim*] of Isaac, and the God [*Elohim*] of Jacob. And Moses hid his face; for he was afraid to look upon *Elohim*."

Referring to this incident, Stephen said:

> "And when forty years were expired there appeared to him in the wilderness of Mount Sinai an angel of the Lord in a flame of fire in a bush ... This Moses whom they refused ... did God send to be a ruler and a deliverer by the hand of the angel which appeared to him in the bush." (Acts 7:30,35)

There can be no question as to the conclusion to be drawn from the comparison of these passages. It was an angel who appeared to Moses, and it was this angel who spoke of himself as the *Elohim* of Abraham, Isaac, and Jacob. Another illustration of the same kind may be mentioned. When Israel reached Sinai the law was given to them. The record of the event states, "And when the voice of the trumpet sounded long and waxed louder and louder, Moses spake, and God [*Elohim*] answered him by a voice" (Exodus 19:19) ... "And God [*Elohim*] spake all these words" (20:1). Turning again to Stephen's defence, we find him saying, "This is he that was in the ecclesia in the wilderness, with the angel which spake to him in the Mount Sinai, and with our fathers, who received the lively oracles to give unto us" (Acts 7:38). He also refers to Israel receiving the law by the disposition of angels (Acts 7:53), and Paul says it was "ordained by angels in the hand of a mediator" (Galatians 3:19); and again, "If the word spoken by angels was steadfast, and every transgression and disobedience received a just recompence of reward, how shall we escape?" (Hebrews 2:2).

It is therefore a fully justifiable conclusion that the angels are *Elohim*. They are beings through whom *El* works. They "excel in strength", they are His hosts, "ministers of His that do His pleasure" (Psalm 103:20,21). The strength in which they excel is His. They are thereby so in rapport with Him that they may be identified with Him, a vast plurality, moved by one great power – *El*.

It will be necessary later on to consider another application of *Elohim* in passages which relate to the future, and where the name is associated with the name *Yahweh* – *Yahweh Elohim* (see page 222). The principle of interpretation will be the same, and it need not detain us further now.

The first use of the term *Elohim* in the scriptures is in accord with what has been considered. "In the beginning *Elohim* created the heaven and the earth" (Genesis 1:1). Thirty times in this one chapter, or thirty-three times if we include verses 1-3 of the second chapter, are creation and various matters connected therewith attributed to God or *Elohim*; including, of course, the passage, "Let us make man in our image". In the light of the foregoing there can be no difficulty in applying the term, nor in interpreting the plurality associated with the single verb. *Elohim* created the heavens, yet they (the heavens) declare the glory of *El* (Psalm 19:1). The personalities concerned were the angels, the power was that of God. That men are in the image of the angels no one is likely to question, except it be for the current ideas of angels' wings, a conception which is quite foreign to the scriptures. No one would mistake a winged angel for a man. The popular conception arises out of references to symbolic creatures, the cherubim and seraphim, which are supposed to be angels, although there is no such association of ideas in the Bible.

'*Elohim*' may be taken as the general term applied to express the mighty personalities through whom the Deity works, and it is found in every kind of reference to His works – in creation, in revelation, and in salvation. A careful study of the use of the term will be the best means of appreciating its place in the scriptures.

It was suggested that it would be advantageous to note a few of the exceptional passages where Elohim occurs, and to that end the following instances may be considered.

1. **Exceeding**. The only occurrence is in Jonah 3:3: "Now Nineveh was an exceeding great city." The marginal rendering gives a truer representation, "a city great of God", or "a city great unto God" (RV margin). This appears to be a Hebraism to express extreme greatness, and extremes of other ideas also. It is carried into the Greek in the record of Stephen's defence where he describes Moses as "exceeding" fair, or as the margin gives it, "fair to God". The same principle will be seen in other cases.
2. **Godly**. "That he might seek a godly seed" (Malachi 2:15). The marginal rendering is "a seed of God". The context will indicate that the idea of the passage is the raising up of "faithful children", Sons of God.
3. **Great**. "And Rachel said, with great wrestlings [margin, wrestlings of God] have I prevailed" (Genesis 30:8). "And the earth quaked, so that it was a very great trembling [margin, trembling of God]" (1 Samuel 14:15). In each case the margin supplies the application of the reference

to Elohim, on the lines indicated above under "exceeding", although in the second case a further application may be, and probably is intended, that God (*Elohim*) was working for Israel, and the earthquake was a part of His work.

4. **Judges**. Two separate references of the kind are found in the Mosaic Law (Exodus 21:6; 22:8,9). In each case the RV substitutes "God" for judges. Some have explained this as really applying to God, but there does not seem much support for this idea. In another verse in the latter chapter it is written, "Thou shalt not revile the Gods [margin, judges], nor curse the ruler of thy people" (Exodus 22:28). The parallelism of this verse requires the alternative word "judge", and indicates that in the other passages judges may be taken as the correct rendering of the word *Elohim*.

   Two reasons may be suggested to account for the usage of the term *Elohim* in relation to human judges. First is the position of the judge, his supremacy as the one who could declare the law, and its bearings upon Israel. Second, the judges were the priests, who were God's representatives amongst Israel; and who, therefore, were addressed as *Elohim*, being viewed as His ambassadors. "Then both the men, between whom the controversy is, shall stand before the Lord, before the priests and the judges, which shall be in those days" (Deuteronomy 19:17).

5. **Mighty**. "Thou [Abraham] art a mighty prince among us [margin, 'Hebrew, a prince of God']" (Genesis 23:6). "Intreat the Lord that there be no more mighty thunderings" (Exodus 9:28). Again, the margin indicates the usage of the word, for we find substituted there "Hebrew, voices of God".

These constitute all the renderings of *Elohim* other than those which are distinctly applicable to God or gods, according to the evident intention in the text, and are useful in indicating the primary meaning which is to be attached to the word. Taken in conjunction with what has been said before, they lead to a clear perception of the ideas which are inherent in the word *Elohim*, a fit name to define those through whom *El* works – *El* the strength or source of the power of the mighty ones.

3 | Hebrew, *Shaddai*

Strong's Number: H7706.

Translation: Always 'Almighty'.

Essential meaning: Burliness and vehemence, thus 'strong ones' and so similar to *elohim*.

IT will be fitting to consider this name next on account of its association with the name *El*, and because of its early appearance in the scriptures. It is a name of the Deity which is particularly connected with patriarchal times, occurring most frequently in the early books of the Bible, or in reference to events of pre-Mosaic history. Like *Elohim*, the word is plural, a fact which must be allowed for in any attempt to understand its meaning. It is the Hebrew word which invariably occurs, where in our English Version we find the name Almighty; and as this is the only way in which the Hebrew is rendered, there will be no difficulty in recognising it wherever it is used.

Shaddai is derived from the root *shadad* meaning 'to treat with violence, to oppress, to attack, to invade, to plunder, to lay waste, destroy'. As *Shaddai* is used only in regard to God, it is evidently intended to express the idea of His power and authority. As an oppressor is such because He possesses the power to carry out His designs irrespective of the wishes of others; so God as the supreme source of all power is the Almighty, whose word and purpose must stand.

The fact that the word is of the plural number is to be explained in the same way as in the case of *Elohim*. There is the *El*, the great power by whom the *Shaddai* are made strong. *Shaddai* may, therefore, be looked upon as another name for the *Elohim*. This can be clearly seen in the first mention that is made of Shaddai. "When Abram was ninety years old and nine, the Lord appeared to Abram, and said unto him, I am *El Shaddai*; walk before me and be thou perfect." On receipt of this message "Abram fell on his face, and *Elohim* talked with him" (Genesis 17:1,3). Thus the Lord (*Yahweh*) spoke through the *Elohim*, saying "I am *El Shaddai*".

Yet there must be some reason for the use of the two terms in relation to them. They are not used by mere caprice, nor to give alternative titles. Having regard to the derivations of *Elohim* and *Shaddai* respectively, it may be concluded that whilst *Elohim*, being derived from *El*, signifies the power of *El* enshrined in those who are so spoken of; *Shaddai* refers to them as those who are commissioned to carry out His behests by virtue of the authority which He has given to them. It is the power of authority, not the power, or force, itself.

The matter may be explained somewhat by taking a human illustration. A ruler may send out his emissaries to perform a certain duty. They may, or may not, be strong. But as they are invested with the authority given to them by the ruler, they are able to carry out his commands by the delegated authority which they have received from him; although in a physical sense they might not have been able to overcome the opposition which their actions would arouse. This will serve to illustrate the idea. The *Shaddai* are omnipotent because they are the representatives of *El* who sent them, and who has invested them with authority. As *Elohim*, they are also possessors of omnipotent power which they derive from *El*. They thus combine authority and power, and by this combination all things whatsoever they may be commissioned to perform they can accomplish.

Shaddai is frequently associated with *El* in the title '*El Shaddai*'. It is never connected with the word *Elohim*. Thus on the first occasion in which it is found we read, "I am *El Shaddai*". An examination of the passages where this combination is used will show that it is associated with the manifestation of the power of God in the over-ruling providence which works through angelic ministers for the accomplishment of God's purposes.

Thus, when God spoke of Himself to Abram as *El Shaddai*, He said, "Walk before Me, and be thou perfect, and I will make

My covenant between Me and thee, and will multiply thee exceedingly" (Genesis 17:1,2).

So also when Isaac sent forth Jacob who had obtained the birthright, with all that it signified in connection with the covenant, he said, "And *El Shaddai* bless thee and make thee fruitful, and multiply thee, that thou mayest be a multitude of people and give thee the blessing of Abraham, to thee and to thy seed with thee, that thou mayest inherit the land wherein thou art a stranger, which God gave unto Abraham" (Genesis 28:3,4).

Further, when God appeared to Jacob at Luz, or Bethel, He said, "I am *El Shaddai*; be fruitful and multiply; a nation and a company of nations shall be of thee; and kings shall come out of thy loins; and the land which I gave Abraham and Isaac, to thee will I give it, and to thy seed after thee will I give the land" (Genesis 35:11,12).

It next occurs in recording how Jacob sent his sons into Egypt for corn, so that the seed through whom this purpose was to be fulfilled might be preserved. It occurs again in a reference by Jacob to the incident at Luz. These are all the cases in which *El* and *Shaddai* are joined, except Exodus 6:3 and Ezekiel 10:5. In the former of these passages we have a confirmation of the suggestion that the name is particularly associated with patriarchal times. The latter reference is in connection with the vision of the Cherubim, where the sound of their wings is said to have been "as the voice of *El Shaddai*". This vision will find its accomplishment when the promises made to Abraham are fulfilled.

---

4 | Hebrew, *Adon / Adonai*

Strong's Number: H113 (*Adon*) and H136 (*Adonai*).

Translation: Always as 'Lord' (uncapitalised) when applied to God.

Essential meaning: 'Lord' or 'Ruler'.

THE above are respectively the singular and plural forms of the same word. Their meaning is easily apprehended by the use which is made of the former in relation to men. It is derived from a root meaning 'to rule', and implies sovereignty or lordship. As applied to God it is always translated Lord, and is represented by that term when it is printed in ordinary type – not capitals.

Adon is also translated as 'Master' (Genesis 24:35; 39:2; Exodus 21:4-8; 1 Samuel 26:16) and 'Owner' (once only in 1 Kings 16:24). Elsewhere it is constantly translated Lord, conveying the idea of lordship, consequent upon possession, or because of the authoritative position of the one to whom it is applied. Thus Abraham was Sarah's 'lord', Aaron called Moses 'my lord' (Exodus 32:22), and the title is frequently applied in addressing kings and other persons in authority.

The use of the plural term in relation to God will afford no difficulty in the light of what has already been considered. The *Elohim*, representing God, become *Adonai*, rulers, or lords. The essential in every such case is the Lord (*Adon*) Himself, and as the power is of Him, the glory and homage are due unto Him.

An early occasion when the single word *Adon* is used specifically in relation to God is a clear illustration of what has been pointed out above. "Behold, the ark of the covenant of the *Adon* of all the earth passeth over before you into Jordan ... the ark of *Yahweh*, the *Adon* of all the earth" (Joshua 3:11-13). The expression, "the *Adon* of all the earth", or "the Lord of the whole earth", occurs six times in all. It speaks of possession, over-lordship, and is a definite indication of why God is spoken of as *Adon*.

The Appendix (page 231) contains a list of the instances in which 'Lord' in the King James Version represents the Hebrew *Adon*. In all the other cases where the word occurs printed in ordinary type (not capitals thus – LORD), the word may be taken as the representative of the plural term *Adonai*.

---

5 | Hebrew, *Elyon*

Strong's Number: H5946.

Translation: The Most High or Highest.

Essential meaning: 'Highest' or 'Supreme'.

ELYON is a word which comes from a Hebrew root meaning 'to ascend'. It follows that the translation Most High, or as twice rendered "Highest", correctly represents the meaning of the term. It refers to the position of the Deity as One who is above all. It is sometimes joined to other Divine Titles, most frequently with *El*, the form being *El Elyon* – *El* Most High. Twice it is connected with *Elohim*, and three times with *Yahweh*. Although it is usually given in the singular, there are a few passages in which it occurs in the plural. These instances are only found in the Book of Daniel – the seventh chapter – the greater part of which is written in the Chaldee language. In each of these references the allusion is to the "saints of the Most High Ones", whereas it should be noted that the little horn is represented as speaking great words against the Most High One, God Himself (compare Revelation 13:6).

6 | Hebrew, *Kadesh*

Strong's Number: H6918.

Translation: 'Holy One' or 'Holy'.

Essential meaning: 'Pure' and 'holy'.

THIS name requires very little in the way of comment. Kadesh means holy; and comes from a root meaning to be clean. Parkhurst says of the word, "To separate or set apart from its common or ordinary to some higher use or purpose". This is the essential meaning of the word. In its application to God it is represented by the expression, the Holy One. In reality there is no word for One as expressed, but as the Hebrew is invariably in the singular it is convenient to express it as the Holy One. Once or twice we read of holy ones, but that is in a different application and does not refer to God.

7 | Hebrew, *Yahweh*

Strong's Number: H3068.

Translation: 'The LORD'.

Essential meaning: 'He who will be'.

THIS, the Memorial Name of the Deity, presents features of special interest. It is essentially "the Name"; it is for this "Name's sake" that many of the things referred to in an earlier section have been done and other things promised. Around it circle the most interesting phases of the purpose of the Deity.

The circumstances under which it was first proclaimed are suggestive. Four hundred and thirty years after the promises to Abraham had been made the subject of a covenant, the time had arrived for an important development to take place in the long chain of circumstances that were to lead to the realisation of the things promised. Israel had been enduring hard bondage in Egypt. Their cries had ascended on high, and the destined deliverer had been prepared. He was now to receive his commission to lead Israel out of the house of bondage, and in response to a question as to the Name he was to announce as appertaining to the God who had sent him, he was told, as the King James Version expresses it, "I am that I am", which was immediately afterwards paraphrased when "God said moreover unto Moses, thus shalt thou say unto the children of Israel, *Yahweh*, *Elohim* of your fathers ... hath sent me unto you; this is My Name for ever, and this is My Memorial unto all generations". Shortly afterwards God spoke again unto Moses, "I am *Yahweh*, and I appeared unto Abraham, unto Isaac, and unto Jacob by the name of *El Shaddai*, but by My name *Yahweh* was I not known to them" (Exodus 6:2,3). The name *Yahweh* thus became associated with a purpose with which Israel's deliverance from Egypt was connected.

The declaration of that purpose takes us back to Abraham with whom the covenant was made. When the promise became a covenant by means of its typical ratification, God said, "Know of a surety that thy seed shall be a stranger in a land that is not theirs, and shall serve them; and they shall afflict them four hundred years; and also that nation, whom they shall serve, will I judge: and afterward shall they come out with great substance. And thou shalt go to thy fathers in peace; thou shalt be buried in a good old age. But in the fourth generation they shall come hither again, for the iniquity of the Amorites is not yet full" (Genesis 15:13-16). "In the same day the LORD made a covenant with Abram, saying, Unto thy seed have I given this land" (verse 18). By the incident referred to above and which were connected with a definite stage in the purpose, the name has become associated with that purpose and covenant, and is, therefore, a covenant name.

With this fact in mind we may consider the translation as it appears in the King James and Revised Versions. In the text of both it is shown as "I am that I am". Orthodox professors have used this rendering as a proof of their doctrines of the Trinity and the pre-existence of Christ. They base their arguments on the fact that when Christ was in discussion with the Jews, He said, "Before Abraham was, I am" (John 8:58). The argument is, at first sight, plausible, but when carefully considered is found to be entirely unsatisfactory. It takes no cognisance of the fact that this was not the only time that Jesus used the words, "I am". On two other occasions in the same chapter are the words used (verses 24,28). In each of these cases the translators have inserted the word 'he' after them – rightly so. An examination of the context will indicate the idea which is associated with that pronoun. In the seventh chapter there is a discussion as to the Messiahship of Jesus. Except for the parenthesis of the incident of the woman taken in adultery, that question is pursued all through the eighth and ninth chapters, and the statements, "I am he", clearly refer to the fact that Jesus claimed to be the Messiah. It was that day of Messianic glory that Abraham rejoiced to see. By faith he beheld him seated in the gates of his enemies in fulfilment of the promise which had been given to him, blessing all the families of the earth (Genesis 22:17,18). The statement has no reference whatever to pre-existence. It must also be remembered that Jesus deliberately used language which was intended to mislead those who had already adversely judged His claims, and too literal an interpretation must not, therefore, be attached to some of the expressions used.

The error of the orthodox explanation is still more apparent when attention is directed to the passage in Exodus and the language is examined critically. The marginal rendering of the Revised Version reads, 'Or, I am because I am, or I am who am, or I will be that I will be'. It is generally admitted now that the last of these is the true rendering of the Hebrew. It declares not that God is, but that He will be. It is thus really a Memorial Name, bringing to memory His covenanted promises. There is very little meaning in the ordinary translation. To say, 'I am that I am' is to repeat a self-evident truism, a thing inconceivable in such circumstances as those under which the declaration was made. To say, 'I will be that I will be' or 'I will be who I will be' is a very different matter. None but one who could foretell the future and control all the possible events of that future, could make such a statement. It involves all that we must consider as inherent in the One God. Absolute omnipotence, omniscience, and prescience are involved. There must be power to prevent any untoward accident. It pre-supposes also that there must be a purpose clearly determined. That purpose was involved in the promises made in Eden and to Abraham. Much more was to be declared before the full knowledge of that purpose could be attained by man, but even in those early promises there was sufficient to make the name of *Yahweh* singularly appropriate to designate the God of Abraham. For *Yahweh* is a name which is equivalent to the 'I will be' of the declaration to Moses. The marginal reference of the Revised Version against the title, "The Lord" (Exodus 3:15), reads, 'Jehovah, from the same root as *Ehyeh*' which as the previous note on Exodus 3:14 indicates, means, 'I will be' and is frequently so rendered.

> "Out of over forty other occurrences of this first person, singular number, future tense of the verb, in such a grammatical position as to make it allowable to draw a comparison with this verse (that is, excluding cases where what is known as the *vav conversive*, alters the state of affairs), there is only one instance of ehyeh being rendered 'I am' in the KJV. We have 'I will be' twenty-seven times, and the remaining occurrences

represented by 'will I be', 'I shall be', 'shall I be', 'though I be', 'should I be', etc." (*The Christadelphian*, 1881, page 212)

The following quotation from *Eureka* will help to a realisation of the meaning of the name:

"In the name and memorial thus revealed at the bush, the Deity declared that He would be a person, or persons, not then manifested. He announced to Moses that He was the Mighty Ones who had appeared as three men to Abraham, and as a host to Jacob; but that at a future period He would manifest Himself in others, even in persons of the Adamic race. Hence in view of this new manifestation, and to keep it constantly in remembrance, He imposed upon Himself the name of *Ehyeh*. 'I will be'. And this name of the Deity was to retain its import in a certain time hidden in the future. The time when it shall no longer be memorial is not yet arrived. It is to continue for the *Olahm* – for that epoch when 'He Who is, and Who was, and Who is coming', shall come with the clouds, and every eye shall see Him; and all the tribes of the earth shall wail before Him (Revelation 1:7). When this terrible crisis is passed, the ascription of chapter 16:5, 'Thou art righteous, O Lord, Who art, and wast, and **shalt be**', will be anachronous, for it will be no longer 'shall be' on earth, seeing that He will then be here, and reigning on Mount Zion and in Jerusalem, and before His ancients gloriously." (*Eureka*, Volume 1, pages 98,99)

The first use of this name in the scriptures (Genesis 2:4) is suggestive of the significance which has been indicated. As, however, it is there joined with the word *Elohim*, it had better be reviewed when this combination of names is considered. From the time of Abraham the name frequently occurs. This is what might be expected, seeing that the covenant had then become a foundation truth in relation to the purpose of God.

This fact, however, raises a difficulty. In referring to the Memorial Name, God said, "I appeared unto Abraham, unto Isaac, and unto Jacob by the name of *El Shaddai*, but by My name *Yahweh* was I not known to them" (Exodus 6:3). Yet in the records of the lives of these men frequent allusion is made to *Yahweh*. It is said, for example, that "Abram called on the name of *Yahweh*". It was "by *Yahweh*, the God of the heaven and the God of the earth", that Abram caused his servant to swear that he would not take a wife for Isaac of the daughters of Canaan, and it was to *Yahweh Elohim* that the servant prayed. Such an apparent discrepancy calls for consideration. Many suggestions have been made in regard to it. It would seem that the name was known as a name, but that its memorial character and meaning were not perceived or declared in patriarchal times. There are gradations in the meaning of the word "know", one of which is defined as "to learn, to be informed, to learn by experience". The latter definition is specifically connected with the name of *Yahweh* in the passage under notice. After saying, "by My name *Yahweh* was I not known unto them", God proceeded to declare that He would bring Israel out of Egypt, adding "And I will take you to Me for a people, and I will be to you *Elohim*, and ye shall know that I am *Yahweh* your *Elohim*, which bringeth you out from under the burdens of the Egyptians. And I will bring you unto the land, concerning the which I did swear to give it to Abraham, to Isaac and to Jacob; and I will give it you for an heritage. I am *Yahweh*" (Exodus 6:7,8). It was thus an experimental knowledge which was to be imparted to the children of Israel in the development of events connected with the purpose associated with the Memorial Name. In this sense the Name had not been known to their fathers.

When we proceed to examine the development of the things suggested by the Memorial Name, most interesting matters are brought before us. "I will be who I will be." Who will He be? Primarily He was to be *Jehoshua* (*Yahweh* saves or helps) – Jesus. As the Son of God by reason of the overshadowing of Mary by the Holy Spirit Jesus was "the only begotten of the Father, full of grace and truth". In him the Father dwelt. "Though ye believe not me, believe the works, that ye may know and believe that the Father is in me and I in Him" (John 10:38). "I am in the Father and the Father in me... the Father that dwelleth in me, He doeth the works " (John 14:10). "God was in Christ" (2 Corinthians

5:19). By reason of this he was "Emmanuel, God with us". As such he was the one through whom the effects of sin were to be overcome. He was the seed of the woman, originally referred to in that section of Genesis where the name of *Yahweh* first occurs. The great truth thus declared by and concerning Christ was a development of the *Yahweh* Name, and furnishes the first manifestation of the Memorial, "I will be Who I will be".

But much more than this is involved. The indwelling of the Father in Christ was to be the basis for a further development in the future when, as a multitude which no man can number, the faithful of every age and race will be the temple, or dwelling-place of *Yahweh*. This twofold idea comes out in two statements found in the prophecy of Isaiah. "Thus saith *Yahweh*, the King of Israel, and His redeemer, *Yahweh* of hosts; I am the first, and I am the last, and beside Me there is no *Elohim*" (Isaiah 44:6). "Who hath wrought and done it, calling the generations from the beginning? I, *Yahweh* the first, and with the last, I am He" (41:4). In the first of these quotations the word for last is singular, in the latter it is plural. The comparison will be more striking if the unexpressed and unnecessary words are omitted, thus:

> 'I first, and I last [singular], and beside Me no *Elohim*. I *Yahweh*, first and last [plural], I, He.'

It cannot be imagined that this variation is accidental, or meaningless. It calls for explanation, and the ideas previously expressed supply that explanation. *Yahweh*, the great *El*, is the first. That as we have already seen is the foundation of any doctrine concerning God. Before Him – nothing! After Him – nothing! Out of Him are all things. That being so, whatever may be in the future must be of Him. But though all things are of Him, there are some things which are more particularly associated with Him – the things directly connected with His purpose. These things centre in the Lord Jesus Christ. Hence *Yahweh*, the first, is in His manifestation in the Lord Jesus, also the last (One). He is also the last ones inasmuch as all those who attain to the life eternal will do so as the result of the Divine work in Christ and them. God was in Christ, as we have seen. God raised him from the dead. God calls the saints to His kingdom and glory through Christ. God in Christ reconciles to Himself. God works in the saints to will and to do of His good pleasure. And finally, when they are accepted at the judgment seat and changed from mortal to immortal nature, they will partake of the Divine nature – God will be all in all. Thus He is the last ones in them, and will be universally so when the end shall come. Thus the *Yahweh* Name contains within itself the declaration of the purpose of the Deity, and is the Memorial of that purpose.

The usage of this Name in the scriptures can be followed without difficulty. Whenever the words LORD or GOD occur in capitals the Hebrew is *Yahweh*, except in the instances given in the Appendix below (page 230) where the name *Yah* is used. *Yah* is an abbreviated form of *Yahweh*, and is the form in which it occurs when it is used as an element in the name of a man, e.g., Jehoshaphat ('*Yah* will judge'), and Isaiah ('*Yah* has saved').

8 | Hebrew, *Yahweh Elohim*

Strong's Number: H3068, H430.

Translation: 'The LORD God'.

Essential meaning: 'He who will be mighty ones'.

THE name of *Yahweh* is constantly associated with other terms, the most usual being the combination *Yahweh Elohim*. Together they mean He who shall (or will) be Mighty Ones, and may be taken as an exposition of the foregoing ideas concerning the multitudinous manifestation of the *Yahweh* name.

The first occurrence of *Yahweh Elohim* is very suggestive. "These are the generations of the heavens and of the earth when they were created, in the day that *Yahweh Elohim* made the earth and the heavens" (Genesis 2:4). It is in the section thus commenced, and which reaches to Genesis 3:24, that sin and redemption are referred to for the first time. The combination is constantly used in this section, whereas it only occurs nine times in the remainder of the book of Genesis. Such a remarkable fact must be intentional. The entrance of sin into the world marked the apparent failure of the work of the *Elohim*. Man, who had been created in their image failed to reflect their moral likeness, and was sentenced to return to the dust from which he had been formed. But the failure was not to be the end. Indeed, God's purpose cannot fail, and that truth is involved in the very title used. "I will be mighty ones", it declares, and in the section it is indicated how this shall be.

> "I will put enmity between thee and the woman, and between thy seed and her seed; it shall bruise thy head, and thou shalt bruise his heel." (Genesis 3:15)

It was not much in itself, but later revelation enables us to construct the plan whereby the man whom *Yahweh* made strong for Himself (Psalm 80:17), was the Arm of *Yahweh* to bring salvation to a multitude who should attain unto more than Adam forfeited by his sin. He lost life and the possession of a perfect human organisation. They attain unto life eternal and a participation in the Divine nature.

> "In him the tribes of Adam boast
> More blessings than their father lost."

They will then constitute *Yahweh Elohim*, having been called out from the mass of mankind to be a people for the Name (Acts 15:14).

The use of these two names in combination may easily be traced. Wherever the words LORD God occur in this form, i.e., LORD in small capitals, the original will be *Yahweh Elohim*. Where on the other hand it is Lord GOD, it is as the equivalent of *Adonai Yahweh*. If this simple guide is noted, it will be apparent which of the two combinations is used in the original Hebrew.

---

9 | Hebrew, *Yahweh Tzevaot*

Strong's Number: H3068, H6635.

Translation: 'The LORD of Hosts'.

Essential meaning: 'He who will be a multitude', used often with reference to an army.

THIS is a somewhat similar title to *Yahweh Elohim*, except that it depicts the *Elohim* in a particular phase of their work. Sometimes it is given in the longer form *Yahweh Elohim* of hosts, whilst in other instances we have *Elohim* of hosts. The word rendered 'hosts' is '*sabaoth*', which comes from a root meaning 'to mass', whether it be an army or servants, but particularly the former. It is defined as a mass of persons, especially regiments organised for war; and it is constantly associated with such an idea when it is used in relation to God.

Although this is contrary to the usual ideas of God current in the world, it presents no difficulty where the Truth is understood. "*Yahweh* is a man of war; *Yahweh* is His name" (Exodus 15:3). His warfare in the future will be accomplished by His agents, the *Elohim*. In the past the angelic hosts have been used by Him in such ways. They now encamp (as a military host) around them that fear Him, and deliver them (Psalm 34:7). One of them described himself as the Captain of *Yahweh*'s host (Joshua 5:14). The future will see other, and greater, illustrations when *Yahweh* "shall go forth and fight against the nations as when He fought in the day of battle".

The first occurrence of this title is 1 Samuel 1:3,11 in connection with the birth of Samuel. Although Samuel was to be a prophet his work was that of saving Israel from the hands of the Philistines. Thus it is recorded, "So the Philistines were subdued, and they came no more into the coast of Israel; and the hand of *Yahweh* was against the Philistines all the days of Samuel" (1 Samuel 7:13). The next reference is in the same book where the Philistines having invaded the land, Israel sent for "the ark of the covenant of the Lord of hosts" (1 Samuel 4:4). The object in view was that they should be victorious in battle; hence the reference to *Yahweh* of hosts is in full accord with the circumstances.

In the days of David, the warrior king, the title is of frequent occurrence. It was used by David in his conflict with

Goliath (1 Samuel 17:45). It was also used when God made a covenant with him (2 Samuel 7:8; 1 Chronicles 17:7).

In the Psalms it is *Yahweh* of hosts who is to deliver Jerusalem (Psalm 24). It is *Yahweh* of hosts who is referred to in association with the time when the heathen shall rage and the kingdoms be moved (Psalm 46). Jerusalem is His city (Psalm 48:8).

An interesting illustration of the use of the title is found in the prophecy of Haggai, where it occurs fourteen times in two chapters, five times in the first and nine in the second. The subject matter of the prophecy will explain the frequent usage. "I will shake the heavens, and the earth, and the sea, and the dry land; and I will shake all nations and I will overthrow the throne of kingdoms, and I will destroy the strength of the kingdoms of the nations" (Haggai 2:6,7,22). It is the work of the saints in the post-Resurrectional epoch in the time when the kings of the earth shall make war with the Lamb. Then the saints as the *Elohim* of hosts in the *Yahweh* name will constitute "the armies of the heaven" following the word of God (Revelation 17,19).

10 | Hebrew, *Abiyr*

Strong's Number: H46.

Translation: 'The Mighty One' or 'The Mighty God'.

Essential meaning: 'Might', from the root idea of a powerful bird in flight.

THIS title, which means 'strong', 'stout', or 'mighty', is derived from a root 'to soar' or 'to fly'. It is only translated 'mighty' and 'Mighty One', although sometimes expressed as 'The Mighty God'. It calls for no particular comment, as the idea conveyed is inherent in the English word 'Mighty'.

11 | Hebrew, *Tzur*

Strong's Number: H6697.

Translation: Usually 'Rock'.

Essential meaning: A cliff or a sharp rock.

THE primary meaning of this word is a cliff or sharp rock (figuratively it stands for a refuge). These meanings will illustrate its application when it is used as a title for God. It is sometimes used in reference to pagan gods, not as indicating what they were, but what their worshippers believed them to be.

---

12 | Greek, *Theos*

Strong's Number: G2316.

Translation: God.

Essential meaning: Deity.

THE principal title of God in the New Testament is *theos*, consistently translated in the English version 'God' or 'god', unless the term is used idiomatically. Parkhurst says of it: "The most probable [derivation] seems to be that which deduces it from the verb theo, to place." He quotes an old writer as saying: "It is probable that *theoi*, the Gods, were so called from *thesis*, position or placing, for the ancients took those for gods whom they found to move in a certain regular and constant manner, thinking them the causes of the changes in the air, and of the conservation of the universe; these are the Gods (*theoi*), which are the disposers and formers of all things."

In the Septuagint Version of the Bible the word constantly occurs as the Greek representative of the Hebrew *Elohim*, thus substituting a singular for a plural noun. This action of the seventy is sanctioned by the New Testament. There may seem some inconsistency in this, but as we have seen the plurality expressed by *Elohim* is a very different idea from that which would have been conveyed to the Greek mind by the use of the plural *theoi*. This would have suggested a number of independent gods, whereas the *Elohim* of the Old Testament are all dependent on, and workers for the One God who is the sole source of their existence and power. Hence, no doubt the use of the singular Greek to represent the plural Hebrew – it emphasised the unity of the Deity. From what has been written concerning *El* and kindred words, and the derivation of *theos*, there will be no difficulty in apprehending what the title implies.

With the foregoing indications, and the exceptions noted below, it will be easy to recognise all the occurrences of *theos* in the New Testament.

1. **God forbid**. It is most unfortunate that the Greek words used should have been so rendered. The expression merely implies "by no means", or "certainly not", as we might express it. Found in Luke 20:16; Romans 3:4,6,31; 6:2,15; 7:7,13; 9:14; 11:1,11; 1 Corinthians 6:15; Galatians 2:17; 3:21; 6:14.
2. **Warned of God**. The word used means 'to be called' or 'named', but was sometimes used to signify a divine oracle, in which sense it is used in the passages noted. In Hebrews 8:5 the same word is translated "admonished of God". Found in Matthew 2:12,22; Acts 10:22; Hebrews 11:7.
3. **Answer of God**. The word in Greek is closely related to that rendered "warned of God". It denotes a divine response or revelation. Found in Romans 11:4.
4. **Would to God**. 'I wish' is the radical meaning of the word. The introduction of the name of God seems to have been done to emphasise the expression. Found in 1 Corinthians 4:8; 2 Corinthians 11:1.
5. **God-speed**. The Greek has *chairo*; it is a salutation (i.e., 'hail' or 'rejoice' or 'be glad'). Found in 2 John 10,11.

There are a few instances where *theos* occurs in the Greek, but no reference to God is found in the English versions:

- **Acts 7:20**. Exceeding fair, Greek 'fair to God'. This is an illustration of a Hebraism in Greek. The speaker was a Hebrew whose words are recorded in the Greek language. A reference to the cases cited elsewhere will indicate the application of the term.

- **2 Corinthians 1:12**. Godly sincerity (RV, 'sincerity of God').
- **1 Timothy 1:4**. Godly edifying (RV, 'dispensation of God').

13 | Greek, *Kurios*

Strong's Number: G2962.

Translation: Usually 'Lord'.

Essential meaning: Supreme authority.

THE root idea of this word is that of authority and supremacy – a controller. Its applicability to God is apparent. It is almost invariably translated Lord, when applied to God (but once translated "God" in Acts 19:20), and when used in reference to men, lord, master, or sir. Its use scarcely calls for comment.

It is equal to the Hebrew *Adon*, but is also used as the equivalent of *Yahweh* in quotations from, or references to, the Old Testament. In the Septuagint it answers to several names or titles of God (*Adonai*, *El*, *Elohim*, *Eloha*, *Tsur*, *Shaddai*, and *Yahweh*). It is likewise used in relation to Jesus (the Lord, the Lord Jesus Christ, etc.). In James 5:4 there is an allusion to the Lord of Sabaoth, which is equivalent to *Yahweh* of hosts in the Old Testament.

In the following cases the word Lord will be found representing other titles than *kurios*:

- '*Rabboni*' (meaning 'teacher' or 'master') in Mark 10:51.
- '*Despotes*' (meaning 'one who has unrestricted authority and lordship over another') in Luke 2:29; Acts 4:24; 2 Peter 2:1; Jude 4; Revelation 6:10.
- It is put for where there is no Greek in the phrase 'the Lord of Glory' in James 2:1.

14 | Greek, *Pantokrator*

Strong's Number: G3841.

Translation: Almighty.

Essential meaning: All-mighty.

THERE are but few occasions where this title is used in the New Testament. It is the equivalent of the Hebrew *Shaddai*. Whenever it occurs it is rendered either Almighty or Omnipotent. It is found in a number of passages; a reference to what has been written in relation to the Hebrew *Shaddai* (page 211) will enable its meaning to be ascertained, so that further comment will not be necessary.

Appendix to Section 3

Biblical occurrences of selected titles of Deity

Occurrences of the term *Eloah*

- Deuteronomy 32:15,17.
- 2 Chronicles 32:15 ('no god of any nation').
- Nehemiah 9:17.
- Job 3:4,23; 4:9,17; 5:17; 6:4,8,9; 9:9,13; 10:2; 11:5-7; 12:4,6 ('God bringeth abundantly'); 15:8; 16:20,21; 19:6,21,26; 21:9,19; 22:12,26; 24:12; 27:3,8,10; 29:2,4; 31:2,6; 33:12,26; 35:10; 36:2; 37:15,22; 39:17; 40:2.
- Psalm 18:31 ('for who is God ...'); 50:22; 114:7; 139:19.
- Proverbs 30:5.
- Isaiah 44:8 ('is there a God ...').
- Daniel 11:37 ('nor regard any god') and all three occurrences in verses 38,39.
- Habakkuk 1:11; 3:3.

Occurrences of the Chaldee term *Elah*

- Every occurrence of 'God' from Ezra 4:24–6:18 and from Ezra 7:12-26.
- Jeremiah 10:11.
- Every occurrence of God from Daniel 2:18–6:26.

Occurrences of the title *Shaddai*

- Genesis 49:25.
- Numbers 24:4,16.
- Ruth 1:20,21.
- Job 5:17; 6:4,14; 8:3,5; 11:7; 13:3; 15:25; 21:15,20; 22:3,17,23,25,26; 23:16; 24:1; 27:2,10,11,13; 29:5; 31:2,35; 32:8; 33:4; 34:10,12; 35:13; 37:23; 40:2.
- Psalm 68:14; 91:1.
- Isaiah 13:6.
- Ezekiel 1:24.
- Joel 1:15.

Occurrences of the title *El Shaddai*

- Genesis 17:1; 28:3; 35:11; 43:14; 48:3.
- Exodus 6:3.
- Ezekiel 10:5.

Occurrences of the title *Adon* (other places where 'the Lord' is in lower case represent instead the plural, *Adonai*)

- Genesis 19:18.
- Joshua 3:11,13; 5:14.
- Judges 6:13.
- Nehemiah 3:5; 8:10; 10:29 ('our Lord').
- Psalm 8:1,9; 45:11; 97:5 ('the Lord of the whole earth'); 110:1 ('said unto my Lord'); 114:7; 135:5; 136:3; 147:5.
- Isaiah 1:24; 3:1; 10:16 ('shall the Lord'),33 ('Behold, the Lord'); 19:4 ('saith the Lord'); 51:22.
- Daniel 10:16,17,19; 12:8.
- Hosea 12:14.
- Micah 4:13 ('the Lord of the whole earth').

- Zechariah 1:9; 4:4,5,13,14; 6:4,5.
- Malachi 3:1.

Occurrences of the title *Elyon*

- Numbers 24:16.
- Deuteronomy 32:8.
- 2 Samuel 22:14.
- Psalm 9:2; 18:13; 21:7; 46:4; 50:14; 73:11; 77:10; 78:17; 82:6; 83:18; 87:5; 91:9; 92:1; 107:11.

Occurrences of the title *El Elyon*

- Genesis 14:18-20,22.
- Psalm 78:35.

Occurrences of the title *Elohim Elyon*

- Psalm 57:2; 78:56.

Occurrences of the title *Yahweh Elyon*

- Psalm 7:17; 47:2; 97:9.

Occurrences of the title *Eloah Illai* (the Chaldee equivalent)

- Daniel 3:26; 4:2; 5:18,21.

Occurrences of the title *Kadesh* with reference to God

- Leviticus 11:44,45; 19:2; 20:26; 21:8.
- 2 Kings 19:22.
- Job 6:10.
- Psalm 22:3; 71:22; 78:41; 89:18; 99:3,5,9; 111:9.
- Proverbs 9:10; 30:3.

- Isaiah 1:4; 5:19,24; 10:17,20; 12:6; 17:7; 29:19,23; 30:11,12,15; 31:1; 37:23; 40:25; 41:14,16,20; 43:3,14,15; 45:11; 47:4; 48:17; 47:7(×2); 54:5; 55:5; 57:15; 60:9,14.
- Jeremiah 50:29; 51:5.
- Ezekiel 39:7.
- Hosea 11:9.
- Habakkuk 1:12; 3:3.

Occurrences of the title *Abiyr*

- Genesis 49:24.
- Psalm 132:2,5.
- Isaiah 1:24; 49:26; 60:16.

Occurrences of the title *Tzur*

- Deuteronomy 32:4,15,18,30,31,37.
- 1 Samuel 2:2.
- 2 Samuel 22:3,32,47(×2); 23:3.
- Psalm 18:2 (translated 'strength'),31,46; 19:14 (translated 'strength'); 28:1; 61:2; 62:2,6,7; 73:26 (translated 'strength'); 78:35; 89:26; 92:15; 94:22; 95:1; 144:1 (translated 'strength').
- Isaiah 17:10; 26:4 (translated 'strength'); 30:29 ('the mighty one'); 44:8.
- Habakkuk 1:12 ('O mighty God').

Occurrences of the title *Pantokrator*

- 2 Corinthians 6:18.
- Revelation 1:8; 4:8; 11:17; 15:3; 16:7,14; 19:6,15; 21:22.

Scripture Index

Exodus

Leviticus

Numbers

Proverbs